SAYED KASHUA is the author of the novels *Dancing Arabs, Let It Be Morning*, which was shortlisted for the International IMPAC Dublin Literary Award, and *Exposure*, winner of the prestigious Bernstein Prize. He is a columnist for *Haaretz* and the creator of the popular, prize-winning sitcom, Arab Labor. Kashua has received numerous awards for his journalism including the Lessing Prize for Critic (Germany) and the SFJFF Freedom of Expression Award (USA). Now living in the United States with his family, he teaches at the University of Illinois.

"Being a Palestinian who was born and raised in Israel, Kashua is an embodiment of the Israeli-Palestinian conflict. If he only was a little less sincere, perceptive, and talented he would have probably been able to co-exist with himself. *Native* is a book that will make you lose most hope in the power of national processes but, at the same time, will leave you in awe of the incredible force of humanity, humor, and some damn good writing."
ETGAR KERET, author of THE SEVEN GOOD YEARS

"Kashua's columns are conversational, confiding, anecdotal, centered on the rituals and trials of bourgeois life . . . While his writing is rarely explicitly political, a sense of uprootedness lurks."
NEW YORKER

"By turns funny, angry, and moving, Kashua's 'dispatches' offer revealing glimpses into the meanings of family and fatherhood and provide keen insight into the deeply rooted complexities of a tragic conflict. A wickedly ironic but humane collection."
KIRKUS REVIEWS

"Startling and insightful . . . Kashua's subtly shaded, necessarily complex, and ultimately despairing account of the tensions within his homeland, 'so beloved and so cursed,' is bound to open the eyes and awaken the sympathies of a new swath of loyal readers."
PUBLISHERS WEEKLY

NATIVE

Dispatches from a
Palestinian-Israeli Life

SAYED KASHUA

Translated from the Hebrew by Ralph Mandel

SAQI

Published in Great Britain 2016 by Saqi Books

Copyright © 2016 Sayed Kashua
Translation © 2014 *Haaretz*

Sayed Kashua has asserted his right under the Copyright, Designs
and Patents Act, 1988, to be identified as the author of this work.

The author owes a great debt of thanks to *Haaretz*, which published the
columns in this collection in their original form.

First published as *Ben Haaretz* by Keter Publishing House in 2015.

ISBN 978-0-86356-196-2
eISBN 978-0-86356-186-3

A full CIP record for this book is available from the British Library

Printed and bound by CPI Group (UK) Ltd, Croydon, CR0 4YY

SAQI BOOKS
26 Westbourne Grove
London W2 5RH
www.saqibooks.com

To my wife, Najat; and my kids: Nai, Emil, and Neil

CONTENTS

INTRODUCTION

It's been about a year since I left Jerusalem and came to Urbana-Champaign, Illinois, with my wife and three children. We celebrated the anniversary by preparing homemade hummus and frying falafel. By now we know where to buy the right products for making food that approximates the taste of home. My younger son, who arrived here at the age of three without knowing a word of English, asked for another portion of falafel. I sliced a pita in half, stuffed it with a few falafel balls, added a slice of tomato and cucumber, and dampened the contents with some tahini sauce. "Wow, Daddy," he said after biting into the pita avidly, and added, in English, with a midwestern accent, "This taco is really good." And I knew I had an idea for my weekly column.

When I started to write a weekly column in the Israeli newspaper *Haaretz*, more than ten years ago, I was still living in Beit Safafa, a Palestinian neighborhood of Jerusalem, with my wife and my firstborn daughter. Since then, I have become the father of two more children; I moved from the eastern to the western part of the city; governments have come and gone; wars have broken out, died down, and erupted anew; and I churned out a column every week.

Writing a weekly column can be a real nightmare. Some days I found myself wandering the streets of Jerusalem and mulling aloud, "What will I write about this week?" If I was apprehensive that I had nothing to write about, or felt that the last column I'd written was not very good, I sank into depression. When I knew I'd written a good piece I was delighted, even if it was about missiles being fired into the country.

Writing the column became a way of life for me. As soon as I sent one column to my editor at the newspaper, I started to think about the next one. I didn't look for a thought or an idea; I looked for a feeling. The method I adopted was to write about what had moved me most that week. I honed my senses and pursued emotions—fear, pain, hope, desire, anger, happiness. My promise to myself was that I would convey those feelings to the reader by means of personal stories. I tried to be honest and to tell the truth as I perceived it, even though what I wrote was sometimes complete fiction.

During the past decade I've written about almost everyone I know. I have very few friends left: people started to keep their distance from me or went silent in my company, for fear that what they said would end up in the paper. I made my wife's life a misery, and the lives of others in my family, by exploiting them shamelessly if I thought it would help me write a better column.

Mostly, though, I think I tried to survive the reality around me through words, to create order out of the swirling chaos and find an inner logic in what I saw and experienced. The column gave me space to apologize, cry out, be afraid, implore, hate, and love—but above all to look for hope and make my life a little more bearable. That's why I went on writing it: in the hope that in the end all would be well and that all one has to do is write one's life as a story—and find a happy ending.

Sayed Kashua
June 2015

NATIVE

PART I

WARNING SIGNS

2006–2007

WARNING SIGNS

April 7, 2006

To: Editor, *Haaretz* magazine
Re: Sayed Kashua's column

Dear Sir,

Well now. This is of course not the first time I've had occasion to send a letter to the editor of a newspaper on which my husband, who goes by the name Sayed Kashua, is employed. And like the letters that came before, this one, too, is a formal warning. If my demands are not met, I will have no choice but to resort to legal measures.

Your correspondent, my husband, is a chronic liar, gossip, and cheat who unfortunately makes a living by distorting the truth and creating a highly unreliable picture of reality. I am astounded that a newspaper that is considered respectable, like *Haaretz*, goes ahead and publishes my husband's abusive articles without bothering to check the accuracy of the material. How can you not have a system, even minimal, that checks whether the columns of your esteemed correspondent might be libelous and constitute grounds for a whole slew of lawsuits?

The law firm I've contacted assures me that 90 percent of my husband's columns that were published in your paper contain grounds for lawsuits whose favorable outcomes are not in doubt. Until now I have avoided filing such suits, as I am not greedy like my husband, your correspondent, who has proved beyond a doubt that he will balk at nothing to make a living. Knowing my husband's character as well as I do, I am not surprised at his behavior. However, I am amazed that your paper's many worthy editors are unaware of the gravity of the situation.

As a condition for terminating legal procedures, I demand that your distinguished newspaper publish a crystal clear apology in a place that's at least as respectable as the one you provide for your immoral correspondent. The paper's readers need to be aware beyond any doubt that the picture my husband paints of his family life is a crude lie and has no basis in reality.

Almost every week, my husband impertinently, and with your backing, creates a monstrous picture in which I usually play the lead. This abuse has to end, and because there is no way to communicate with the nutcase who has hospitalized himself in my home, I am asking you, who bear exclusive responsibility, to put a stop to this vile smear campaign.

As his readers realize, my husband suffers from a serious addiction problem—by which I do not necessarily mean alcohol and other substances, but an addiction to lies and fabrications that have become an inseparable part of his daily life.

He reached new peaks in his last column, when he described me as an irritable, grumpy woman who wishes him dead and says things like "May worms eat his lungs." Of course, I never spoke any such words. It's all the product of the hallucinations and perversions of his feverish mind. Not to mention the other aspersions he casts on me—but this is not the place to repeat them, in order not to offend the public's sensibilities.

It's altogether baffling that my husband uses swear words as a regular tool in his writing. The only conclusion is that your editors don't bat an eyelash at the unbroken string of obscenities.

His descriptions of me cause me no end of grief and trouble. I find myself being forced to provide answers and explanations to my circle of acquaintances, at work, in the neighborhood, and within the family. I am bombarded day and night with questions about groundless accusations that are published in your serious newspaper. As long as I alone was the target of his barbs, I bit my lip and decided to restrain myself in order to keep up an appearance of domestic harmony. Lately, though, my husband has been undermining his children's routine as well: his daughter and firstborn child is also having to come up with answers and explanations to the parents of the other children in her kindergarten. Last Purim, tears welled up in my eyes when one of the mothers wanted to know—based on material published in your paper—whether my mother, whom your correspondent calls "my mother-in-law," is really a witch whose only goal in life is to get me away from my husband.

I don't understand why family matters, irrespective of whether they are reliable, have to be published in newspapers, still less in a newspaper like *Haaretz*. By the way, I want to take this opportunity to inform you that I am joining the list of those who are canceling their subscription to your paper, and I call on everyone with common sense to follow my example and that of many others who do not allow this defective product into their home.

I am not one of those people who like to go public with family disputes, but in this case, and in the light of past experience, I am well aware that this is the only way to stop the malicious smear campaign. It is my fervent hope that you will follow the path of previous newspapers that received formal warnings and acceded to my request to fire my husband instantly.

The reading public needs to know that my husband—and I am speaking here as a professional with many years of work experience in a psychiatric hospital—is afflicted with any number of personality disorders. In jargon, his condition is officially described as a borderline personality who suffers from a number of behavioral disorders, of which the most serious, perhaps, are paranoid personality disorder, induced delusional disorder, and severe narcissistic damage. The reading public needs to know that my husband suffers from recurrent attacks of delusions—graded as level 4 on a scale of 5—which are becoming increasingly grimmer as he grows older.

Here's one small example out of many, just to illustrate what I mean. Recently, my husband has convinced himself that he is an Ashkenazi of Polish descent whose parents—both of whom are in fact still alive and living in the village of Tira—are Holocaust survivors who came to this country on an illegal immigrant ship in 1945. Esteemed editors and readers, my husband, your correspondent, has been wandering the streets of Beit Safafa, the Palestinian neighborhood of Jerusalem where we live, telling passersby that he's the only Ashkenazi in the neighborhood. He gives his address, when requested, as "Beit Safafa Heights."

I very much regret having been dragged into this series of verbal abuses in the pages of the newspaper. It is unnatural, but in view of the deteriorating situation I am left with no choice. I ask the readers' pardon.

Yours sincerely,
Sayed Kashua's wife

P.S. Please publish my letter anonymously.

HIGH TECH

June 1, 2006

"So, what are you going to do today?" my wife asked when I woke up.

"What do you mean?" I replied, not getting her drift. "Go to work, as usual."

"Don't tell me you forgot."

"What?"

"I don't believe it. For the past week I've been telling you that there's a holiday in the kindergarten today. You never listen. Do you know how many times I told you?"

"What holiday is that?"

"I don't know, the school's announcement says Aliyah Day."

They're overdoing it in school, I thought. Bilingual, all right, *'ala rasi*, my choice, respect all the religions, the two languages, the two narratives of the two peoples. I respect all that, despite the endless holidays in the school. But Aliyah Day, *rabak*, for heaven's sake?

"Who celebrates Aliyah Day?" I shouted. "What kind of cynicism is it to celebrate Jewish immigration?"

"Daddy," my daughter cut in, "the kindergarten teacher said it's the day when Jesus went up to heaven."

"Ah, yes?" I calmed down. "Well, we have to respect that."

Fine. It's been a while since I spent quality time with my daughter, and Ascension Day can be a terrific opportunity for bridge building. "We'll have a fun day," I said to my daughter. "We'll celebrate the ascension right."

So I could have the car, we all left together: first we dropped off the baby at his crèche, which thank God is not bi-anything and follows the Muslim calendar for holidays, and then we took Mom to work.

"Are you hungry?" I asked my daughter when we were alone in the car, and drove to the restaurant in the Botanical Garden on the Hebrew University's campus. "You see?" I explained to my daughter, brimming with pride at the education I was giving her as we attacked a salad and cheeses. "This garden is filled with flowers, trees, and plants from the *whole* world."

"I want to walk around in the garden. Can we, Daddy?"

"Uh," I said. The thought of a hike wasn't especially appealing. "Isn't what you can see from here enough? Look, there are ducks in the pond."

"No, Daddy, let's walk a little."

"All right, finish eating."

After five minutes of walking, I was cursing myself for the dumb idea of eating in the Botanical Garden. "And what's this, Daddy?" my daughter asked, stopping next to every explanatory sign.

"Aren't you tired?" I asked her.

"No, this is really fun. Look at this, Daddy, so pretty and yellow. What does it say?"

"Maybe we'll go to the mall? I'll buy you ice cream."

"Yummy, ice cream."

I drove to the mall. There's actually something I have to buy, maybe at long last I'll change the fluorescent lamp in the bathroom. It hasn't been working for a year, and I moved the reading light there.

"Daddy," my daughter said as we waited in the line of cars that were queued for the security check, "can I speak Arabic now?"

"What do you mean?"—I turned around to her—"Of course. You can speak Arabic whenever you want and wherever you want. What are you talking about, anyway?"

The security guard looked through the window and I smiled at him. "What's happening? Everything all right?" he asked, so he could check my accent. Before I could say, "Good, thanks"—two words without the telltale letters "p" and "r"—my daughter chimed in with *"Alhamdulillah"*—everything's fine.

"ID card, please," the security guard said.

"You hear, sweetie," I explained to my daughter as we entered a do-it-yourself store, "it's fine to speak Arabic everywhere, anytime you want, but not at the entrance to a mall, okay, sweetie?"

I bought a fluorescent lamp, a wastebasket for my office, and a shoe rack. "We'll surprise Mommy," I said to my daughter, who was thrilled by the shoe rack. She knows as well as I that Mom has wanted a shoe rack since she was born. I received a large carton. The salesman said that assembling it was not a problem. You don't need any equipment, he added, except a Phillips screwdriver. I hope I have one on my penknife, I thought, because that's the only tool I have in the house.

Excuse my French, but *kus shel ha'ima* of the do-it-yourself store and the same to that salesman's mother. They're sons of bitches and so is their shoe rack. Who needs a shoe rack, anyway? A million years we got along without it, so what for? I'll show my wife what for. Two hours I've been fighting my Swiss Army knife and their crappy screws, totally baffled by the instructions page, it's all coming out ass-backward, I'm sweating like a mule, and my fingers are blistered. "Very simple assembly," *'alek*, you believe it. My back has seized up and I'm broiling with irritation.

I try to remember that my daughter is next to me and not swear too much. And they have the nerve to take money for it. I'll sue them, the shits. And this Ascension Day, too, where did they dredge that up?

Okay, I have to relax, start from the beginning. There's still three hours to go before I pick up my wife from work. Inhale deeply, one step at a time. I spread a newspaper on the floor and on it put the different-size screws, the nails, and the pieces of plastic, according to the instructions, according to the numbers.

Perspiration drips from my nose straight onto the forehead of Olmert addressing congress. I actually saw him on TV—it was on all the news channels, live, emotional—extending a hand to peace, and all the Americans giving him a standing ovation. So what if at the same time he killed four Arabs in Ramallah? But what do I care about Olmert now? Shoe rack; three hours.

That's the good thing about the Jews, that's what I like about them—promises. They're good talkers. "Half an hour to assemble it, of course it's not complicated?"

At 3 p.m. I drove with my daughter to pick up my wife. "Well, how was it, fun?" she asked. I said nothing.

"Daddy got you a surprise."

"Really? What?"

"It's a secret," my daughter said.

At home the shoe rack was fully assembled: handsome, cognac colored, standing in the correct corner. The carpenter cost me 100 shekels for a quarter of an hour.

"Did you do it?" my wife asked. I nodded my head affirmatively. She gave me a kiss.

"But, Daddy," my daughter said, "you said it's wrong to . . ."

I lifted her up in the air to make her stop talking, and whispered in her ear, "Today it's allowed, today is Aliyah Day."

HEAD START

July 7, 2006

The telephone jangles me out of sleep. My head is pounding and I almost trip and fall when I get up to answer.

"Are you still sleeping?"

"No, I'm working," I reply to my wife. "Is anything wrong?"

"No. I just wanted to tell you that the battery in my cell is dead, so don't be alarmed if I don't answer."

Wow, what a headache. What time is it, anyway? I check the wall clock: 10 A.M. What day is it? Sunday. Yes, Sunday. What did I do last night? I try to do a mental replay, to make sure, like after every evening of drinking, that I didn't do anything really bad. It seems to me that I did do something, based on what I manage to remember.

I didn't drive back, I know that. I gave the keys to the neighbor. I invited him because I knew that by the time the France-Brazil soccer game ended everything would be one big blur. I didn't go out for the game, I went out for the alcohol, and I needed a lot of it. I went out deliberately to get drunk. Who won? I'll check the Internet in a minute.

Horrible nausea assails me. I go to the bathroom, bend over, stick my head into the toilet bowl, but nothing comes out. Who just called? There was a phone call a minute ago. Ah, right, it was my wife, from work. What did she want? *Wallah*, hey, France won, but I'll check, I'm not sure.

Strong black coffee will help, I tell myself, knowing very well that it won't help. I only hope I didn't bug the barmen last night at the Lab. And if I did, I hope they'll forgive me—they know me a little. I was probably nice once, I hope. But they have to understand that I had to. This time I really had to. I think we're talking about four vodkas and three beers.

I have to stop this. How can I work now? I have so much work, but all I want is to go back to bed. No, I mustn't, the coffee will help for sure, I'll take an Advil, I have to work.

The coffee only aggravates the nausea. I'll try a cigarette. I light one up as I turn on the computer. The screen is slow coming up. The antivirus announces that the computer is under threat. The phone rings. Probably my wife—it seems to me she called before—let's see what she wants.

"Hello," I say, and connect to the Internet. Right off, the home page declares that France won.

"This is the kindergarten," I hear the kindergarten teacher say. The start of a sentence that has zero chance of ending well. "The baby has a fever, he's been crying all morning, he doesn't eat, doesn't drink, just cries. We tried to call his mother, but she's not answering her cell phone."

My wife has the car. She doesn't answer her cell, it goes straight to voice mail. I'll take a cab. I check my wallet—empty. I drank until the last shekel yesterday. From information I get the number of my wife's work and call over and over, but the line is busy. It takes a quarter of an hour until I get through to someone and am given the number of the requested department. I dial for another quarter of an hour—no answer.

My head is bursting, the baby must be screaming now. "Hello." I wake up the neighbor from last night's binge. "Yes, I'm home," he says in his half-sleep, "but I can't drive. If you want, come and get the key and take my car. It has a baby seat."

In the parking lot I remember the call I got from my mother half an hour before the game. "I called to say that everything is all right," she said, "except that someone burned your brother's car." It's true that torching cars has become routine in Tira. But my little brother? What could he have done? Why would someone want to burn his car? "It was probably someone he fired at work," my mother said. I became livid. Someone was trying to hurt my little brother.

At 2 A.M. they were awakened by the explosion of the car's gas tank next to the house. Luckily, a few neighbors came to help and they were able to keep the flames from reaching their home. He fired someone. A good enough reason in a crime-ridden town. I can hardly think of an Arab locale in Israel that isn't like that.

"Don't you think I want to?" my little brother said on the phone when I shouted at him that he has to leave that horrible place, get out of there. "Where would I go?" he asked. "And what kind of work would I find somewhere else? Do you think it's easy? I'm dying to get out of here, do you think I want my son to grow up here? I think about it all the time. But where?"

My son is crying. His eyes are red and his face is burning. I hug him and feel his body heat. "Come to Daddy. Come to Daddy, sweetie. Everything will be all right." He leans his head on my neck and bawls.

The clinic in the mall was open. You have to watch him closely, the doctor said. It's important for him to drink, otherwise he'll dehydrate. She recommended a sweet liquid and wrote the name on a piece of notepaper. "It's not subsidized," she said. I have yet to encounter anything in life that makes me sadder than a crying child. He usually likes the petting corner in the mall. I take him there, and a small smile flits across his face. "Wab," he says, seeing a rabbit, and then following the parrots with his eyes.

I hate to see animals in cages. Nevertheless, I decide to make a purchase from the store opposite the petting corner. Two birds, a

cage, sand, food, and a toy. I pay with a credit card. I put the cage
next to the baby in the car and he grows calmer. When we get home
I try to get him to drink something. Milk, water, ice cream that he
loves, but he doesn't want anything. I force an Acamol—the local
equivalent of aspirin—down his throat. He cries a little and almost
immediately falls asleep opposite the cage. I put him to bed and
go back to the birds. I give them water and food and slice a loquat
for them, but they don't eat. They just stand on the plastic branch,
trembling.

I, THE JURY

July 14, 2006

What am I doing here? The question grabbed me and wouldn't let go.

It's as though I'd just woken from a weird dream in which I'm sitting in a fancy restaurant among a lot of rich American Jews, some of them very familiar, who I didn't know are Jewish. I probably saw them on TV at some point. They look important in their elegant attire, they speak articulately, they flash self-aware smiles. Stars. In the dream I was sure that huge deals, of which I just had to be a part, were being hatched around the table. This must be the way it works: a Friday evening dinner in a fancy restaurant among people for whom money is no object. I have to cut down on the drinking, I remind myself, my dreams are getting weirder by the day.

"Yes, thank you," I hear myself say, and smile at the waitress who refills my glass. I awaken from the dream, after going with it, and give my head a vigorous shake, trying to remember whom I met in that restaurant. Noise with an American accent assaults me from the left. Turning my head, I see Jeff Goldblum, the tall hunk from *The Fly*, sitting right next to me. He speaks softly and moves his head with measured motions.

"You must try Yarden's pinot noir," someone tells me, swirling the wine in his glass like a pro.

"What? Sure, pinot noir, sure." I try the pinot noir and remember that I'm here as a judge. Actually as part of a jury, which is a little less distinguished, but I've always wanted to be on a jury and face the court at the conclusion of the deliberations, declaring, "Not guilty."

A judge is a judge, it's a prestige thing, even if it's a judge at the Jerusalem International Film Festival. Indeed, here I am, sitting next to the Fly in a fancy restaurant. And not just next to him. Around two hours ago, I sat next to Debra Winger in a screening at the Cinematheque. And not by chance—deliberately. I'm a judge, just like her. Half an hour before the film I joined her for a beer in a café. Well, okay, I drank beer, she drank soda water, and we weren't exactly alone. All right, she doesn't know my name, either. Okay, it's possible she doesn't know what I look like, because she never turned toward me even though we were together for something like three hours without a break. Still, I'm on the jury, just like her, and I'm pretty sure that with nineteen movies in eight days she'll end up sitting next to me and will cast a glance my way for sure. This is only the second day of the festival.

"How's the pinot noir?" the voice next to me asks, still swirling the wine.

"Excellent," I reply, and nod my head. This is only the beginning—it looks as though I'll be at more cocktail parties and meals during the week of the festival than ever before in my life. I love doing the *dawin* thing, posturing, posing as the rich guy whenever I get the chance. I can strike up a conversation about Yarden Winery's 2002 pinot noir without understanding the least thing about it. I was made for a false life. I have a shirt and trousers that are just the thing for events like this. They're old, yes, but still cut it. Though now that I think of it, it's not becoming for Debra and Jeff—I think I can use their first names; after all we're colleagues—to see me in the same clothes every day. Maybe I'll buy something new.

So far I've used my social-events clothes twice at the festival: today and yesterday evening, at the opening. But yesterday I sat far from the VIPs; I didn't go down to the front rows, even though I had a reserved seat there. But I wasn't sure and I didn't want to get into a quarrel with the guards and have to swear to them that I'm a judge and that they should let me through. I sat with the simple folk, far back. It actually worked out for the best, because my colleagues didn't see what I was wearing.

"Yes," I say to the waitress, "I think I'll have the bass," my tone intimating that the bass and I are old friends.

The opening was nice. Two cabinet ministers, a deputy mayor, and others delivered impassioned speeches. They talked about the importance of culture, especially in Jerusalem. My friends Jeff and Debra also went onstage. Jeff spoke in Hebrew, read "shalom" from notepaper, and didn't forget to wish for the speedy release of Gilad Shalit, whose name he also read from notepaper. The audience applauded.

A bunch of white balloons were released and were carried eastward by the wind. Then came a display of fireworks, inflicting a frightful warlike noise on Sultan's Pool, the outdoor venue of the festival's opening film, where a giant screen had been erected below the Old City wall.

"More pinot noir?"

"Yes, please," I say, flashing another smile at the waitress.

What am I doing here? The question resonated in my mind all the way to Beit Safafa. It's just a dream, and it's lasting the whole night. Debra was sleeping next to me. "Did you see the images from Gaza?" she asks me in Arabic, with a village accent. I raise my head from the pillow and look at the crying woman. "There was a baby there, it was on Al Jazeera."

"*Bihyat*, Debra, come on, let me dream," I implored my wife in English.

HAPPY BIRTHDAY

August 25, 2006

"Excuse me," the nurse said, holding a syringe, "whose girl is this?"

"Mine," I replied.

"Then, please, only the mother should stay with the baby. This isn't a place for children, and anyway the girl shouldn't have to see things like this."

She's right, the nurse, the girl shouldn't see things like this. I kissed the baby, who lay limp as a rag in his mother's lap, at the same time checking whether his fever had gone down. It hadn't.

"Come on, sweetie," I said, taking my daughter's hand. On the way out, she gaped at a young man who was hopping on one leg and leaning on a paramedic, who said, "Car accident." I felt her grip tighten. "Don't be afraid," I said to her, "nothing happened to him, it's for the insurance."

The waiting room at the emergency clinic is packed, mostly with families. My wife called to say that it would take time—blood and urine tests, throat swab. "You two go home, she needs to go to bed. I'll take a cab." It was 10 P.M., two hours after our daughter's bedtime. But she's not tired, she said, she can wait a little more.

I was happy to stay. The baby worried me. Since his vaccination three days earlier, his temperature hadn't been below 40 degrees Celsius (104 degrees Fahrenheit). Acamol (the local aspirin), Nurofen, cold baths—nothing had brought down his temperature by more than one degree, and then only for an hour. During the first two days we were told that it was side effects, then that it probably wasn't.

What's certain is that we can't go on like this any longer. The last two nights were one big nightmare. Nonstop crying, screaming in the cold baths, and above all, your heart breaks at the sight of a suffering infant. We were referred to the emergency clinic, which was supposed to be more convenient than the hospital ER.

"Daddy, will you cancel my birthday party?"

"Why would we do that?"

"Because my brother is in the hospital."

"No, no, we won't cancel, he's just having tests, he's not staying there."

Last year we canceled her birthday party at the last minute because the baby was hospitalized. He's a champ, my baby, touch wood, he has an impressive hospital record. I can't think of anything that hasn't messed up in him. What was it last August? Ah, yes, the circumcision. Four days in the hospital because of bleeding from being circumcised. What can I do, that's how he is. My friends say he's an extreme child, that he got it from me. If a side effect of vaccination is a temperature of 38 (100.4) for 48 hours, he'll do 40 for 96 hours.

Leaving the waiting room, my daughter and I went outside. We watched ambulances coming and going. In the quiet between the ambulances I could hear my son screaming, feel his head about to explode. I know that wailing, that bellowing. I called my wife to find out what happened.

"They took a blood sample," she reported. "Didn't you go home?"

"No, I'll wait. I want to know what's happening. Call me as soon as the results come in, okay?"

I wanted to move away from there, from the noise of the crying. "There's a kind of mall here," I said to my daughter. "Want to go?" She nodded her head yes and we walked to The Center. I haven't been here for a million years, maybe not since high school. There used to be a movie theater, I recall.

Most of the people in The Center were ultra-Orthodox Jews, or Haredim as they're known. In fact, other than the vendors in the booths for sweets, ice cream, and skewers of meat, there were only Haredim. Happy little kids and pregnant women. "I want those snakes," my daughter said, pointing to a booth packed with boxes of sweets. Taking a bag, she put in a few gummy snakes and some butterflies.

Not a pleasant place—tremendous noise and ominously dense crowds. Still, I needed cigarettes. I asked for two packs, even though I hoped that the night would turn out to be shorter than it was shaping up to be. As I was paying I noticed a row of small bottles of liquor, like on planes. "Can I have one bottle?" I said to the vendor. "Actually, make it two." I stuffed them into my pockets and we left. My daughter chewed on a snake on the way back to the clinic, and said that if she does have a birthday party she wants to bring snakes like these to the kindergarten.

"Hello?" I said, answering the phone and feeling my pulse accelerate.

"The blood test is normal," my wife said, "we're waiting for the urine."

My daughter and I sat on the steps of the blood bank, she with her bag of sweets, me with the whiskey. "Yo, Daddy, what's that?"

"Whiskey."

"Why is the bottle small? Is it for kids?"

The whiskey helped. Too bad I didn't buy a threesome. I felt somewhat calmer. It'll be all right, I told myself, probably something viral, like they said, nothing serious. That's how it is with infants: sick all the time, a high fever is nothing; 40 for them is like 38 for an adult. I repeated to myself the reassurances I'd heard on the subject.

"Daddy, I'm tired," my daughter said, rubbing her eyes with her hands.

"If you want, I'll show you something interesting. Come on," I said. I took her to the car—she was thrilled with the idea of a seat that folds back and becomes a bed. I opened the windows and sat beside her. She asked for music, too, and in no time was asleep.

"Well?" I said on the phone.

"Nothing, he's not giving urine. And he won't, either, because he didn't drink anything. I'm tired, I can't go on."

"Do you want to switch? You and the girl go home. I'll stay here with him."

"Fine, I'll be right out."

A few minutes later, my wife emerged with the baby. "Well, did he pee?" I asked.

"No, the doctor said it doesn't look serious and that we can come back tomorrow for the other tests."

"Good," I said, even though I wanted to be done with it, the sooner the better.

"I don't feel well," my wife said. "My head hurts and I feel something in my throat."

"Probably just tired."

"I think I'll call the children we invited for tomorrow. I can't go through with it."

"What? She'll go nuts."

"There's no choice, we'll put off the birthday party until September."

"All right," I said, and picked up my daughter from the front seat. She woke up for a second in a fright, her body shaking. "Shh . . . It's me, sweetie, it's me."

HOLIDAY IN TEL AVIV

September 8, 2006

"Everyone up," I surprised the family at 6 A.M. "We're going on a holiday." It was a last-minute thing. Hunched over the computer, I'd looked for a vacant room. I'd tried a few close-to-home hotels here around Jerusalem. No luck. So I tried Tel Aviv and found a room in the Sheraton. A first holiday in Tel Aviv, could be nice.

"Where?" my wife asked.

"Tel Aviv. The Sheraton."

"Have you lost your mind? Who goes to Tel Aviv for a holiday? A quarter of an hour from Tira. We might as well go to your parents."

"I've already reserved. What's the matter with you? Sheraton, beach, boardwalk. We've never been there."

My wife was persuaded mostly because she would rather do anything than stay home. Even Tel Aviv. On top of which, I'd promised my daughter a summer vacation but we hadn't gone. So we'll take her to a hotel in Tel Aviv, she'll swim a little in the pool, a little in the sea, and no one will be able to sue us for breaking a verbal agreement. How does my daughter know anything about Tel Aviv? But the fact is that as soon as I told her about the trip a smile spread across her face and she went immediately to pack her bathing suit. "Right on. Tel Aviv. Right on."

I hardly know Tel Aviv—it's a well-known Jerusalem syndrome. I have a friend who, whenever he goes to Tel Aviv, puts a sign on the back windshield: "Excuse me, I'm from Jerusalem." Thanks to the sign, he says, even the traffic cops forgive him when he drives in the public-transportation lane or makes an illegal U-turn. True Jerusalemites already get lost on the Ayalon Freeway into the city, like me. But before leaving I checked out all the map sites on the web carefully. Get off the freeway at Rokach, turn left, and basically just keep going until you see the hotel.

"Here it is," I said, "this is the hotel."

"Hey, you know what, we've been here before," my wife said.

"What are you talking about? When?"

"What's the matter with you? This is where I had my hair done for the wedding—you don't remember?"

The truth is that I didn't really remember. It was a long time ago, I was very young, and I remember that one morning I got up and was told I was married. I remember being very surprised. I'm still surprised.

"I can't believe you don't remember," my wife said, a bit hurt. "The day before the wedding we rented a dress and I got a hairdo in the Sheraton as a gift, right?"

"Sure, sure, of course I remember. Okay, you take the kids and I'll find a parking place, all right?"

Gradually the images began to return. I'd gone home the day before the wedding. I remember it was the middle of winter and I had no trouble finding a hall, because Arabs hardly ever get married in winter. Even the proprietor was surprised. We settled on the next day. At home, my father gave me NIS 5,000—around $1,250—because I didn't have a shekel to my name. For a suit and a dress, he said. Someone in the family took us to a store in Tel Aviv, where we rented the cheapest dress they had and I bought an ugly black suit. I remember that from Dad's 5,000 we had about 50 left and used it to buy socks. Because we really needed them.

On the day of the wedding, I remember that only my friend Yonatan came to Tira first thing in the morning. Ah, yes, and also that we drove to Tel Aviv with the bride. After that, darkness. I

remember nothing. I was young, and in those days I didn't stop at
alcohol.

Finally, here I am, a parking place, where that ugly round
thing is that you drive under on Hayarkon, next to the gas station.

In the lobby the children were happy, my wife a bit less. I
picked up a kid and went to reception. "Hello, I reserved a room,
name of Kashua."

"Kashuach, I don't see anything."

"Kashua, with an ayin. I made the reservation around two
hours ago."

"Okay, maybe it hasn't updated here. Just a minute. How was
that again?"

"Kashua, with an ayin at the end."

"No," the polite receptionist said. "I don't see anything. Who
did you talk to?"

"The reservations center, the number on the Internet."

"Okay, one moment, sir. Sayed?"

"Exactly."

"All right, they wrote Yehoshua. I'll correct it immediately, sir."

My children are wild about hotels, mainly because unlike the
house, hotels have cable TV and the children's channel. As far as
they're concerned, stick them in front of the TV on a soft mattress
for hours and they'll be happy. It was too hot to go to the beach, so
we stuck them in front of the TV and went out on the balcony, me
to smoke and my wife to settle accounts.

"So, this is how you trick us? Bring us to a hotel in Tel Aviv
so you can play the family man?"

"What are you talking about? I'm sorry I didn't have time
during the summer vacation. You know how overloaded I am."

"How many meetings do you have today in Tel Aviv?"

"What are you talking about? I'm here for a bit of a holiday
with the kids before school starts."

"Tell me, how many meetings did you schedule?"

"All right, two, that's all, only two. What of it? You have the pool, the sea, restaurants."

"I can't go on like this."

"What do you mean, 'like this'?"

"Alone."

"But what can I do? Am I working for myself? You know it's for an apartment. You think I enjoy this work? That I don't want to be home with you and the kids all the time?"

"But you stress us all like this."

"What can I do?"

"Do you remember our wedding?"

"Of course, yes. We came here, no? To the hairdresser."

"Yes, but that's not what I mean."

"What, then?"

"Nothing. Forget it."

"Well, *bihyat*, fine. I know we didn't do it the way others do, that it was fast, but so what? You know how all those people who plan weddings years ahead disgust me. So what?"

"No, no. That doesn't really bother me, either."

"What, then?"

"I don't know if you remember, but I remember very well that in the week we got married you sent an article to the paper."

"Oh, really? Sounds strange."

"That's how it was. You said the same thing then."

"What did I say?"

"'I'm not doing it for me. It's for us. We have to buy a home.' Remember?"

"I don't remember."

I didn't remember.

I STAND ACCUSED

September 15, 2006

"Hello."

"Yes, Dad, what's up?"

"Tell me, do you read the reactions against you?"

"Sometimes. Why, what happened?"

"People are canceling their subscription because of you, that's what they're writing. Be careful, in the end they'll shut down the paper."

"No, it's not because of me. It's Gideon Levy, the guy who writes about the West Bank, he's the wild man."

"No, it's you, too. I read about it all the time in the comments."

I find it hard to believe that anyone would actually cancel a subscription because of something someone wrote in the paper. First of all, from my experience with other companies, like satellite TV, Internet, and cell phones, it's very hard to cancel a subscription. Angry and determined, you call customer service and start off aggressively: "Hello, shalom, I want to cancel my subscription now. This minute." Usually they say, "One moment, sir," and then another person comes on the line and you say, "I want to cancel my subscription," and she passes you on, until they're sure you're determined to cancel.

At that point they transfer you to the person in charge of cancellations—it's almost always a woman who speaks in dulcet tones, is well educated, has a master's in psychology at least, but is also a hussy. She'll absorb your anger, channel it to the right places; she will understand you, sir, and will empathize with your rage at the company you subscribe to. She will also engage you in a pleasant conversation, at the end of which, somehow, at least in my case, instead of canceling I upgrade and choose a new package that locks me in for three more years.

So I hope *Haaretz* has an expert in subscription cancellations. In fact, from what I read, the paper should have an automated attendant that can transfer an irate caller to at least ten cancellation experts. "If you want to cancel because of an editorial, press 1. If you want to cancel because of Amira Hass's columns about the occupation, press 2. If it's because of the Arab, press 3. For Gideon Levy you can cancel automatically by hanging up."

But seriously, please don't cancel your subscription because of me. I'm crazy about you, I love you, and I'm so sorry. I apologize from the bottom of my heart. I've lived in fear since rumors reached me that angry people are canceling subscriptions. Even if it's just two, it's *Haaretz* subscribers—how many are there, anyway? Please stay, you don't have to read the stuff, do what I do, jump straight to the All in the Family column. Please.

I admit that I made a mistake. I should never have yielded to temptation and written about that accursed war. But I want to make it clear here, once and for all, even if I pay for it dearly: I was forced to write what I did. It's not really my opinion, but I was threatened with murder if I didn't write that. Well, I'm not afraid anymore, and if it comes down to subscription cancellations I am ready to risk my life on the altar of free expression.

Yes, that's how I am, I swear to you, you can even ask my wife. I was totally in favor of the war, by which I mean in favor of Israel in the war against the axis of evil. *Bihyat Allah*, in God's name, ask my wife, she caught me a few times shouting in a dream, "Flatten! Pulverize!" And I, who thought I was living in a democracy and could express my opinion of the war, walked around the village speaking publicly about my feelings and my desire to see Beirut destroyed as long as one person feels threatened in this country.

By the way, I'm also in favor of mashing Gaza. The fact is, did anyone see that I wrote something about that? Nothing. Why, what's changed? They kill left and right there. But I didn't write that I'm against, because I wasn't threatened with murder over Gaza. Only over Lebanon.

Here's what happened: One day, after I gave a talk in the village about Hezbollah's crimes and ended by expressing a wish to see Nasrallah's head skewered on a pole in Rabin Square—I swear to you, this is what happened—suddenly in the middle of the night, which was an especially dark one, there was pounding on the door. *Boom, boom, boom.* My wife woke up in a fright and the children started to cry. "Who is it?" I shouted from behind the door.

"Arabs! Open up! The house is surrounded. Open up or we'll break in." As soon as I turned the key a bunch of genuine Arabs pounced on me—I could tell they were Arabs because of their smell. The children and my wife screamed in panic. Two bearded guys jumped on me and two other bearded guys started kicking me hard all over, in the face, in the ribs. And the children and my wife were standing there, scared out of their wits, watching the whole thing. "Are you in favor of Israel in the war?" someone asked, and punched me.

"Yes, I am in favor of Israel, yes," I shouted, and burst into the national anthem. The punches and kicks didn't deter me, I insisted on my viewpoint and didn't yield. The only reason I gave in was that they seized my children and threatened them with weapons. I said, fine, we'll do as you want, just leave us alone. They brought me two pre-written columns—one about pilots, the other about tank crews—made me read them aloud, and demanded that I publish them verbatim, unchanged, in the next two weeks.

I faxed the columns to the paper on the spot, in the middle of the night, as they were. The copy editors corrected mistakes of "b" instead of "p." I didn't touch the material. My plan was to call the paper in the morning and explain. But the Arabs, may their names be expunged, weren't as dumb as I thought, the snakes. They took one of the children as a hostage and said they would release the child in two weeks, only after making sure that their virulent propaganda was published.

By the way, and this is the time to point this out, the editors of course refused to publish the columns, because they conflict with the paper's views and policy. It took a secret meeting, in which the higher-ups were made to understand that a child's life was in danger, before they agreed to publish the columns. Thank God, the child was released by the kidnappers and told us he'd been held in a room filled with children of *Haaretz* employees. Some of them—for security reasons I won't make their names public—have been held in captivity since the start of the first intifada.

In the meantime, at the urging of the security authorities, I've moved to a settlement and have a bodyguard. But it's clear to me that my life is in danger. We're talking about bloodthirsty fanatics who are certainly lurking in a corner and waiting for the right moment to pounce. But contrary to the recommendations of the security officials, I decided to publish the true story here, for you readers, well aware that I am risking my life. I can take anything, only not someone canceling a subscription because of me.

UNSEAMLY

October 13, 2006

Thursday went like a dream. In the afternoon I turned in material that was due for submission, and the boss spared me no words of praise. You know, all it takes to make me happy is a little pat on the shoulder. But it was more than that: I had this good, all's-right-with-the-world feeling the whole evening. I smiled at the children and tried to cajole my wife into going out with me, but she didn't want to. "Go by yourself, but don't come back late," she said, and really meant it about my going out. She seemed to revel in my happiness.

Everything flowed. I sang in the shower. The mirror smiled at me, too: the three-day-old stubble looked quite becoming, and I decided not to shave. The deodorant didn't burn my underarms. My favorite shirt and pants were clean and ironed and gave off a freshly laundered scent. It doesn't happen a lot, but when I inhaled deeply my lungs seemed to be free of mucus and my stomach wasn't bloated.

I started to believe that beauty really is a matter of inner feeling, that it's "what you project." Otherwise, what's the scientific explanation for the fact that I saw a world-class hunk opposite me in the mirror? All the folds fell into place, suddenly they only added charm, all the bulges I always hated somehow coalesced into an almost perfect whole—even the gel worked wonders for my hair.

"Well, well, well," my wife said as I emerged from the bedroom, fully dressed. "A bridegroom. Come back fast, I'll be waiting for you."

A delightful kiss on the cheek, then I tossed the car keys into the air and set out to conquer the nation's capital.

The car surprised me by starting on the first try. Nick Drake whined a depressive song, but I couldn't handle that, so I ejected the CD and turned on Army Radio's music station. It was playing "London Bridge," a rhythmic number, at the request of some unit in the north, a new song by a noisy girl that I was hearing for the first time, but it suited me and I sang along, all but dancing in the seat.

At the first traffic light I looked straight ahead, smiling, knowing that the gorgeous girl whose BMW was in the lane next to mine couldn't take her eyes off me—that was my feeling. I didn't return her gaze.

At the next light we stopped together again, and I knew she'd done it on purpose, so she could run her eyes over me again. And because I'm not only a hunk but also a sensitive guy, I allowed her, in my honor, to look to her right and nod her head at some building contractor who was talking on a cell. It didn't spoil my sense of victory. "Sex Machine" on the radio restored my confidence, and the perfect parking job, two meters from the bar on Ben Sira Street, showed that my star was still in the ascendant.

It was still early, and I grabbed the best spot at the bar to observe the room. Terrific music was playing in the background, the beer glided down my throat, smooth and cool, and a cigarette only heightened the pleasure. I moved gently to the rhythm of the music—calculated shoulder motions of someone who is hip to the beat, but without overdoing it. Quickly the place started to fill up. I'd arrived at the perfect time, everyone stopped to look at me. Two women, friends, sat down next to me, intentionally of course. I looked straight ahead. "Excuse me," I said to the barman, "another one, please. Thanks."

"I hope I'm not disturbing you," I heard the woman on my right say, and I turned toward her. What eyes, *ya'allah*, I felt a bit flustered.

"No," I replied, trying to keep my cool.

"Is it you?" she asked.

I knew she'd recognized me; I extended a hand and introduced myself.

"Yo, I don't believe it. I pictured you totally differently. No, I'm surprised. Favorably, I mean. I thought you were a lot more . . . different. My girlfriend said it was you, but I didn't believe her. Yo, what am I prattling on about? I'm Netta, I just adore reading you."

"Thank you so much," I said, and sipped my beer.

I tell you, it's all a matter of inner feeling, there's no such thing as exterior beauty. Fact. Within less than a minute we toasted each other and talked about Jerusalem, about her studies (final year in med school, wants to specialize in gynecology). She said I was incredibly modest, she never thought I was so young. And she's way on the left, too, even though she grew up in a right-wing home, she has an Arab girlfriend at the university, it's really hard to be an Arab woman here. "We need more people who think like me, so Arab women will feel liberated." I went along by playing the avowed feminist, what's it to me.

She accidentally knocked her lighter off the bar, and when I, a true gentleman, bent down to pick it up, I felt it happen. For sure, I tore my pants, I felt the seam in the back rip apart. My face turned red. I only hoped she hadn't heard the tearing sound. I sat back up—don't think she noticed. Glancing around, I didn't see any amused faces. I reminded myself that not everyone was looking at me all the time, as I imagined.

"Is something the matter?" she asked, as I tried to regain control of my trembling body.

"No, nothing," I said, and lit her cigarette.

"I feel like something strong," she said, and ordered a Scotch.

"Not for me," I said, and asked for another beer. I have to stay in control.

The country is really crap, she said, and added that she knows why I'm sad, it's because of the children in Gaza who have nothing to eat. I nodded my head.

"What a pretty song, I really feel like dancing. Are you game?"

"No," I said, forcing a smile. "I get embarrassed."

I watched her dance, surrounded by a group of guys. She signaled for me to join her, but I shook my head no. With subtle movements I tried to feel the back of my pants without anyone noticing. I couldn't find the tear. I hoped it wasn't obvious; still, I sat at an angle that hid the area as much as possible. It's only midnight, and my bladder is starting to get angry. No more drinking tonight, that's for sure.

Netta came back perspiring, ordered another drink, and gulped it down. "Hey, you don't feel like dancing?"

"No, excuse me."

"What, do I bug you?"

"Absolutely not, not in the least. I'm a little bit . . ."

"Maybe we can go out for some air, it's hot in here."

"Uh, I'm afraid to leave my seat, you know how it is here."

She sat down. "Yo, I feel really dumb. Sorry I came on to you like that. You probably get that all the time."

Okay, no one ever came on to me before, but I just nodded my head, then ate my heart out when she paid and left. For three hours I sat nailed to the bar stool, cursing the pants and the day I bought them. I tried to avoid unnecessary movements, otherwise my bladder would have been done for. Three hours without ordering anything, just waiting for everyone to scram so I could get up and go to the washroom. One table was left, a nitwit couple who were making out. The barman had already folded the chairs and was about to lock the cash register. "Want anything else? I'm closing down."

Beat it, you little shits, so I can finally piss. As though anyone cares that my pants are torn. As though anyone can even see anything in the dark. But I can't bring myself to get up. I'll hold it in a bit longer. The barman disappeared and finally the last couple left. I rushed to the washroom. "Don't come in, I'm cleaning," the barman shouted.

I ran to my car but it wouldn't start. There is a problem with the 4 on the keypad. You have to wait three minutes before the next attempt. I cursed, looked left and right in the alley, got out of the car, and, with my face to the wall, unshackled my body.

"Disgusting," I heard someone say, and like an idiot I automatically turned my head.

"Yo," I heard a woman's voice from a large group. "It's that Arab journalist—what's his name?"

"Kashua."

HAPPY HOLIDAY

October 27, 2006

Holiday eve. A puppy's whines resonate through the house. From the living room window I can see the animal on the neighbors' roof, a rope tied around its neck, standing on the cement parapet and crying.

The cell phone rings once and then stops. The screen says, "Dad." Probably checking to see if I'm awake.

"Yes, I'm up."

"All right, I'm coming."

At the last minute, my parents and two of my brothers changed their plans; instead of going to Sinai on the second day of the holiday, they've decided to leave before dawn. "You'll make the holiday rounds with your brother," my father requested before we started to transfer the presents from his car to mine. "Look after Grandma, all right? Are you sure you don't want to go to Sinai? Too bad, the kids would have a great time."

Again Tira, again midnight, holiday eve, hard to sleep. I'm no longer sure whether the cause is the sleeplessness that's been attacking me lately, the oppressive no-exit feeling I get every time I come home, or the fireworks, which are still going off noisily. Tomorrow's a holiday. It will begin officially after the dawn prayers, and until then one doesn't even wish people a happy holiday, unlike in Judaism, where the eve of the holiday is the main thing. It's Eid al-Fitr, one of two Eids we have, and the children have no other way to celebrate than by buying firecrackers and letting them off in the streets all night.

I don't blame any culture, education, or interior ministry for this. Not anymore. I don't think anything can help now. I know I'm a defeatist, a feeling that's intensifying within me over time, but I also know that it's not the same pessimism that's always gripped me. I feel we've crossed a red line and I no longer see how it's possible to salvage anything here. Oy, Tira, what have we come to—hard times, oy, oy, oy.

Holiday morning. The children wake me quite early. The dog on the neighbors' roof is still wailing; my daughter is already in her holiday dress.

"What do you say, Daddy?"

"Very pretty. Happy holiday."

"Mommy, make me two braids."

"Happy holiday," I greet my wife. "My parents left at night, I'm going to check up on Grandma."

Grandma is irritable. She's an irritable person and has not been pleased by almost everything my parents have done since they got married.

"Happy holiday," I bellow into her ear, so she can hear me. Her sight is pretty much gone as well.

"Did you see what your mother did? Took him to a hotel for the holiday. Who goes for a vacation on the holiday? Just throwing their money away. And what for? Left me here alone. Soon guests will come and there's nothing in the house."

"They organized everything, it's all ready for the guests," I shout, and start to arrange her room in case guests come. Fruits, cookies, coffee in a Thermos—my mother prepared everything before she left. "I'll buy chocolates, too," I shout, "something good so you'll be pleased." I went to the grocery store below the house and was back in two minutes.

"Who is it?"

"Me, Grandma."

"Did you see, they went on the first day of the holiday and left me alone, just to throw away money, for no good reason. They didn't prepare a thing, your brother bought everything."

"It's me, Grandma, it's me."

"Ah, I thought you were your brother."

This will be the first time that one of my brothers and I do the round of holiday visits. Usually we start earlier, but my brother was out late in some mall in a nearby city and isn't up yet. At 9:30 I decide the time has come to wake him, because I want to get home before dark. "I'll be ready in half an hour," he promises from his sleep.

I count sixteen presents in the car. Sixteen houses that we need to visit, one after the other. The holiday rounds. I run through my mind the unchanging map of visits we've made twice a year ever since I can remember. We will follow the exact same order as always, starting in the east and finishing in the west of the village—city—I always forget that this is a city.

"You should have seen what went on here last night," my brother says immediately after our holiday greeting. "Thousands of people in the streets, a huge traffic jam, I've never seen anything like it. Incredible. The streets were full until one A.M."

"Okay, you'll follow me?"

I know in advance what awaits us in every home we'll visit. The stories are the same stories, very little changes over a year. I even know what will be laid out on the tables in each of my relatives' houses, and in what order. I know who will serve cake and who will offer ice cream. I'm familiar with the taste of the cookies in each house, know where there are cashews in the bowl of nuts and seeds, and know the percentage of cashews in each house. "Did you manage to get any sleep?" I mumble to myself as we enter the first house.

"Did you manage to get any sleep?" my cousin asks me as we shake hands. "Tires screeching and firecrackers going off until four in the morning. What is it with this place? How can people live like this?" The truth is that I don't know how people can live like this.

"What's the story with those masked guys?" my cousin continues. "Dozens of guys in masks wandering through the streets, what is that?"

"Yeah, I saw them," my brother says.

It really is depressing, the holiday here, it really gets me down hearing about people firing live ammunition from cars, just for the fun of it, and I freak out when I hear about three people who were shot dead in the middle of the street on the eve of the holiday in nearby Jaljulya. What will become of us? The weight on my chest is ferociously heavy and won't let up.

"All right," I say after a quarter of an hour of stories and tales from last night, "we have to get going. Have a happy holiday."

Everyone gets up after me, and for an instant I feel that I am playing the role of the father of the family, the one who makes the decisions. "Just a minute," the same cousin says, and gives my daughter a bill from his wallet. "*Eidiyah*," it's called, money for children, holiday allowance. My daughter takes the money, says thank you, and stuffs the bill into her holiday purse. She gives me a happy smile that takes me back thirty years in a flash, and I see immediately that everything is fine here. Nothing has changed.

INSTEAD OF A STORY

November 17, 2006

I have a hankering to write something smart, for a change. Maybe a short story with a dark atmosphere and a vague ending. Something that will leave an impression. The readers will be gaping in astonishment when they finish, the smokers will light up a cigarette and grab their heads, the others will consider starting this minute. A serious writer has to be drunk for a story like that, but I don't have anything in the house. I looked already—nothing. I looked in the freezer, in the cupboards, under the sink. Nothing. I've been clean for quite a while.

It's pretty late now, otherwise I'd rev up the car and go to get something. But at this hour I'll have to go to the center of town to find a store that's open.

"Hello?" I'm calling a neighbor.

"Yes, what's happening? Is everything good?"

"Yeah, fine. What, did I wake you?"

"No, no."

I know I did, but I don't really care. "Tell me, do you by any chance have anything to drink?"

"Now?"

"No, I'll just take it home. I've got writer's block and I need something for a serious story, a long story. Do you have anything?"

"I'll check, I don't know."

"Check. I'm coming over."

He had remnants of Finlandia at room temperature. I have nothing to mix it with. We don't even have ice in the freezer. My wife is sleeping, otherwise I'd blame her. It's not enough vodka for a serious story. Sorry, you'll have to settle for a mediocre story, same as me.

Readers, I have a lot to tell you, and I'll start with the good things. Last week, I discovered, happily, and contrary to my fears in the past few years, that I have not yet lost the ability to cry. And I'm not talking here about teary eyes or crying from drunkenness; I'm talking genuine weeping, serious sobbing, rivers of tears like only children can produce. I was watching the Arab news channels, I saw bodies of small children, and I cried. I didn't get angry, I didn't get upset, I just cried for hours on end. At some point I switched the channel and watched the tenth rerun of some Egyptian comedy, but the tears flowed unbidden.

Only the sound of the steps of my family returning home got me up from the sofa. I rushed to the bathroom, washed my face, and ran with a towel to open the door when the bell rang. My daughter was first in, but instead of the usual leap and kiss, she threw her schoolbag on the floor and threw herself on the sofa morosely.

"What happened, sweetie?"

"I don't want to go to school."

My wife came in with the baby on her shoulder, stuff running out of his nose down to the rim of the pacifier. Without thinking twice I wiped it with the towel on my shoulder. He started to scream.

"What did you do?"

"Nothing. What?"

"Why are you wiping his face with a towel that your parents stole twenty years ago from the Dan Panorama Hotel?"

"Excuse me, at least my parents went to hotels, not like yours."

The boy cried. I held out my arms to him, but that only made him tighten his grip on his mother and turn his back on me. God only knows what she bribes him with. "What happened to you?"

I asked, swinging my head in the direction of my daughter, whose face was buried in the sofa.

"She doesn't want to go to school," my wife said in English. Now that the girl is fluent in Hebrew, too, we speak English when we don't want her to understand. The only trouble is that we both speak really crappy English, and the little we know doesn't help us understand each other, as I'm from south Tira and my wife is from north Tira, two different worlds.

"Why, what happened?" I asked, still in English, trying to use a north Tira accent so my wife would understand.

"She thinks she's dumb," my wife replied in the language our daughter didn't understand. "She says they handed out different workbooks to the advanced pupils in the class."

"What, what, what?!" I shouted in a southern accent that brought out my loutish side. "Why, who is more *mitkadem*, more advanced, than my daughter?"

"I don't know, that's what she says. I don't know whether it's serious or just a show."

"What do you mean, 'a show'?"

"I don't know, it doesn't make sense. We're sending her to an open, non–achievement-oriented school. There's not supposed to be competition among the children."

"Did she say who the advanced kids are?"

"Yes."

"Jews or Arabs?"

"According to what she said, they're all Jews."

"Fuck, I knew it," I shouted in English. "How do you say *konspiratzia* in English?"

"Conspiration," my wife replied. She's from academe, after all.

"Exactly. Conspi-screw-them, I tell you."

"What are you talking about?"

"I read about it, it's called the ignorance policy. It must have been Azmi Bishara or Emile Touma, I can't remember now. They tell you 'open education' so the kids won't learn. But it's only the Arabs who don't learn in the end. It's preplanned, all the way back from Basel."

"Fine, fine, but tell me, why are your eyes so red and swollen?"

"No, it's nothing, must be from the computer. I wrote all day, don't ask."

(The truth is that the continuation of the story was very sad and prompted my wife and me to decide on drastic changes in our lives. We were both the best students in school, she in northern Tira, I in the south. However, we only met in Jerusalem and swore already then, twelve years ago, that we would not let our children experience a childhood like ours. Believe it or not, there are things I still can't reveal. So in the meantime I'm concluding the story with an ending that's fictional. Partly.)

My heart broke to hear my daughter say, after she picked herself up from the sofa, that she thinks she's dumb and there are children in the class who are better than she is. I gave her a big hug and explained to her that the important thing is that she should be herself, that she mustn't look at others, and that we prefer her just as she is, and that even if she's dumb we won't kick her out until she's eighteen, unless she finds a groom when she's fifteen. She smiled and I kissed her and explained to her in a gentle, warm tone of voice that if it's true I could only blame the genes she got from her mother. My daughter kissed me back, asked, "What are genes?" and said that in the car Mommy said the same thing about me.

STAGE FRIGHT

January 19, 2007

A black grand piano stands on a low stage; parents take their places in the hall. The teacher walks onstage, program in hand, welcomes the guests, hopes that they will enjoy the music, and emcees the event.

"The first to play will be the youngest girl," the teacher says. I give my daughter a pat on the head and her mother gives her a kiss. I start the small video camera just before the teacher calls her name and invites her onstage. My daughter walks slowly, head bent to her chest and her gaze on the ground. She ascends the stage and sits down in the wrong posture, and through the camera I see the tremor that shoots down her back.

In the morning, my daughter had called from the school office, crying, and asked me to come and take her home. When I picked her up she cried and said that the other kids had made fun of her. I'm not sure that was accurate—children seem to know that parents are sensitive when it comes to "They made fun of me in school."

Sometimes it seems as though all parents are certain that their children are victims of abuse by other children. Somehow it seems that all parents are certain that they themselves were victims of abuse in school, and they will not allow this to happen to their kids. Even though children can also be the cruelest group imaginable, especially the cutest of them.

"Well, then, shall we go home?"

"Don't know. Maybe some other place?" the child asks.

My daughter smiles and rushes to the empty swings before anyone gets there ahead of her. Like me, she too is surprised to discover that Gilo Park can be so empty that there is no need to wait in line even for the coveted swings. There were two families in the park on Sunday morning. A group of English-speaking children, some of them blond and the others appearing to be of Indian or Pakistani origin, were playing together, while their parents sat on the stone base that surrounds one of the playgrounds. I sat on a wooden bench at a safe distance and glanced at the two cars in the parking lot. Both had white license plates.

I always envied them, the owners of the cars with the white plates who can be seen around Jerusalem. I always wanted to be one of them. We call them UN, even though UN are generally foreign correspondents with leased cars and yellow plates. UN is effectively a term for every foreigner who is ready to pay three times the going rental rate for an apartment.

I look at the UN-niks and their children. Foreign kids always seem to be more polite, even though they are precisely pummeling one another. Now that I think of it, if I had managed to restrain myself until the age of twenty-five before getting married, I would have had a reasonable chance of catching some UN-nik woman from a respectable French paper. Everything would look different then. It always seems to me that my life would look completely different if I didn't have to take care of the rent.

My daughter looks at the English-speaking children, who look back at her. She gets off the swing and runs over to me. "Daddy, what are they saying?" she asks angrily.

"Nothing. They're playing. They didn't say anything."

"Are you sure they weren't talking about me?"

"No, they weren't talking about you."

My daughter goes back to her swing. The mothers call their children and they all move to a different playground. I see that my daughter is bending her head down and has given up pumping her legs, which she does when she wants the swing to take her as high as it can. She is sitting there and waiting for the momentum to die.

"They just wanted to play on different things," I tell her, and with my hand remove the hair that has fallen across her face.

She pushes my hand away and pulls the hair forward again. "I want to go," she says, and walks ahead of me to the car.

We have about an hour before the doctor's appointment. There's no point going home now. I'll drive around a bit and then we'll go to the clinic. "I want you to know that you can hardly see anything anymore," I tell the child, who is sitting quietly in the backseat. I look in the mirror and see that my words have not persuaded her. "You'll see, by evening nothing will be left," I say without thinking too much, and immediately realize that I made a big mistake—I should not have mentioned the word "evening," which probably made her even more uptight. The best thing is for me to shut up now. I put on a CD I know she likes and drive around aimlessly.

Two elderly, elegantly attired women are sitting on the chairs opposite us in the clinic. They wear lovely, glittering earrings, and bracelets rub together on the wrist of one of them.

"Too bad for his wife," one of them says.

"Yes, truly, *haram* on her, a good woman, truly *haram*."

"It's at three, right?"

"Yes, but I can't go, it's already hard for me, you know. I will go to her later."

"No. You have to go because of poor Fanny. I want you to know that she came with me to the funeral and twice to the shivah."

"Yes, she really is a pure soul."

"What does she have, chicken pox?" the lady with the bracelets asks as she screws up her eyes and gazes at my daughter. "It's not so terrible, sweetie, a week or ten days and it's over."

"It's not chicken pox," the doctor says after ascertaining that, apart from the face, there are no spots or sores on the rest of the body. "Did you change soaps?" the doctor asks, and the child shakes her head. "Cream? A new pillow? New sheets? Because it's an allergy to something—you don't remember what you put on your face, sweetie?"

"No," the child replies.

"Fine," the doctor says. "I'll prescribe her drops against allergy. It makes you a bit drowsy, so if you see that she's sleepy, it's because of the medicine."

"She has an event this evening," I say.

"Then it's best to give it to her before she goes to sleep," the doctor replies.

"Daddy," the child whispers to me. "Ask her if I can put on makeup in the evening."

"Not a good idea, because it might make things worse," the doctor says, and addresses my daughter: "You don't need makeup; you are very beautiful as you are."

Now she fell asleep, which is excellent, because she has to be fresh for this evening, the first concert she is taking part in. For more than a month she has been waiting for this day, only to wake up in the morning and discover that her face is covered with red sores.

"She went to her room to sleep an hour ago," I told my wife when she got home from work.

"Very good," she said. "We'll give her another half hour and then wake her up. The babysitter will soon be here."

We were both ready for the concert when we woke her. The babysitter was playing with my son in the living room, and he laughed loudly, before he cried. My daughter immediately ran to the closet and took out the dress she had been keeping for this evening. Pink stockings, red dress, a necklace with a small butterfly. "Mommy, make me braids," she asked, and then ran to the mirror and bristled at the result.

DO YOU LOVE ME?

March 2, 2007

"Can you come here for a minute?" I call my wife over to the study.

"What do you want from me? I need to clean the house," she says with characteristic patience.

"I have nothing to write about so I'm interviewing you this week. So don't talk about cleaning because it could make me look like a chauvinist."

"Why are you interviewing me?"

"I don't have anything else."

"Okay, ask whatever you want."

"What do you want to talk about?"

"Nothing. Ask your questions if you have any."

"Do you love me?"

"Yes."

"Liar."

"This is not a professional interview."

"You don't have anything important to say to the newspaper?"

"You ask, I'll answer. What do you want from my life?"

"How are things at work?"

"I hate work, it's awful."

"They're going to read this."

"What, you think they don't know? I like the patients. But I hate the system."

"Careful, your bosses will see this."

"I don't care. We work like crazy and don't get anything in return. No financial reward and no possibility of advancement. It's like running in place."

"For our readers' sake, name your place of work."

"I can't. Generally speaking, I'm a social worker."

"Congratulations, you have a new welfare minister. What do you think of your new minister?"

"I don't know, I've seen his picture. What's his name—Bougie? The one who was in tourism, no?"

"What do you think of him?"

"All I know about him is that he had a thing with Bar Refaeli."

"Do you love me?"

"Yes, I answered you already."

"Why?"

"I forgot. Now you ask, after twelve years?"

"Then you don't want to get divorced?"

"No."

"Why not?"

"No complaints."

"Really?"

"I don't know. Right now it's not marriage that's bothering me, I'm not thinking about you. What bothers me is work. Work and school."

"What about school?"

"I want to continue studying. But will I ever have time to continue?"

"What do you want to study?"

"I don't know whether to continue with social work or try something new."

"Like what?"

"A profession with a normal salary and better conditions."

"Like what?"

"Automotive mechanics or insurance appraisal."

"*Wallah*, a mechanic—then I could interview you as the first female Arab auto mechanic."

"Yeah, you could take a picture of me with grease on my hands under the car."

"But why does the financial compensation concern you so much?"

"Why? You ask why? Because on the first of every month you start yelling right after you've called the bank."

"Just because of my yelling?"

"For one thing. If I end up living on my own one day, how will I support myself, not to mention the children?"

"Wait a second—so you do want to divorce?"

"No, but if you die, let's say."

"Tfu, tfu, tfu . . . What's the matter with you?"

"Okay, you don't die. You stopped writing, they figured out that you had no talent, you fell apart, you had a breakdown, you tried to kill yourself and were left with brain damage. What will become of me?"

"There's insurance, isn't there?"

"How much can that be? And you haven't bought any private insurance. How much do you think the National Insurance Institute is going to give me?"

"All right, all right. Let's leave work and school aside for now. What do you say about the political situation?"

"What, the country? It's a mess."

"Be more specific."

"I don't have any special insights, but generally speaking, it's bad to be an Arab."

"And to be a Jew?"

"Doesn't seem so great, either."

"Would you marry a Jew?"

"No."

"That's racism."

"It's not racism, it's because the country is corrupt."

"What does a corrupt country have to do with marrying a Jew?"

"The same reason that I don't want our daughter to marry a Jew."

"You don't? And I actually thought . . ."

"For what? We don't have enough troubles? Why cause yourself more troubles from the start, things are tough enough."

"What about love?"

"A person has to make a choice before he gets to the stage of love. From a young age he should know that it's not an option."

"You think our daughter knows that she mustn't fall in love with a Jew?"

"Yes."

"Where are you getting this from?"

"She doesn't play with them in school. You want her to marry them?"

"Who said she doesn't play with them?"

"She did."

"Why?"

"She said that the Jewish kids don't let her play with them."

"That's not true."

"That's what she says. That she approached a few girls from the Jewish group and they wouldn't let her participate in their game."

"That'll change in adolescence."

"Then we'll talk to her."

"What will you tell her?"

"That she mustn't marry a Jew or a Christian."

"Christians are out, too?"

"Obviously."

"Why?"

"Again, because it's hard enough anyway, so why ask for trouble? Why create problems? What does she know from Christians?"

"What about love?"

"I follow the head, not the heart."

"Is that what you did when you married me?"

"It was a winning combination, head and heart."

"Liar."

"Don't write 'liar.'"

"Why?"

"Why? Who are you to write that I'm a liar? I have to pay the price just because you can't come up with anything for your column?"

"What do you think about the column?"

"Don't leave it, don't give it up. I love your column."

"Really?"

"Sure. You write rubbish, you work one hour a week, and you get double what a social worker who works her ass off gets for a whole month."

"That's why you love me?"

"No. I could have found someone who makes a lot more."

NOUVEAU RICHE

April 13, 2007

"Aiiiiiii!" A piercing scream reverberated through the house and woke me in a fright.

"It's Mom," my daughter said. "She's in the bathroom."

"What happened?" I shouted, rushing in a panic to the bathroom and trying to open the locked door. I attempted to batter it in with my shoulder, like in the movies, but the door stayed put. "What happened, are you all right?" I shouted, and tried the shoulder thing again.

"No," she said. "I'm not all right. Do we go abroad once a year?!" she yelled from behind the door.

"What's with you? What are you talking about?"

My wife emerged, her face flushed with anger, holding a newspaper. "This is what I'm talking about," she said, thrusting the paper into my face. "About this," she repeated, pointing to a headline: "Arab Screenwriter Spends NIS 300,000 a Year."

"Oh yes, that," I said, scratching the back of my neck. "That's why you're screaming? You gave me a real scare."

That morning the paper had an article listing the weekly expenses for certain Israeli personalities, to which I had been asked to contribute. The editors told me I would get a bit of money for it, so I agreed. Afterward they called and asked about other family expenses, and one of the things I told them was that my wife and I take a trip abroad every year at a cost of 2,000 euros.

"In addition," the paper wrote, "he vacations with his wife four to five times a year at a cost of NIS 3,000 each time." The truth is that the article made me smile a little. And don't think it's not true—I really did tell the paper those things. The publication is quite reliable. I was the liar.

"Four to five vacations?!" my wife protested. "On holidays you take us to Tira and call that a three-thousand-shekel vacation?" Then she laughed: "The only reason we go there at all is to save money. Food, drink—everything is at your parents' expense."

The article made me—unlike my wife—happy. Until then, I was afraid that I would end up as the poorest one in the survey. Somehow I inflated my spending in order to occupy a place in the middle. It never crossed my mind that in the end I would lead the list, with NIS 300,000 a year. Not only did I lead, I won by a knockout. Just so you'll get the picture, the person in second place spends NIS 169,000 a year.

"All right," I said. "So I blew things up a little. What's wrong with that? What's better, for people to think we're poor or for them to know we're rolling in it?"

"If you ask me," she replied, "it's nobody's business how much we spend, and especially how much we don't spend."

"Okay, that's already a different question," I said.

My wife and I have different worldviews. What she calls private, I call the public's right to know. Maybe I overdid it a little, but so what? Exaggerations have become a way of life, particularly when it comes to people's economic situation—otherwise, how can you survive? On the days when my overdraft reaches a level that prompts the bank to call and ask when I'm going to cover it, I can sit with friends in the evening and feed them stories for hours about how I'm trying to make up my mind about which new car to buy. It's always between the latest Volkswagen Passat—"people say it's terrific"—and the BMW 3 Series: "because you can't go wrong with that." In the months when my bank account is balanced I indulge myself by calling up real estate agents to ask about five-room apartments in Jerusalem—"but only in Old Katamon and Baka."

I don't know if there's a connection, but I've just remembered a childhood story, or maybe more accurately a secret, that Grandma once told me. In those days right after the war, after her husband was killed, leaving her with a stack of orphans, there was nothing left to eat in the house, she said. She, who would never ask anyone for help, left the kids with her eldest daughter and went out at dawn to work in the fields for pennies, not returning until dusk. But, she said, no one knew what she and the children were going through: she never allowed anyone to pity them. She would fill the cushions with shreds of newspaper and plastic bags, and when the neighborhood women came to call on a Friday they heard rustling sounds when they sat down on them. "Oh," Grandma would say apologetically, "I hid a bundle of money in there. It's a good thing you came or I would have forgotten about it."

MY INVESTMENT ADVICE

April 27, 2007

For two days now I have been sitting at the computer without a word coming out. My head is bursting from nerves and the kids are keeping their distance from me, because I have the look of a madman in my eyes. And why? Because of a crappy column that appears after articles about steaks and barbecuing tips for Independence Day. Does it really make any difference to anyone what I will scribble there? Why can't I take it lightly, try to enjoy it? Because that's how I am. I wasn't made for pleasures: I always miss them. "It seems to come to you easily, naturally"—that drives me up the wall every time I hear it. "How long does it take you, an hour?"

Well, in fact, no, sometimes it seems like an eternity, sometimes it reaches a point where I hear comments at home like "Make up your mind—either me or the column."

Nothing happened this week. I have the feeling that not only is nothing happening in my life, but nothing is happening in this village I'm stuck in. Which is good: it's considered an achievement to find a boring village where there's no news. You pay an extra NIS 200 a month for that. Because what good news can come out of an Arab village, anyway?

For a few hours now, the neighbors have been cleaning their new car. Their little boy is sitting in the driver's seat blowing the horn. I have to get out of here, I have to find a place where things happen, a place where all you have to do is look out the window or step outside and straightaway you encounter an interesting face that will be grist for the writing mill. A place where you can sit, have a cup of coffee, read the paper, and watch the passersby.

I live in a desert. In the past two days I have visited every possible place in the village—the barber, the butcher, the greengrocer—and nothing happened, they were sparing with their words. Everyone seems to be at least as engrossed in how to escape as I am.

No good writer can emerge in a place like this. How could he? I need a true city, not a toy village near a city that looks more like some dreary settler outpost than a city. And just to pour salt in the wound, I spent the whole week wandering around Istanbul with Orhan Pamuk. What makes Istanbul holy, as opposed to Jerusalem, is the fact that it has whorehouses and nightclubs. How can anyone write in a city that doesn't have a tavern?

"I wouldn't live in Switzerland," idiots will say arrogantly. "It's boring there. Nothing happens—not like here, where there's something new every day." What's new already? Even the war has looked the same for the past hundred years. But never mind the war, if there were whores in the holy city.

You know what? That's what Zionism is for me: to think that the country is interesting, that Jerusalem is beautiful, and that Tel Aviv is lively. True, in Tel Aviv there are at least whores, but whores of a type you can't write a word about, because you can't exchange a word with them unless you studied dentistry at the expense of the Communist Party twenty years ago.

Ah, the phone is ringing at last. At least something's happening here.

"Allo."

"Hello, have I reached the writer and journalist?"

"No."

"Isn't this the phone number of Sayed Kashua?"

"It is."

"Can I speak to him, please?"

"Speaking."

"Oh, it's you?"

"Yes."

"Hello, I wanted to ask if we could interview you for a special program we're doing for Independence Day."

"Sure. When?"

"If you have a few minutes, I'll be happy to ask you a few preparatory questions."

"I have all the time in the world."

"So, to begin with, I really wanted to ask you how Independence Day makes you feel, as an Arab and a citizen of the country."

"Shit."

"Could you, um, maybe elaborate a bit?"

"Yeah, sure. Independence Day makes me, as an Arab and as a citizen, feel like shit."

"I understand, but could you, let's say, explain why? Is it because you don't have a sense of belonging? Because of the discrimination? Can you . . ."

"It has nothing to do with belonging. What does belonging have to do with it? I feel bad here in general, without any connection."

"And Independence Day, I imagine, adds to the feeling of depression that you feel as a citizen of the country."

"That's right."

"Can you be more specific?"

"Yeah, sure. On Independence Day I feel bad and depressed, and on top of it the kids are out of school."

"I don't understand."

"I am saying that they bother me on Independence Day, I have to be with them the whole day."

"And what do you actually tell your children on Independence Day? What do you say to them on a day like this?"

"I tell them to hightail it into the living room. Sometimes I swear at them."

"Ah. Another question we're asking all the participants in the special: If you were prime minister, what would you change in the country?"

"I would invest in whores."

"Excuse me?"

"Yes, that's what I would do, without a doubt, invest in whores."

A ROOM OF MY OWN

May 11, 2007

This week I found a room. Last year I rented a small one for work, but then it was for a month. I went there only four days a week for two hours each time at best. But now it's an entirely different story.

I can no longer write at home. As of this week my room has officially become a child's room. Everyone is pleased: the children, who don't have to be together anymore; my wife, who complained all last year about how crowded it was getting—"Why are you buying the child a ball, where exactly will I put it? So what if it's only a tennis ball?"—but mainly me.

I've always felt that a room in the right place, with the right view, is what separates me from the great work I've always wanted to write—something else, something unforgettable, that thing for which everything I've done until now has been only a rehearsal, that thing that's hard for me to define, but whose smell I can recognize.

I now have a room in the center of town, between the *shuk* and the pedestrian mall. I feel like someone from my father's stories about Naguib Mahfouz, whom my father saw sitting in the same café in old Cairo, at the same time each day, at the same table, with a glass of tea, observing real life. So here I am in an old building that could be beautiful, and under my very nose real life is going on. Soon I'll be able to observe it. All that's left is to paint and to change the lock, and then all my life will be before me.

I had a feeling that the painter wanted too much. After all, it's only a medium-sized room that has to be painted white, not including the ceiling and woodwork. So NIS 1,000 sounded like too much, especially because of those cardboard signs on every traffic light in Jerusalem: "Paint your house for NIS 1,400." But I didn't start looking for another one because finding a painter who was available was exhausting. They were all busy, and they sent me from one to another; only the fifth one I tried could begin work the following day.

"Are you crazy?" said my father on the phone when I consulted with him. "NIS 1,000 for what? How much does five liters of paint cost, NIS 100? Why not do it yourself?"

"I don't know," I replied. "He also promised to change the lock."

"What's wrong with you? It's the easiest thing in the world. Don't tell me you can't change a lock!"

It's unbelievable how easy it is to find a store with tools and paint in the middle of town. I was walking down the street, thinking, "Where will I find paint?," when I came upon a hardware store with a nice salesman who provided me with paint and a roller. Noticing my inexperience, he also told me about mixing, squeezing, and dealing with corners, and told me how simple it is to change a lock. The whole business cost about NIS 200.

"Oh," he said, before wrapping it all up, "do you have masking tape?"

"No. What's that?"

Okay. First, he says, every lock has three screws. I took a screw, stuck it in the middle hole of the new lock, and prepared to tighten it. Then I saw the door has holes for only two screws. Lucky the store is close.

"You must have an old one," said the salesman. "You have to change the whole thing. Easy as pie. First remove the small nail that holds the doorknob."

I could see the small nail that holds the doorknob, but three cuts out of about ten on my hands were bleeding. All my fingers hurt; I couldn't hold the screwdriver; its shape was etched in burning red on my palms. The small nail, the one holding the doorknob, didn't budge.

"Dad?" I phoned.

"*Nu*, did you finish painting?"

"Almost," I replied.

"I told you, it's nothing."

"Tell me, Dad, is there a trick to removing the nail from the doorknob?"

I don't know why, but my father got very angry and didn't answer. He then shouted over the phone: "Tell me, did you drive to your office?"

"Yes, why?"

"Because I suggest that your wife drive you to work. Why? If you can't pull out a nail from the doorknob, then I'm not sure you can remember where you live." Before hanging up, I heard him shouting: "How did I get such a child? Am I sure he's mine?"

I lit a cigarette and leaned against the window in my new room. It was afternoon and ten meters below me lots of people were rushing around; from above I had the impression that they really didn't have anywhere to rush to.

THE NEXT BIG THING

July 6, 2007

For two hours I've been sitting in front of the screen and deleting the same sentence: "I don't have anything to write." Occasionally the emptiness feels unpleasant, so I type out songs from the radio, then select and delete. I hate these weeks when I know beforehand that I won't have anything to write about, only I didn't insist on my request last week to go on vacation. It won't happen again next week, I promise myself, I'm going on vacation. It's not that I'll pack a bag and fly abroad, or even go to some beach. No, just a vacation from the newspaper, which means intense work on scripts. Shooting will start soon. It'll soon be over. I know I've been hearing that sentence, "It'll soon be over," for the past two years, but this time it has to happen. There's no choice.

In August they'll be shooting some extra sequences for a television series I wrote. This time it looks serious, there's already a board in the production room that's divided into slots. It lists days for rehearsals, photography, editing. All ahead of the big thing that's known as a television series. I'm working on final script revisions, trying to adjust it to the spirit of at least three different people. Sometimes I forget my own personal taste. But that's not always important, certainly not now. They'll soon be shooting; everything has to be ready. On top of which, if I really had the personal taste that I insist I do, I'd probably never have become involved in this long, exhausting adventure that began in early 2004. I don't have personal taste, or at least it's not clear to me. It's changeable. It's response dependent. I've never been able to distinguish between good and bad, especially in writing.

This is the first time I've worked with other people. Scary. Suddenly the characters have clear faces, suddenly the sentences that are written have a human voice. There's a director, there are actors, cinematographers, producers, and editors, and scariest of all—a viewing audience. I've never been so uptight, which is another regular statement with me, but I mean it every time anew. I've never been so uptight. Sometimes, in very specific moments, when I revise a sentence or imagine an actor speaking it, I brim with optimism and think it's going to be good, even excellent. Most of the time I think it's going to be horrible, that I will regret having done this for the rest of my life. That I will suffer from episode to episode, from week to week, until it's over. And then, too, for sure I'll have to abstain from life, sink into a funk for half a year at least, do tiresome inner stocktaking in the hope that afterward I'll emerge more bitter and maybe a little smarter.

Sometimes I conjure up in my imagination a result that's so gloomy that I'm not sure which will make me sadder: broadcasting the series or scrapping it. The most insulting thing that can happen is to compromise, after all a lot of money went into producing this thing, after all it's considered an Arab slot, so it'll be broadcast without any consideration for quality, somewhere amid the niche programs, which are just that: programs not intended for viewing. It scares me to be a filler in a half-hour slot on Friday or on Saturday afternoon.

I really have no way of knowing; all I can do is wait and see. They'll soon be shooting—it's no longer in my hands. Now I'm typing a song that leaps to mind: "What did you do with it, they ask, how did you squander it all, you had a chance and now you'll have to start all over again."

Sometimes I imagine people rushing home with their bags from shopping at noon on Friday, and all at once the streets empty out. I picture families at home, cafés full of card players and narghile smokers in East Jerusalem, and other places that are air-conditioned, where decaf is served. Construction workers drop what they're doing, housewives take a break from preparing the Sabbath-eve meal, patients in wheelchairs pack a hospital lobby. Soldiers at checkpoints invite the people in line to join them for half an hour. A fixed weekly truce will be declared in Gaza. Everyone's waiting for the end of the commercial, which for the first time in the history of television costs more than a prime-time commercial in the right season. Parents shush their children and children hush their pets, and suddenly, all across the Middle East, we hear, "Shh. It's starting."

YES, I DON'T WANT TO

September 7, 2007

No one takes me seriously. Everyone thinks I'm being funny all the time. The truth is, this is not everyone's problem, it's mine. I can never say no. Lately I've been thinking that it's a genetic thing, or maybe cultural, even though I know that culture and economic status are no less genetic than Down syndrome.

I inherited, was taught, or simply developed an inability to be unequivocal with my no's. When I entered the Jewish world, meaning when I started to work for Jewish bosses, who were usually older than me, whenever there was something I was asked to do, but didn't want to, I said "*insh'Allah*," which is the politest word I can use with someone who is older, to say, "I don't want to." Jews treated *insh'Allah* as though it means yes. But it doesn't. When an Arab says, "*Insh'Allah*, I will come at five o'clock to fix the faucet in the bathroom," he is actually telling you: Forget it, I don't have time, call another plumber. That's how I found myself, owing to a mistaken use of *insh'Allah*, washing dishes in a restaurant that I happened to eat in, leaving the university, and becoming the sex slave of the owner of a steak joint who was on the far side of sixty.

"So, you're meeting me in the storeroom later on?"

"*Insh'Allah*."

Afterward, when I found out that *insh'Allah* has different meanings in other cultures, I switched to "I don't think I want to."

Still, politeness is politeness, and I really, but really, cannot say no. Certainly not to a Jew. It's a caste thing.

After the boss in the restaurant was arrested for some illicit financial activity, I started to rehabilitate my life. I reenrolled in the Bezalel Academy of Art, taking photography courses and enjoying every minute. When the time came that I needed money for paper and developing materials on a scale that I could no longer ask my parents for, I started to look for work in the profession. I went to the editor of a local paper with a portfolio and a camera slung over my shoulder, and asked if he needed freelance photographers.

"Photographers we don't need," he said, and asked, "Tell me, are you an Arab?"

"Yes." I nodded my head.

"Can you write?"

"Yes."

"We are looking for a reporter on Arab affairs, what do you say?"

"I don't think I want to," I replied.

Following this wrong use of "I don't think I want to," I found myself getting heart attacks in Gaza and Jenin, crying with hungry children, fleeing from snipers from both sides, interviewing wanted individuals and settlers, and trying to escape from helicopters. When the war stopped being sexy, I found myself interviewing models and dog barbers, writing about television, cars, nightlife, restaurants, pimps, and whores.

A good few years passed until I adopted the rejection statement "That's not for me." I rehabilitated my life, wrote books, saved up money, and got a girlfriend.

"Do you want to get married?"

"That's not for me."

"Is there a big hall in the village?"

"That's not for me."

"A thousand guests?"

"That's not for me."

"Honeymoon in Antalya?"

"No, that's really not for me."

"A child?"

"That's not for me."

"Another one?"

"That's not for me."

"What about a third?"

"No. I don't want to. Do you hear? I don't want to."

"Fine, fine. Since when have you become so unequivocal?"

"That's it. I don't want to."

With the powerful put-down assertion "I don't want to," I wrought miracles. I worked only in jobs that I wanted to have. I wrote only what I wanted. So simple. How had I survived without the words "I don't want to"? I wrote a screenplay and a television series that I wanted to write, and then I started to get a lot of calls from producers and big agents. A real success story. Until recently, when people who don't take no for an answer started to approach me.

Already in the first meeting with the first producer who offered me a job writing a telenovela, I whipped out the put-down response that had saved me in recent years: "I don't want to." With producers and agents, it turns out the word "no" is not an option. It's like in *The Godfather*—you can't say no to a serious producer. At most you can hit him with an *insh'Allah* and pray he will leave you alone.

Five producers to whom I said "I don't want to" came back with "No is not an option." Suddenly my "no" is being defied. "Sure you want to, but you just don't know yet that you want to"—that's another sentence you often hear from businessmen with plenty of money.

"Ah, really? So you are saying that I do want to?"

"Sure you want to."

"*Wallah*, I don't know, because the truth is that I don't feel so comfortable, and anyway I don't have time . . ."

"Do you want fifty thousand dollars?"

"Yeah, sure, that's something I really want."

"So you see that you want to?"

"You were right."

"Okay, within a month I want a musical for a huge production starring all the children's heroes."

"Insh'Allah."

"I take it you have no trouble composing music, either?"

"Insh'Allah."

THE BICYCLE

September 12, 2007

Shabbat morning, a nice day, an opportunity to take the hike I've been postponing for years. This hike, the walking, even if it's not fast, don't even mention running, is what will repair all my body systems. It will regulate my breathing, refresh my bones, and breathe new life into muscles that would not pass the test of any standards institute.

My body has long since turned into a neighborhood trash bin. During the past two years the situation has begun to worry me. I don't know, maybe it's my age, and maybe it's because I find myself often visiting my parents in hospitals—and this though my father is considered an athlete and my mother swims several times a week. I have recently begun to see my back, my muscles, my lungs, and, of course, certainly my liver as apparently essential things. For the time being, I can't and don't want to stop drinking and smoking, because it's a shame, I tell myself, to work hard now, to suffer, to torture myself, to go into withdrawal, and then in another year, or a month or two weeks or so, a war will break out and I'll find myself without sedatives.

I wore shorts. I discovered that the closest thing I have to sports shoes are Crocs, and I stood for a long time in front of the shelf and wondered whether to take the pack of cigarettes, until in the end I decided to do so. I can get drunk just from the clear mountain air. I parted from my family as though I were about to embark on a pilgrimage by camel all the way through the desert to Mecca, and I was on my way.

I walked very slowly. After ten minutes I already regretted the whole idea. Not because I was tired, not at all, more because of the thought: What am I really doing? Is this what will save me from cardiac arrest? A relaxed walk on a pleasant Shabbat morning?

But I have to start somewhere, and signing up for a health club is the most terrible mistake I could make, I know I'll never go there. Moreover, all those in the know say that you give up after the first month, and they all recommend: "Start by walking in the neighborhood, then you'll see if you're serious."

I'm not serious, never have been, but I won't give up now. At least when I walk under the heading "Save your heart from an approaching heart attack," I have a good enough reason not to be at home, and to enjoy quiet and freedom from the children for an hour. All right, maybe half an hour.

Believe it or not, slowly but surely I discovered the wonders of walking. In fact, I completely forgot that I was on a journey, and I sank into pleasant hallucinations and thoughts that at that moment seemed brilliant to me. Wonderful ideas that I felt were coming from my heart and would probably not have been able to ascend to my brain without sufficient healthful oxygen. I became immersed in a magical world, I saw feelings, and while I was walking I already managed to translate them into words.

And when I looked at the watch I've never worn I discovered that an hour had passed since I left the house. I took a moment to look around and found myself on Bethlehem Road, on the more southerly part of the street, in Baka, lovely houses—even their dark history did not disturb the serenity. Passersby and just plain religious people wearing gleaming white Shabbat clothes were walking around, mothers and happy children. Only when I stopped dreaming did I realize how tired I was, and I could feel my heart coughing. I was hot and perspiring in a way that you never perspire in Jerusalem.

A wooden bench on a shady street was the suitable solution for the turmoil of my body. A pleasant breeze cooled the perspiration and caressed my skin. Very tired, I tried to regulate my breathing and realized that I would need an hour of rest before I could retrace my steps. I was almost envious of a smiling boy who approached the bench on his new bicycle, although I'm not sure that riding in Jerusalem would be easier than walking. The boy looked at the road and stopped suddenly. At first he tried to smile, and only then did I notice that a policeman was getting out of a van and approaching the bicycle.

"Whose bicycle is that?" asked the policeman in Hebrew. The boy, who had a frightened look mixed with his smile, didn't know what to answer. "*Bicyclet?*" said the policeman, trying out his Arabic. "Whose?"

"Mine," answered the boy in Arabic, "my *bicyclet*."

The policeman waved the boy away, grabbed the bicycle, and started to examine it from all sides. "Where did you take the bicycle from?"

"The bicycle is mine," replied the boy in Arabic.

"Why are you lying?"

I almost got up from the bench; my heart was beating harder than during the walk. For a moment I remembered that I had gone out without an ID card, without anything, only with walking clothes, and I sat back down.

"Where are you from?" asked the policeman, and then again in Arabic. "What are you doing here?"

The boy was silent and looked around. Other children from Baka stood and watched the show, like me. Some came closer, one boy smiled and licked an ice cream while the policeman checked the number on the bicycle.

"Where did you take the bicycle from?" said the policeman, repeating his question.

The boy answered in Arabic, which only I understood completely: "My father bought it for me. I had a birthday."

"Abui, abui?" replied the policeman, and some of the children found that funny.

"If you want to call him, I know his number," tried the boy, but the policeman didn't understand.

"Does anyone here know Arabic?" asked the policeman, looking in my direction.

"No." I shook my head, got up from the bench, and ran as I've never run before, all the way home.

VOX POPULI

September 28, 2007

"Hello?"

"Hi. May I speak with Mr. Sayed Kashua?"

"Speaking."

"My name is Bassam, I am from Nazareth and currently live in Jerusalem. I hope I'm not disturbing you."

"No, not at all."

"First of all, I wanted to tell you that I love your writing. I follow your articles and usually am very pleased with them."

"Thank you very much. Thank you."

"You used to write longer stories, right?"

"Right."

"So what happened? You stopped?"

"Nothing happened. No reason."

"I want to ask you something, if I may."

"Go ahead."

"The papers prevent you from writing about politics, don't they?"

"Not at all. No."

"No? Because let me tell you, I and a few of my friends who are also acquainted with your writing are surprised that you have stopped writing your political views. Is it because of censorship?"

"No. There is no censorship."

"Then what happened?"

"About what?"

"You mean to tell me that they give you total freedom to write whatever you want?"

"Totally."

"And this is what you choose to write?"

"Yes. Why? Is something wrong?"

"No. Not at all. I was just sure that your writing was censored."

"Why?"

"Because all you write about is how you got drunk, about your wife, and all sorts of other nonsense."

"I don't get it."

"Well, don't get me wrong, sometimes it's funny, but I thought they were not allowing you to write about Arabs and about the war."

"No, it has nothing to do with my writing. I can write whatever I want."

"And this is what you want?"

"Umm . . ."

"Well, it's a bit surprising. To tell you the truth, I am surprised."

"What about?"

"Finally there's a platform for an Arab in an Israeli paper and this is what he writes?"

"No, umm . . ."

"Don't we have other problems right now, other than your hangovers and your conversations with your wife?"

"You're right."

"You have to make better use of the platform you were given."

"Right."

"Good-bye."

"I only wanted to tell you that you're right and thank you for calling."

Ya'allah. He is absolutely right, this man. My body is trembling with shame. I feel my face burning red with embarrassment. What an idiot I am! Truly. Starting this week I'm changing everything. That's it. A new era. I don't care anymore. From now on I'm giving it to everyone. That includes the government, the settlers, all of them! I need to write about Olmert and Rice. I'll show them this week. Okay, first I need a drink, so I can calm down. I must concentrate. So I can give it to them for what they did this week. My God, what on earth did they do this week?

The hell with it! For once I've not been reading the papers, I've not been watching the news, and the only websites I surf are related to culture and cars. No, this man is right. I'm disconnected. Enough! From now on, I'm on it. Hang on, wait a second, okay? Sorry, I just called my father. I wanted to ask him if anything of interest happened this week, but he didn't answer.

Never mind. What can I write about?

I've got an idea. I'll dial *42.

"Hello?"

"Hello, Bassam?"

"Speaking."

"This is Sayed. We talked just now."

"Hi there."

"I wanted to tell you once again that you're absolutely right and that from this day on things will be different."

"I'm glad that I could be of some assistance."

"No, really. Thank you. I just wanted to ask: For this week's column, what do you think I should write about? I mean, what can serve our purpose as a national minority?"

"Well, a lot of things. First we have this business with the Syrians and the North Koreans."

"What about them? Can I write about that?"

"Clearly, it's an example of political persecution. Not only of the Syrians, but of the entire Arab public. Please write that Israel and America allow themselves to be the world's policemen."

"Okay." I wrote that down. "What else?"

"There's this thing about the poverty and hunger in besieged Gaza. And of course there's always the ongoing assassinations that nobody even talks about anymore. And there's also Olmert's so-called easement of the Palestinian situation, although in practice he hasn't removed even one roadblock. Write that it's all part of a disgusting media manipulation."

"Okay."

"What else? Let's see . . ."

"I think I have enough for one week. Tell me, Bassam, may I call you again next week?"

"Sure. Be my guest."

"Okay. Thank you very much. Thank you."

PART II

FOREIGN
PASSPORTS

2008–2010

FOREIGN PASSPORTS

May 22, 2009

The older I get, the more of an Arab I become. I don't know whether it's because of the new belly, or maybe the cheap haircuts in the eastern city, but I do know that my national identity is more blatant than ever. Lately I can hardly get past a security guard without showing an ID card.

Well aware of the new profile I've developed as a usual suspect, I took great pains to prepare for my encounter with Ben-Gurion Airport. I went to a Jewish barber for twice the price. I washed the car inside and out, and almost hung an aromatic freshener in the shape of a Star of David from the mirror. I put on the polo shirt I'd asked my wife to buy me as a birthday present. I slipped on my shades, uttered the prayer for a safe journey, and set out for Ben-Gurion.

I waited in the line of cars at the entry gate. The cars moved ahead one after the other, the guard barely glancing inside and gesturing to the driver to go ahead. Until my turn came. The guard held up his hand for me to stop. "Where are you arriving from?" he asked, looking straight at me. I knew that if I said Jerusalem the story wouldn't end well. I've never been able to pronounce the city's name in Hebrew without making mistakes. Jerusalem is the nightmare of every posturing Arab. In addition to the "r," there is also a "u" and too many consonants. I thought of saying I was arriving from Tel Aviv, but that would be a risk, because if it didn't work and I was asked to show an ID card, I would be both an Arab and a liar, and that could morph from a check to an interrogation, if not an actual arrest.

"Jerusalem," I muttered in a low voice.

"ID, please," the security guard said, looked long and hard at my details, and, still holding the ID, signaled me to pull into the bay on the right, shut off the engine, and wait for someone to come over to me. Ten minutes later, a security man came over and, after a check, wished me "a pleasant flight." The situation must be serious, I thought as I drove to long-term parking. Generally I get through that checkpoint easily. And I even arrived in a Citroën, which I'd bought especially for the checkpoints. God in heaven, who ever saw an Arab driving a Citroën?

The shuttle bus dropped me off at the entrance to the terminal, along with the other long-term parkers. Another guard was standing at the entrance. Pulling my suitcase, I walked with the others, reminding myself not to look at the guard like I always do. A kind of glance of expectation to be arrested. I lowered my head and tried to be natural. But naturally, I looked suspicious to the guard. "Sir," he called to me, and I smiled like an idiot when he signaled me to go to the Arab detectors.

I came out clean, was released, and entered the terminal, anticipating a day packed with security guards. If I hadn't managed to get by the two guard posts where they work with their eyes, God knows what awaits me inside when I'll be asked to show my passport.

"What's the origin of the name?" the guard asked as he flipped through my passport in the line ahead of the airline counters.

"Arab," I replied.

He marked circles on white stickers and asked the usual questions. "Did anyone give you anything to take with you?" I answered no to everything, even though I always have the suspicion that maybe my wife stuck something into my bag in order to settle some score with me. "Suitcase to the baggage X-ray machine," the security man ordered. I complied gladly. Everyone goes through X-ray, irrespective of creed, race, or gender. X-raying is the beautiful side of democracy.

But not everyone goes through without a hitch. When my small suitcase arrived on the other side of the machine, another security guard stuck another sticker on it and instructed me to proceed to the security-check counter opposite. What could she have seen on her computer screen? I wondered. All I'd packed for this short, two-day trip was a shirt, two pairs of underpants, and socks. I don't take a computer to the airport. An Arab with a computer is nothing less than an agent of Hezbollah.

The security woman at the counter asked me to open the suspicious bag. I complied proudly. I have underwear and socks that are designated exclusively for the airport. Hugo Boss and Calvin Klein. To impress the guards. An Arab, yes, but an Arab with class. I came out clean. The security woman said I could close the bag, which I did, and then she took out a kind of orange plastic handcuff and locked it on to the handle of the bag, like a bracelet.

My body temperature shot up. I felt dizzy and had difficulty breathing. I looked around at the other counters and didn't see anyone with a bracelet like mine. I knew people were looking at me, I knew I was marked. A feeling of being cruelly insulted seized me whenever someone passed by and looked at the orange bracelet, driving daggers into my heart. I'd been to the airport dozens of times before, and this was the first time I'd encountered a flagrant bracelet like this. Trying to choke back tears, I continued on the Via Dolorosa to the plane.

"Go to counter fourteen," the security woman before the entry to the duty-free area told me. Only people with bracelets were there. A security man took my passport and boarding pass, waved them, and asked, "Who wants them?" I came out clean, put on my shoes, put the belt back on my pants, and went on to passports. A security woman with a boy and a girl who were holding notebooks and looked like schoolkids asked to see my passport. "B-3," she said, and the girl with the notebook exclaimed, "Wow, I thought it was G-2 for sure."

Released, I stood, head bowed, in the passport-control line. "Sir," the policewoman behind the glass snarled at me, and handed me back my passport, unstamped, "this is not for Israelis!" With a scolding finger she pointed to the illuminated sign above her stand. I looked up and discovered that I was in the line for foreign passports.

SAYED'S THEATER

February 1, 2008

It was as though I'd always lived here, in New York City, even though this was the first time I'd dared to fly to America. I arrived in the big city late at night. Everything looked so familiar. A Pakistani taxi driver took me from JFK Airport to midtown Manhattan. White steam rose from manhole covers in the streets, homeless people huddled by subway vents to get warm, young African Americans drove SUVs with music blaring, and a drowsy Latino hotel clerk directed me to a modest room on the fifth floor.

I was afraid of the hotel and I was afraid of New York City. If what I'd learned from the movies was right, I knew that any minute a gang of thugs armed with baseball bats and pistols would break into my room, make off with my computer and my money, and leave me bleeding on the floor, unable to call 911. I finally managed to fall asleep in the menacing hotel after remembering that Spider-Man lived nearby. I saw him hanging from threads, darting through the city's skies, and flitting through the window to save me from the cruel marauders.

My anxieties faded when I went down for breakfast to a small storeroom called the "dining room." I discovered that pretty much all the guests looked more or less like me: tourists looking for somewhere cheap to stay who were impressed by promising photos on the Internet and found themselves in a place out of a Hitchcock movie. I took an American coffee and went outside for a smoke. I'd

prepared myself for nippy weather but hadn't imagined how cold
New York could be. A cloudless sky and an ear-freezing cold that
burned the lungs with every drag on the cigarette. I wound my
scarf tightly around my neck and buttoned up my jacket. No way
the cold was going to stop me from finishing my morning smoke.

Just like in America, women strode by quickly, a Starbucks
coffee in one hand and a newspaper in the other. Nearly all the
Americans were carrying a Starbucks cup. On the opposite sidewalk
was a fire hydrant of a kind I thought existed only in Spike Lee
movies. Even the fire escapes, which descend from one landing to
another, zigzagging from right to left and left to right, are real, an
inseparable part of the local cityscape.

I didn't stay long in New York City, just one day. Actually, I
flew in from San Francisco solely in order to make the trip back to
Israel with someone I knew, a woman who had come for a family
wedding. I wasn't up to flying that distance on my own. So a one-
day wait in New York—what could be bad? I crushed my cigarette
underfoot, touched my frozen ears to make sure they hadn't fallen
off, and stuck out a thumb for a taxi. Within a second a yellow cab
with an ad on the roof pulled over. From my notebook I read out the
address of my first meeting, on the Upper West Side. Seventy-Ninth
Street and Amsterdam Avenue, I told the driver with an American
accent I noticed I had adopted and hoped did not sound out of place.

I arrived five minutes early. Because of the no-smoking laws
championed by the world's tobacco-manufacturing superpower, I
decided, despite the cold, to suck on another Marlboro from the
duty-free before entering the café. I had a feeling the guy wouldn't
show up. Why should he? Who am I that he should want to meet
me? But it was too important for me not to try to be at the right
place at the right time and verify firsthand that he didn't show, even
though I knew it was a waste of time. The gloveless hand holding
the cigarette became a solid lump, making the work of getting the
cigarette into my mouth torture that made me want to kick the

habit now. I'd managed only two drags when I saw him, taller than I had imagined, looking like the photos I was familiar with, the most recent of which was probably twenty years old.

Philip Roth entered the coffee shop and I hurried in after him.

"Mr. Roth?" I said behind his back as he was taking off his heavy coat in the entrance.

"Sayed?" he asked.

I nodded. We shook hands.

"Nice to see you," he said, and invited me to sit at a window table.

Great—what now? Here I am, sitting in a Manhattan café-restaurant with a French name, across from Philip Roth, whom I so much admire. What are my chances of not screwing up? And what, exactly, does screwing up mean in this case? What was I expecting, anyway?

"So you're enjoying New York?" he asked, perusing the menu. I nodded silently.

"First time?" he asked, and I nodded again, certain that nodding was the right way to cover up shallowness and lack of literary talent.

"So, what do you want?" he asked.

I didn't know where to begin. What do I want? For him to autograph my copies of his books, to tell me everything about Portnoy, about Zuckerman, about Operation Shylock, about Mickey Sabbath's theater, about how he got started, about how it was with Saul Bellow. What do I really want? I know very well what I want. I want to know what it's like to feel like a public enemy, how a writer copes with attacks from the very people he belongs to. All I really wanted was for him to tell me how to deal with that kind of criticism, how to live with the feeling that the people who are closest to you have become your persecutors. I wanted to ask him how he'd felt when the entire Jewish American leadership attacked his work. What had he done then, and what's it like now? But how do I even begin?

I was pondering the matter with consternation when he shattered my profound soul-searching.

"So, what do you want?" he repeated, and just as I opened my mouth to ask a question of universal import he broke in: "They have very good breakfasts here. Would you like one?"

"Uh," I said, emerging from my reverie. "I want tea, I guess, tea with mint, if they have that here."

RABBIT MONSTER

March 21, 2008

Salon du Livre, Paris

Hello, my sweet daughter,

I got your letter by e-mail, but just as I started to write to you the computer crashed. So I'm writing to you through the paper; in the end, as its slogan goes, *Haaretz* is not what you thought.

As I promised, I will tell you all about Paris. The French have a long, tasty bread here, like the baguettes in Israel but without that sweet challah taste. They have wonderful food here that you can't get in Israel. Yesterday evening, for example, I ate snails! People here are very fussy about food. It's not like with Mommy—no one in Paris would ever say, "Like it or lump it" about food.

There are really beautiful buildings and a lot of sculptures, gardens, and amazing museums. When you visit Paris, you will understand that what they teach you in school about Jerusalem is just not true. Jerusalem is not a beautiful city or an important one.

There's a train system in Paris called the Métro, and it travels under the ground to every place in the city. I can't figure out the Métro and always get lost or take the wrong direction and find myself on the other side. But you know what's great about Paris? That the other side is terrific, too, so I hardly ever cry about making a mistake.

There was one late night when I wanted to be alone for a while. I left the restaurant where I'd been sitting with everyone and decided to walk around the city without knowing where I was. There are a lot of lights here, which is why Paris is called the "City of Light." I walked and walked and saw pleasant, smiling people who were going out, and then suddenly it started to rain hard and I wanted to get back home. It was late and the Métro wasn't running anymore. I thought that in such a big, crowded city the Métro ran all night, but I was wrong.

Taxis in Paris aren't like those in Jerusalem—at a certain time of the day you just can't find one. Well, I got lost and looked for the hotel all night, and finally, when I was tired and wet and all hope was gone, I sat down to rest on a piece of cardboard next to a huge pillar and fell asleep. When I woke up in the morning a miracle happened: next to the cardboard I found a cup of tea and four coins, which are called euros in Paris.

There are many writers here, whom I meet all the time—very important writers, some of whom you and your brother read and like. Etgar Keret, for example, who wrote *Dad Runs Away with the Circus*, and Rutu Modan, who drew the pictures for the book. Also Meir Shalev, who wrote a lot of books that you really liked. They're all here, like me, because there is a book fair. A book fair is a really huge place that has a great many books.

People in Paris love to read. In the morning, when I arrive at the fair, there are hundreds and maybe thousands of French people—men, women, children—with smiles on their lips, waiting quietly in a long line in order to enter the hall where the books are. You should see how they stand in line—you won't see anything like it in Jerusalem. No one asks, "Who's last?"

One day I was also standing in line to enter the fair, when suddenly an author who writes in Hebrew showed up and saw me. He laughed, put his hand on my shoulder, and said, "Tell me, when are you people going to learn?" He thought it was laughable, so I laughed with him. "Come, come," he said, and I followed him to the front door, bypassing all the people. He went up to the guard at the gate and spoke the magic words, "We are from Israel," and the guard immediately opened the big gate and let us enter the magic cave filled with books.

There are so many books—for children, too. Books with pictures like you don't see in our stores. People walk among the stands, read and browse, eat and drink, bands play happy music, and there are shows with delightful puppets. It's lovely in the magic cave; people are happy and glad. But, you know, everyone is afraid of one small corner in the cave. They say that according to legend a scary monster lives there. So people are afraid—they enjoy everything but keep their distance from the corner with the big monster. Some people take the legend a little more seriously and decide not to come to the book cave at all.

You know how I don't like monsters and tell you all the time that they're only in fairy tales and there's nothing to be scared of, right? So I decided to check out the story about the monster. Very slowly I approached the cave, which had "Israel" written on it in big letters, and I remembered that the magician who opened the gate for me used the same word. Even though I don't believe in fairy tales and don't believe that monsters exist, I was still a bit frightened, because even if there are no monsters, sometimes they show up in dreams.

Well, I looked into the entrance of that cave and didn't see a monster. I saw nice people smiling and talking, drinking coffee and looking at books just like in the other corners of the magic cave. My legs were shaking, but I decided to go in and talk to the monster. "Hello," I said, and immediately took a step back, but nothing happened, in fact just the opposite: the monster wasn't a monster at all but a cute little rabbit with green eyes and white hair, and it answered, "Hello to you, too."

In no time, the monster—I mean the rabbit—and I became fast friends. We had a lot of things in common. I had the feeling that this monster was more like me than all the other people I met in the cave. I could speak the monster's language and understand every word it said. Amazing how people think the wrong thing sometimes. Weird how people turn a rabbit into a monster, don't you think? So I asked the cute rabbit in its language if I could ask a small question that might be a bit personal.

"Sure," the rabbit said with a smile.

"Why do people think you're a monster?"

"Oy, oy." The rabbit sighed sorrowfully, and with tears in its eyes told me that a curse has hung over it since birth. An evil magician from a far land robbed it of one power: the power to lie. As long as the rabbit speaks the truth it's cute and sweet, but as soon as it starts to lie it becomes an ugly, frightening monster. Like in the story of Pinocchio, but in this case the magician was evil, and instead of a long nose he decided that the rabbit would become a monster.

"So what do we do?" I asked the rabbit, and rubbed its fur.

"Speak only the truth," the rabbit replied, and added, "Come, come with me."

I went with the rabbit to another lovely place, with a stage, lights, and cameras. Other people like me were there, too, not frightened. The rabbit went onstage and put on a really terrific show. Everyone applauded happily, and a man with a camera on his shoulder asked something in a magic language I didn't understand, because I understand only the language of the rabbit, and the rabbit said, "We are looking for peace." And then, suddenly, the skies clouded over and the rabbit started to change colors. Realizing what was happening, I ran as fast as I could. Others stayed, but I ran and ran, and the gates were closed, and I don't know how but I suddenly remembered the magic words and shouted, "I am from Israel." The gate opened and so I was able to save myself.

HOME AGAIN

May 30, 2008

I'm tired. What I really want is to go to bed. It's midnight now, and I'm sitting brokenhearted in Berlin. Oy, Berlin, Berlin, young and beautiful, bursting with life, white clouds smiling sadly in its skies.

One last night alone. Tomorrow morning I fly home after a two-week tour. I miss my wife, my daughter, and my son. This is the longest tour I've ever done, and the hardest, too. I don't have much to write other than words of longing. I'm sitting in a pretty ritzy hotel in the center of Berlin, and all I can think about is the moment when I will get home. I'll hug the children and apologize to my wife for an ill-considered, inconsiderate trip, cry on her shoulder that I promise never to abandon them again like this, never to leave her alone, and beg her to forgive me my wrongs.

That's it, I'm ready to swear that I will not go on a long trip to anywhere. I will not go, certainly not alone. There's no way I'll put up with suffering like this again, no matter how important the trips are to promote my work. I will not yield to temptation. I will remember the cruelty of the parting, the fire of the longing, and I will politely refuse everyone who invites me.

"How are you feeling?" was the way I started every morning, with a text message to my wife.

"Missing you" was the regular reply.

"How are the children?" I added immediately, wiping away a tear of longing.

"Waiting for Daddy," my wife answered back.

"Kiss them for me and tell them Daddy loves them."

"I love you," she wrote every day anew.

Now that I think about it, I haven't heard her utter that phrase—"I love you"—for the past ten years. I received it mainly in text messages when I was abroad. Oh, my wonderful wife, tomorrow I will be back laden with the many presents I bought as compensation for your anguish and as therapy for my guilt.

I can already imagine how I will enter the house tomorrow afternoon and we will embrace mightily. The children will enjoy their presents and she and I will sit hugging each other until the next morning. Tomorrow afternoon—come fast! My patience has run out. Although tomorrow afternoon my daughter has a hobby group, so I'll have to postpone the prolonged embrace. I hope my wife drives her and doesn't ask me to, even though I usually take her. No, she wouldn't ask something like that; I'll have just landed, she won't force that on me, she'll know I'm very tired. If she insists, I'll take my daughter—it's not so terrible, it's just an hour. Then, when I get back, we'll sit hugging each other.

She'll probably want to get the children bathed right away, because they usually go to sleep at eight. I hope she won't ask me to make supper. What, she can't do it? That's just not fair. I got up at the crack of dawn, flew four hours, took the girl to her group, and now she's asking me to scrape together a meal? Fine, it's not so terrible. How long will it take to make supper? It's just smearing on some cheese, and if I decide to pamper them I'll scramble a couple of eggs. No big deal.

She'll put the children to bed and then we'll sit hugging each other and I'll give her all the presents I bought her in New York City and Berlin. Ah, but for sure she'll ask me to unpack first, separate colors from whites and get it all ready for the washing machine. "You know why I hate your flights?" she'll certainly ask, as she customarily does when I get home from a trip, and will reply, without waiting for an answer, "Because of all the laundry you bring. Five machines it takes."

By the time I'm done organizing the clothes, she will have showered, and when she comes out she'll say I stink from the flight and that I'd better not dare get on the sheets without first scrubbing myself with bleach, because she changed them just yesterday. I will take a shower, and when I come out she'll be yawning, eyes half shut. "Those were two hard weeks," she'll say. "I have to sleep. Don't make noise, all right?"

The next morning I'll wake up into the tumult of getting ready for the day and will naturally be part of it. I will forget room service completely and make my own black-mud coffee with a teaspoon of sugar, and it won't be brought directly to the bed by a young blond German woman. I won't give her a tip and she won't give me an angelic smile and say, *"Danke schön."*

We'll barely manage to exchange a few words in the morning, because my wife will certainly want to beat the traffic getting to work. She'll ask me if I can drop off the children and I will say yes, because what chance do I have, after two weeks in the Western world, of daring to pamper myself? I know from experience that it takes me pretty much a whole month after returning home before I dare to say no.

I'll take the kids and then go to my study. There I will sit and weep over my bitter fate and torment myself over the course of my life again. I'll smoke, I'll drink tons of coffee, and I won't have written a word before it's time to pick up the kids. My wife will call from the car and ask me to pick up something to eat because there's nothing in the refrigerator. What can I do, those were two busy weeks and she had no time to shop. "You know," she'll say, "it's not easy being alone with the two of them." I will try to think where in Jerusalem they have Viennese schnitzel, and when I realize that there is no such place I will buy falafel with a few fries on the side.

She'll come home tired after an exhausting day, ask whether our daughter has homework, and then send me to quarrel with her about her daily hour of piano practice. "I don't have the strength," she will say; "the piano was your idea, not mine." In the end, the girl will play for less than half an hour and I, as is my custom, will forgive her. Then showers and supper, and before she goes to sleep I will bring her the presents in bed, smiling as I hand them to her.

"I missed you," I will say, and she'll smile, too, as she opens the first package.

"*Ya'allah*," she'll exclaim, disappointed. "Every time the same perfume?"

NEW DEAL

June 27, 2008

In exactly two hours I am due in the lawyer's office to sign the contract for the apartment. I'm scared like never before. Okay, maybe I'm exaggerating, because at the end of September 2000 I was more scared. I was scared when I got married, too, and when my daughter was born, and I was hysterical at the birth of my son and even more scared during the operations he had. So allow me to rephrase: in another two hours I'm going to sign a contract to buy an apartment and I'm pretty darn scared.

"What's to be afraid of?" my friends ask. "A mortgage is natural, what's the matter with you? Investment in real estate is the best investment in the world. Be happy." So I'm trying to be happy, but it's not working. Real estate investments never interested me. I want a home, not an investment. I don't believe in investments; I've always been too lazy. People can say what they want about real estate, I can promise them that property prices will start going down exactly two hours from now.

I'm not an expert on the economy or, heaven forbid, the global market. I don't understand the first thing about it. As far as I'm concerned, the prime rate is the number of households that are watching television in the peak hours, after deducting the percentage of Arab households. In any event, I can promise you scientifically that real estate prices will tumble, crash. A home will cost a quarter of what it does now, and the renovators will start handing out floor tiles free. It's a known fact: if I invest in something, it crashes. The lesson of a lifetime's experience. That's always been my luck. By the time I started working in television and was so thrilled at signing an agreement in dollars, the dollar rate jumped off the Empire State Building. I still remember the day I signed that contract, when I preened like a peacock and told everyone who would listen, and some who wouldn't, that from now on I was getting a salary in greenbacks.

"Mortgage," what a scary word. A twenty-five-year mortgage. Still, once I get the mortgage I'll feel more Israeli than ever. I know that people take out mortgages everywhere, but still, I grew up in a family where taking out a mortgage was considered to be on a par with being drafted into the Israeli army.

"Dad, what's a mortgage?" I asked whenever I saw an article about mortgage holders being thrown into the street, penniless.

"A mortgage, my son," the communist would answer after lengthy reflection, "is a debt because of which poor people have their home taken away."

"What, a mortgage is a Nakba, Dad?"

"Exactly, a Jews' Nakba."

Since making the decision to buy an apartment, I've been drowning in a sea of notebooks, contracts, and calculators, scribbling numbers nonstop, trying to understand the scale of the disaster, but to no avail. Time and again I call the bank, the accountant, the lawyer, the bank again, calculating it all supposedly down to the last shekel, even though I know I don't have a clue what I'm doing. But there's something comforting about writing down numbers, subtracting, adding, checking percentages. On my wife, at least, it left the impression that finally I'm becoming a serious person, at last connecting to reality and knowing what we pay for electricity, water, and municipal tax, and, above all, how much we pay our cellular-phone company.

"What?" I found myself shouting in the grocery store. "Coca-Cola costs seven shekels? For what?"

No more Coke, period.

One of the great things that's happened since the onset of the mortgage process is that I'm smoking less. Even though with all these numbers and percentages dancing before my eyes the temptation to suck on a cigarette is tremendous, almost like the desire for a cigarette after sex, I'm holding back. Two packs a day times 16 shekels each is almost 1,000 shekels a month for cigarettes. In the meantime, I'm down to one pack a day and I've stopped having sex.

"You hear, sweetie," I said to my daughter last week when I drove her back from the conservatory, "maybe we'll stop the piano lessons, what do you say?"

"Why, Dad?" she asked, surprised. After all, we've been fighting over this issue every day for the past two years, and I'm stubborn and don't let her miss home practice. Not, heaven forbid, because I wanted her to be a pianist, but because I wanted her to be one of those white people who, when they grow up, complain about how their parents made them play an instrument. What can I tell you? Everyone I've heard complaining about having a hard childhood because of music lessons grew up to become more successful than those who didn't. I didn't want her to grow up feeling different from her Ashkenazi friends. They'll complain about the violin; my daughter will complain about the piano. That's what I call equal opportunity.

"Listen," I said to her, and thought about the 1,000 shekels a month we were paying for her lessons and hobby groups. "I'll tell you why. It's hard to practice every day, so forget it."

"No, Daddy," she said, tears in her eyes. "I'll practice, Daddy. I promise. Every day, like you want."

"What do you mean, you'll practice?" I tried to keep my nerves under control. "Music is for people who aren't good in mathematics. You're good in math, right?"

"Please, Daddy, I want to keep playing."

"Piano is boring, wouldn't it be better to watch television? What's wrong with the Children's Channel?"

"But, Daddy," she replied, "you canceled the cable subscription."

"Terrific," I said, starting to get irritated by my daughter's smart-aleck replies. "I canceled the cable television subscription. Wasn't that for your good? Only for your good. I do everything for you and your brother, and all you do is complain. Fine, accuse me of canceling cable. You should know that you'll only thank me for it when you grow up. These days all the progressive people are throwing out their televisions. Did I throw ours out? No, I only canceled. What's the matter with Channel 1, state TV? What's wrong with an antenna? You know, when I was your age all we had was Jordan TV. And you know what? Things haven't changed much. Just the opposite: Jordan is better than all the channels you like. Complaints, that's all I get from you."

My daughter sobbed in the backseat. Poor kid, why is she to blame? When we get home I will calm her down, I told myself, I will apologize, but I won't backtrack about the piano. Enough—for what? On top of which, she can learn alone if she really wants to.

The car cell rang. My wife's number came up on the screen.

"Hello," she said.

"What happened?" I asked immediately.

"Nothing," she replied, "I just wanted to hear how the lesson went."

I couldn't believe it. "Couldn't you wait another minute until we get home? Didn't we say only in an emergency and even then only SMS? Tell me, am I the only one working here?" I disconnected irritably and without even noticing lit up a cigarette.

TAKING NOTICE

July 18, 2008

That's it, everything is ready. Papers, city permits, bank authorization, land registry, property insurance, life insurance, bill of sale, irrevocable power of attorney, purchase tax, city tax, electricity company, water, cooking gas, and standing orders in the bank. That's a partial list. Early Sunday morning, the previous owners received the final payment, signed off, and handed me the keys to the apartment. My excellent lawyer called it "taking possession of the property," and I was happy, I was so happy, that we could finally start working.

I have exactly two weeks in which to move. I gave my word to the landlord that I would hand over our present apartment at the beginning of August. That shouldn't be a problem: the renovation contractor I hired promised that within ten days, two weeks tops, he'll hand me the apartment looking like new. He promised to start on Sunday. "We won't waste time," he declared. "The minute I get the keys we'll start ripping out the floor, everything is ready. *Insh'Allah*, God willing."

Immediately after taking possession, I rushed to the new place with a notice for the bulletin board in the foyer. The notice is addressed to the occupants of the building, and I worked on it for a whole weekend. "We, the new occupants on the ground floor, apologize in advance for the inconvenience that the renovations are liable to cause you. We promise you that we will do all we can so the work will be concluded *ba'agala uvizman kariv, v'imru amen*—swiftly and soon, now say amen." That was the spirit of the message in one of the drafts I came up with and threw out. The notice is our entry ticket to a new world, a business card, a first impression, and I'm convinced it will seal our fate as kosher neighbors, or abruptly terminate a relationship that hasn't begun.

Should I display full fluency in Hebrew? Will that reassure the neighbors—the fact that the Arabs below are ours? Or maybe they're Circassians or Druze and not really and truly Arabs? Or will the use of highfalutin language mark us as a tribe of weirdos from the Stone Age? Maybe, after all, the style of the notice should be in a contemporary, young-Israeli spirit, to prove beyond the shadow of a doubt that we are liberals, modern, up to date, and socially acceptable. Something like: "To all the neighbors, shalom, *ahlan*, greetings. We hope you will forgive us for the renovation work, we'll do it quickie, terribly sorry, *yalla bye*." No, no. Of course not. Too clever, vulgar, inconsiderate, and not credible. As it is, we're arriving with relatively low loyalty credits, and a notice in that spirit will only add olive oil to the *mangal*, the barbecue.

And the graphics? Should I print the notice? In what font? Should "To the occupants" be in bold? Should I add the line "Re: Renovation work on the ground floor"? A printed notice will lend the text an official character. On the one hand, it will show that this is a family with a computer, a printer, and enough money for ink, which is not the case, though I could easily ask my wife to print a page at work. On the other hand, maybe a handwritten notice would be better, to give it that personal touch and maybe break the ice with the neighbors.

Is my Hebrew handwriting good enough? For hours I worked on the letters of the Hebrew alphabet, trying to remember the inanities I'd heard graphologists utter on television. If I write the letter lamed with a big curve, does that mean I suffer from mental disorders, or is it the other way around? Should I elevate the final zadi in *shiputz*, in the word "renovation," or lower it and

thereby prove that the father of the family is a modest fellow
who isn't looking for trouble with the neighbors? Maybe I'll let
my daughter write it? A notice written by a child will show that
our children are fluent in the language of the occupants and will
reassure the skeptics. But what if they think it's the handwriting of
an adult Arab? Problem. How will they know that it was written
by my daughter? I'll end up looking like a dumb neighbor with
substandard handwriting.

And what about the signature at the bottom? Should I really
conclude with "Please excuse us" and sign it "Kashua family"? Or
is that too fast, announcing the event like that? Maybe without
a signature? Just make do with proof that we are polite and will
maintain quiet between two and four in the afternoon, without
revealing our national identity immediately? On the other hand,
how long will I be able to hide?

All right, maybe a signature with the surname, to let all the
occupants know that there's an Arab family down below, so they'll
have enough time to digest the idea before we move in. We'll let the
rumor circulate; they can talk among themselves, rack their brains
over what to do. There must be one leftist maniac who reads *Haaretz*
in the building—I'm counting on him to calm the rabid opponents.
"No, he's all right, what's the matter with all of you? And his wife?
Marvelous. Apart from that stumble in the Second Lebanon War, I
tell you, he's A-OK. I read him every week. He's not like the others.
My feeling is that he's all right. In any event, our approach will be
to respect him but suspect him."

I couldn't make up my mind about the signature. I tore up
dozens of pages, which overflowed the wastebasket onto the living
room floor, like in movies about frustrated writers, until finally I
arrived at a compromise text. On Sunday, as soon as I got the keys,
I rushed to the new apartment with my wife. The renovator didn't
show, said he was sick and couldn't start until the next day. My
wife became irritated, said she didn't believe him, but I was glad—I

didn't want him to start working before I put up the notice, which I'd toiled over for two full days.

"Tell me," my wife started to ask as I stood next to the notice board with colored thumbtacks that I bought specially and put up the notice, which contained one printed word in the center of the page: "Sorry."

"What?" I replied. "Just a minute, what do you say, is it straight?"

"Yes, straight. Very nice."

"What did you want to ask?" I said, backing up to get perspective and gazing proudly at the notice.

"Tell me, what will we do with the mezuzah?"

LAND OF UNLIMITED
POSSIBILITIES

August 29, 2008

Heartfelt greetings to my parents, brothers, family, and all my dear ones,

How are you? I trust you all feel well and are enjoying quiet, comfortable days. How are my little nephews? Excited about the new school year? What about Amir—has he already bought a lunch box for kindergarten? Oh, what I would give to see him walking hand in hand with Karem to school.

It's only been a week since I left for the new country, but already my heart is filled with longing and the desire to be with you again.

My wife and children send regards and say they miss you very much. We are fine, things are still a bit difficult, but as they say here: all new beginnings are hard. The children are starting to adjust to the new place, they're already sleeping almost whole nights in their rooms.

Gradually we're learning about the new place, the new culture, and the way of life of the inhabitants of this new country. I'd like to be able to tell you that everything is fine, but I don't want to lie: it's quite hard for us here. You know, we were used to one thing and overnight we find ourselves in a different world. It will undoubtedly take time before we feel at home, though I doubt that I ever will. In the end, there is only one home.

With the children it's a different story. They are still young
and perhaps will learn how to cope with the codes of this foreign
land—my wife and I are throwing up our hands from the outset.
What won't we do to ensure a better future for our children.
This place is different from everything we know, so different
that I sometimes feel afraid. I still can't get over the feeling of terror
that seized me the first time I took a shower here. The Jews have
such strong water pressure. Scary. I would say that the water caught
me with my pants down. As far as I knew, only hotels have water
pressure like that, not the homes of ordinary citizens. So there I am
under the showerhead, waiting for the trickle of water like always
for these past thirty-some years, when suddenly a fierce flood bat-
ters my head. And would you believe it: it's been seven whole days
since we migrated and there hasn't been one water stoppage. One
night I got up on purpose to check whether the water pressure was
still terrifying even in the wee hours, and it was.

There's a large garbage bin next to the building—okay, I'm
lying, because I don't want to torture you, but the truth is that there
are two huge garbage bins in front of the building. Each has the
inscription "This bin is emptied on Sunday, Tuesday, and Thursday." At first I thought it was a prank, that bored kids were amusing
themselves with the art of graffiti and had decided to spray-paint a
protest against city hall on garbage bins, of all places. Definitely an
original idea. But no, to my surprise I discovered that what it says is
absolutely true. The garbage collectors really do come three times
a week to empty the bins. Would you believe it—three times! If I'd
had to write something on a garbage bin in our former country, it
probably would have been: "This bin is emptied on the Feast of
the Sacrifice."

Another wondrous thing they have here and we don't is the
mail. We have an address here, not a post-office box number. I saw
a real mailman, like you see in movies, arrive with a bag slung over

his shoulder and distribute mail to the citizens in the mailboxes at
the entrance to their building. An address is like magic. You call up
a fast-food place, give them the address, and within a short time a
delivery person shows up on a moped bringing hot food. The children enjoyed the new gimmick, though at first they didn't believe
it, until one evening I ordered from three different places: pizza,
burgers, and Chinese. All kinds of companies don't dawdle in coming: phone, gas, water, cable TV. You just give them your address,
and that's enough for them to appear as scheduled. You don't hear
things like "We don't know when a technician will be available in
your area" or "Entry into your area has to be coordinated with the
police." There were a few customer-service operators who, when
they heard my name, started to recite the standard response: "We'll
check when a technician will be . . ." But I broke in and gave my
address in the new country, and right away a date for the technician
to visit was set.

It's hard to get used to, but you survive. Every intersection has
signs—slow down, stop, left or right turn—the same ones you see
on the huge page you have to memorize before getting your license
and then never see again. Well, they have plenty of those here, in
blue and red, round ones and triangles. All the streets are paved,
and as if that weren't enough, allow me to tell you that next to them
are lanes for pedestrians, called sidewalks. There are green parks,
lawns that are watered with automatic sprinklers, and olive trees,
which once belonged to someone else, I heard, but here in the new
country they maintain them well, even if they're not theirs. Green
buses pass by, too, and there are stops with benches.

Next to our building there is something strange and scary, a
kind of dugout with a heavy metal door and a peculiar bulky handle.
At first I hesitated, but finally I asked a passerby about it. He said it's
a shelter in which you hide in a war. For a whole night I dreamed
about the shelter next to our home. I managed to fall asleep only

when I promised myself that if a war breaks out, heaven forbid, I will catch the first plane home and hide with you. Please take care of the good room for us.

Missing you very much,
Your loving son

GOOD MORNING, ISRAEL

June 5, 2009

"Second floor," the guard at the entrance to the police station said. She pointed toward the elevator. It was almost noon. Three men were sitting in the waiting room of the Citizen Service Center (Filing of Complaints).

"You're after him," I was greeted by the eldest of the three, a man of about fifty. He pointed to a young man wearing the uniform of a parking inspector who was sitting opposite him. "But it'll take time. So who attacked you?" the older man asked the inspector, resuming their conversation. "Was it an Arab or a Jew?"

"A Jew," the inspector replied.

"How do you know?" the older man pressed him.

"I spoke to him," the inspector answered.

"I don't believe it," the older man said, tilting his head to the side and guffawing in dismissal of the young inspector's words. "A Jew wouldn't do that. An Arab could. They can look right and left"—he looked right and left himself—"and if they don't see anyone they can attack."

I sat quietly for almost an hour, and in all that time the door of the Citizen Service Center didn't open even once. From time to time a citizen entered the waiting room, asked the older man how long he'd been waiting, and when he heard the answer—two and a half hours—uttered a *"Vai, vai, vai"* and left. The inspector said he didn't care, because the wait counted as part of his working hours.

He stretched out across several chairs and shut his eyes. After waiting for about two hours, I had to leave in order to pick up my children from school. They didn't understand why I hugged them so tight.

"What for?" my wife asked when I decided, that evening, to return to the police station. "To tell them that the writing is on the wall?"

The wall clock in the waiting room said 6:30. The door to the unit was closed. Brushing off pita crumbs and bits of pickle from a chair with my hand, I sat down, determined to make the complaint even if I had to wait all night. There were two women in the waiting room, one older, the other young, and also a man, who was pacing back and forth in the small room and shouting into his cell phone: "No. It's not the first time. He harasses them in school, too. Now we're at the police station."

"He's got some nerve," the young woman said, twisting her mouth. "Someone has to teach him a lesson. If not his father, then the police."

The older woman nodded her head in agreement. The man finished his call and addressed the two women with a wink: "I could tell from his father's voice that he's uptight."

I've never asked people in line, "Who's last?" but I started to understand that the two women and the man are one family, so there's only one complaint ahead of me, not three.

The man's phone rang. He glanced at the screen. "It's him," he whispered. He then answered in a different tone, masculine, brimming with self-confidence. "Hello, so what's the story? Is it like that?" He winked at the women again, and they started to smile. "*Wallah*, all right, I don't know what to tell you. Give me a minute, I'll get back to you." He disconnected and turned to the young woman, who was no doubt his wife: "His father wants to wrap it up without complications. What do you say?"

"What do you say, Mom?" the younger woman asked the older. "Dunno. Whatever you say."

"*Ya'allah*," the man exclaimed, and gestured to the two women to get up. "The main thing is we stressed out the father."

The waiting family left; I was alone in the room. I got up from where I was and sat down on a stained chair from which I could see the television screen that was hanging in the corner and was soundlessly broadcasting the State Cup final in soccer. A uniformed policeman entered the room together with a woman who kept wiping tears from her eyes. The policeman pushed open the door to the unit and said to an unseen person, "There's a woman here whose husband beat her." I lowered my head and the woman went in ahead of me. I figured it must be an urgent case and went back to staring at the screen.

Half an hour went by. A young couple in their early twenties entered. The guy was dark skinned, the girl white, her hair completely yellow. He pressed himself up against her, ran his hand over her arms, and kissed her on the neck repeatedly. The game, between Beitar Jerusalem and Maccabi Haifa, started, in the presence of the president of Israel. I tried to keep my eyes on the screen and ignore the couple making out opposite me. Two Ethiopian women came in with three small children. I got up to give them my seat. The door of the unit opened and a young policewoman emerged. "Oho," she cried out, looking at the young couple, "what do you two want to complain about?"

"Our property was stolen," the guy said.

"Not exactly," the girl said in a Russian accent. "My ex-boyfriend took a computer that was both of ours."

The policewoman nodded her head and turned to the Ethiopians. "Are you together?"

"Yes," one of the women replied. "This is my sister and these are my children."

"What are you filing a complaint about?"

"About being hit," the mother said, and pointed to a boy of about ten who was wearing sports clothes and cheap soccer shoes.

"What?" the policewoman said impatiently. "Someone hit him?"

"Yes," the mother replied, "his father almost hit him to death."

"And you?" the policewoman said to me. "What are you here for?"

"I," I said, and my face started to burn, "I would rather tell you inside, if possible."

The policewoman studied me carefully. I was sorry I hadn't shaved or changed the T-shirt I was wearing.

The policewoman disappeared into the room. A few minutes later, an older policeman came out. "The computers crashed," he announced.

"What?" the young man asked. "How long will it take?"

"It could take hours," the policeman said, "there's no way of knowing."

The two young people looked at each other and got up. The policeman turned to the Ethiopians. "Who is the mother of the battered boy?"

"Me," the mother said, raising her hand.

"Ma'am, I am not allowed to question children. Do you understand? Here," he said, handing her a piece of paper. "There's a phone number on this. Call them tomorrow morning and take the boy there. Do you understand, under the law I'm not even allowed to talk to a child? That's why I'm talking to you, not to him. I don't have the authority."

The policeman glanced at the television screen, waited until the Ethiopians had left, and then spoke to me. "The computers crashed."

"What does that mean?" I asked. "That it's impossible to make a complaint?"

"It's up to you."

"I don't understand," I said. "Should I go and come back another time?"

"I can't tell you anything like that. It's up to you. It's your decision."

"Sir." I tried again. "Really, I don't understand what I'm supposed to do."

"I can't tell you. It's your decision. I am telling you that there's an overload and the computers crashed," he said, and went back into his office, shutting the door behind him.

I sat down and looked at the clock. I'd been here two hours, and except for the woman whose husband hit her, no one had entered or come out.

"What, just you?" a man in a colorful shirt that was stuffed into jeans shouted at me. I nodded.

"But the computers crashed," I told him.

"What computers?" The man guffawed. "They always do that." He knocked lightly on the door and opened it. "What happened?" he shouted into the office. I couldn't hear the reply. "How long have you been waiting?" he asked me.

"Around three hours."

"*Vai, vai, vai,*" he said, and looked at the clock. "Listen up, my man. I'm absolutely dying of hunger. Do me a favor. Take my phone number, and text me when you go in. Write it down." He dictated the number to me and I wrote it down.

Beitar was leading 2–0. The battered wife, still wiping away tears, emerged with the policewoman. "So third floor, all right?" the policewoman said to her, and then turned to me: "We're not done, she has to come back to me." She went into the office again, slamming the door behind her.

"I'm sorry," I told my wife on the phone, "but I have to file a complaint."

"The children asked about you," she said, "and I'm tired and afraid to sleep alone."

"*Ya'allah,*" the young man in the colorful shirt said as he returned holding a falafel pita, "haven't you gone in yet?"

"No," I said, shaking my head.

He knocked on the door again, shouted, "What's happening?" and bit into the pita.

The older policeman came out of the office, looked at the screen and liked what he saw. "*Ya'allah*, two–nothing," he said, and turned to the man with the falafel: "What's going on with you? Again you and your ex-wife?"

"What can I do? She won't let me see the kids. I know you won't do anything, but it's for the judge. For sure he'll ask, 'Why didn't you file a complaint?' So here I am again, filing a complaint."

"All right, he's ahead of you," the policeman said, pointing at me: "Come in."

Instinctively I looked around to make sure he meant me.

There were two rooms inside. The young policewoman was in one of them; I followed the older policeman into the other one. "There are no computers," he said as we sat down. "Tell me what happened. Worst case, we'll take it down by hand."

"I'm a journalist," I said for openers, and I saw his expression change. "I work for a newspaper, *Haaretz*."

The policeman stopped me with his hand, checked the computer, and announced that I was in luck. "The computer's back. How long did you wait outside?"

"About three hours. Second time."

"I'm sorry, there's a lot of pressure. You don't know what we go through here. Do you know what a policeman goes through? It's a nightmare. I wouldn't have let you wait three hours. It's not right. So go on with what happened."

"I am also an Arab," I continued. "A few months ago, I moved with my family to a Jewish neighborhood, and this morning my home was attacked with eggs. I came because I am afraid it happened because we're Arabs. You see, I have young children."

"Was it the first time?" the policeman asked, and took my ID card.

"No, about three weeks ago our cars, mine and my wife's, were smeared with eggs."

"Did you file a complaint then?"

"No."

"Why not?"

"Because I was sure it was just kids, I didn't attach any importance to it."

"Too bad, you should have filed a complaint then, too."

"I don't know, I only came because of concern that it's related to our ethnic origin."

"So you think it's because you're Arabs?"

"I hope not."

"You hope it's something else."

"Yes, but I'm afraid it's because of that."

"All right," the policeman said, and started to enter data into the computer. "We'll start from the beginning. This is a serious incident; a complaint needs to be filed. So, from the beginning. You live in Beit Safafa?"

"No," I stopped him. "I live in the western city," and I added the name of the neighborhood.

"Right, sorry," he said, correcting the mistake and continuing to type on the keyboard.

"When we woke up this morning, my wife and I discovered that the window screens in the living room were torn and that three eggs had been thrown. We didn't say a word, so the children wouldn't notice. After they were in school we came back to clean up."

"You cleaned it up?"

"Yes."

"All right, I'm continuing," the policeman said, and asked, "When did you say stuff was thrown at the car?"

"Three weeks ago."

"*Ya'allah*," the policeman said, pressing hard on one of the keys. "I don't have the letter shin. The shin has stopped working. Do you see how it is? They don't even replace a keyboard. All right. It's not so terrible, we'll continue in any case," and he went on typing, leaving a space every time there was supposed to be a shin.

"Excuse me," the young policewoman said, bursting into the room. She was taking down the complaint of the divorced man. "What do I write for place where the offense happened if he called his wife when he was in Talpiot and she answered from Gilo and said she wasn't going to let him see his children?"

"Can't you see that I am with a citizen?" the older policeman yelled at her, and then he turned to me: "They don't know the meaning of work. You can see I'm with a citizen, why do you burst in?"

The policeman handed me a stack of papers, including a sheet titled "Assistance for Victims of Offenses." "You have the phone number of the aid people here," he explained, and apologized that the sheet was in English. "We're out of the Hebrew and Arabic forms. And this is confirmation that a complaint was filed." I looked at the confirmation: "Complaint about damage caused to a vehicle maliciously." The policeman escorted me out. "I want you to know," he said, "that whoever did it is scum."

"What am I supposed to do?" I asked with a look of concern.

"There's no way to know how cases like this will progress," he replied. "In the meantime, look after the children. Don't let them wander about alone, explain to them not to touch suspicious objects. And if, heaven forbid, anything happens, call 100."

"Thank you," I said, and shook his hand. We both looked at the celebrations on the television screen. The fans and players of the victorious team from the country's capital were celebrating the winning of the cup, dancing and singing "Death to the Arabs! Death to the Arabs!"

SUPERMAN AND ME

October 30, 2009

"Excuse me," the guy sitting next to me at the bar said to me in Arabic, emitting a strong whiff of cheap whiskey. "I heard you speaking Arabic on the phone." He swayed a bit and nearly tumbled from the high bar stool. "Are you Arab?" he asked.

"Yes," I answered hesitantly, not being overly fond of having conversations with drunks, but something in the young man's face exuded goodwill.

"I'm really sorry to bother you," he went on, "but I don't know Hebrew and I would really like to ask the bartender for more peanuts. They're all finished," said the young man in a desperate tone, pointing to the empty peanut bowl in front of him.

"Sure," I told him, and asked the bartender to replenish the poor guy's peanut supply.

"Thank you very much," said the drunk Arab, shoving a fistful of peanuts into his mouth.

"Maybe you want a little water to wash that down?" I said to him, hoping he wouldn't be offended—you never know how drunks will react.

"I sure do," said the young fellow, "but I don't know how to say 'tap water.' I don't have money for a bottle."

I ordered a glass of water for him, too. He gulped it down quickly, thanked me, and asked if I could get him another one, which he promptly downed with lightning speed.

"Where are you from?" I ventured to ask, wanting to help him. He appeared to be in great distress. He obviously didn't know much about drinking and had come here to drown his sorrows in alcohol.

"From Deir Debwan," he replied. "A small village. You know it?"

"Sure," I said. "I know it. It's out near Ramallah."

"Right." He nodded, happy that someone knew where he was from.

"So," I asked, "you have an entry permit for Jerusalem?"

"No." He shook his head and asked for more water and peanuts. "I jumped over the fence and ran here."

Well, then. It *was* a mistake to start up a conversation with this drunk. I smiled faintly and looked the other way, hoping that this would signal the end of our conversation and that he'd leave me alone.

"You don't believe me, huh?" he said, and I knew I was in trouble, that I'd have no choice but to get up and leave so as not to let this Arab ruin the one evening a week when I go out to drink a little and forget life's burdens.

"Look down for a second," he said. I ignored him. "Come on," he persisted. "Just look down for a second," he urged, inclining his head toward the legs of the bar stool. "Just look at the floor for a minute, and if you still don't believe me I promise you I'll leave this place right away."

"Fine," I said, huffing with impatience and turning my gaze to the legs of his bar stool and the floor. "Whoa!" I shouted, shaking my head in disbelief when I distinctly saw his stool levitating off the floor at least two centimeters in the air.

"Shh . . . " the Arab quickly silenced me, glancing right and left to make sure no one had noticed. "I don't want anyone else to know about this," he implored in a panic.

"What the hell is that?" I asked, still unable to believe my eyes.

"I'm the Palestinian Superman," whispered the Arab dejectedly.

"What?"

"Just what you heard," he said, sighing ruefully. Then he started telling me how he was a chemistry student at Birzeit University. He pulled out his student ID to prove it. He said it all started with a lab experiment. One day, a colleague brought to the lab the remnants of some substance the Israeli army uses against demonstrators. He ran a few simple procedures, added an acid and a base or two, and put it all together in a test tube. Just as he was stirring it, a supersonic boom from an air force jet shook the lab. Startled, he dropped the test tube and the substance spilled all over his legs.

"The next day," he continued, "I woke up in the morning with a very strange feeling." He said that when he went to open the door of his room, it came off in his hand. When he turned the faucet handle, he pulled up the pipes. When he tried to walk, he found himself passing cars, and when he tried to skip over a puddle, he ended up leaping over the separation fence.

"You're putting me on, right?" I laughed, because it reminded me of a joke about a drunk Superman.

"Not at all," he insisted. "Look." With his eyes he indicated that I should look at the television screen suspended in a corner of the bar, and with just a wink he changed channels, one after the other.

"Whoa, man," I said. "When did all this happen?"

"Just a week ago," Superman replied, still in Arabic, his accent a sure giveaway of his rural origins.

"You know what?" I suddenly lost my patience with the guy sitting next to me. "This is messed up. Really messed up. *Ya'ani*, let's say you really are the Palestinian Superman, the guy every Arab has been waiting for even more than Obama, and instead of saving your people you're sitting here drinking whiskey in a pub in West Jerusalem? Have you no shame?"

My words upset him. "Do you have any idea how happy I was when I discovered my superpowers? That's it, I said, no more settlements, no more stealing of our water, no more tanks, no more fence, no more siege. You understand? After just a day or two of adjustments and getting the hang of my superpowers, I was ready to go to work. Olive trees were being uprooted, so I went out to replant them and . . ."

"Well, and . . . ?"

"Never mind, forget it," said the young man with tears in his eyes. "It's too painful to talk about."

"Speak, man," I said encouragingly, placing my hand on his slumping shoulder and getting him another glass of water. "What happened?"

"The uniform," he wept, resting his head in the palm of his hand. "The uniform killed me. You see, most of the missions I can't perform without the uniform. Look at it." He undid the top button of his shirt to reveal a little of the tight blue suit. "It's skintight. If I do any extra exertion, the clothes disappear and all I'm left with is the tight uniform."

"So? What's the problem with the uniform?"

"As soon as I left the house to go plant olive trees, a Palestinian Authority patrol car picked me up and took me in for a 'talk' in which I was told, in no uncertain terms, that I had to change the colors of the uniform to match the colors of the flag. They wanted the underwear in red, the cape in black, and the rest in white and green."

"What?!"

"The moment I came out of the interrogation by the Preventive Security Forces, a Hamas car came and snatched me away. They wanted the cape to be green, and instead of an "S," to write in Arabic 'There is no God but Allah.'"

"Man," I told him. "Because of that you're ready to give up on your people? Who are those guys, anyway? You're Superman. One puff and you blow them all away. You're above the internal Palestinian conflict, man."

"That's what I thought," he said, and sighed. "Until the neighborhood kids started chasing me with stones and taunting me with the most awful insults."

"Why?"

"Because of the tights," he said. "And they're right, you know. The whole thing is too tight. This uniform was really made for an American white guy and it looks totally ridiculous on me."

"It's tough, yeah." I had to agree with him because I would never go around the village wearing a suit like that, even if it meant I could wrap Aryeh Eldad around my little finger.

"Whiskey?" I offered.

"I'm flat broke, man," said Superman.

"No problem. It's on me."

BAR-SIDE BANTER

January 22, 2010

"I don't know," she continued, shrugging her shoulders and trying to overcome the shudder that seized her when she said the word "Arabs." "I don't know what the solution with them will be, nor do I care if there's a transfer or if they are given a state of their own where they can rot. The main thing is that we won't have to deal with them anymore."

What lovely eyes she has, I thought, trying to decide in the dim light of the bar whether they were blue or green. I couldn't tell; sometimes they looked blue, but with a different tilt of the head, they looked green for some reason. But what difference did it make? The main thing was that she has beautiful eyes and straight brown hair that she pushed away from her face with long, thin fingers.

"Do you understand?" she asked, sipping her drink.

This was the first time I'd talked with a girl who was drinking a cocktail, and I considered it an impressive achievement. I bet it was because of my diet and my black shirt (black looks good on me).

"And it's not that you can say I grew up in a right-wing home. On the contrary," she said, while I camouflaged my attempt to peek at her backside by craning my neck, which had presumably become stiff from sitting bent over at the bar. She had a perfect posterior, that I could swear, with buttocks that were firm and solid when coming in contact with the stool.

"I actually grew up in a leftist home," she went on. "My parents were leftists. Members of the Labor Party. You know what I mean?"

"You don't say?" I said, finding myself surprised at the magnitude of the change she had undergone. With any drinker of beer or whiskey, I would immediately have declared that Labor was never a leftist party, but she—the imbiber of the margarita, or whatever you call the colored liquid in her decorated glass—was allowed to do whatever she wanted. As far as I was concerned, she could also claim that Meretz was leftist and I wouldn't express any opposition.

"I swear to you, my folks were leftists. Only in the last elections did they vote for Kadima. And that was only because of Tzipi Livni. Otherwise only Labor. Dyed-in-the-wool leftists." She giggled, and I smiled back.

"And I remember as a girl in French Hill . . . ," she continued, and I, like some Arab, interrupted her automatically: "You know, that's a settlement."

"What settlement?" she asked.

And I was so angry at myself. Not only did I not want to talk about politics on this magical evening—I mean, that was true, too—but mainly this was all a result of my inability to listen. I've reminded myself a million times to try to listen to people, mainly to girls, when they talk. But I can't. My wife is right when she claims that I consider myself the center of the universe and think the sun rises from my backside, and that I never, but never, attribute importance to what people around me are saying. Like an idiot I had to come out with some wisecrack that would probably destroy a pleasant conversation that was clearly progressing in a promising manner.

"Excuse me," I said, trying to assume the expression of a man listening all the way down to the roots of his hair. "Excuse me for interrupting you. Please continue."

"No," she said with a surprised look. "You said French Hill is a settlement?"

"Yes," I replied in an apologetic tone, "but that's really not important. You know, geography, who cares. What's important is what you feel. Please go on, it was fascinating."

"*Wallah*, I didn't know," she persisted, and with an unexpected sort of movement sat up straight on her stool, showing off a perfect chest. "Are you sure it's a settlement?"

"More or less," I replied. "You know, Jerusalem is Jerusalem. But it's really not important, you were just saying that as a girl in French Hill . . ." I urged her to continue talking about her childhood and to stay as far away as possible from the 1967 borders.

"Yes," she finally went on. "So I remember as a child that I actually didn't hate Arabs. Really, it all seemed so natural. They worked in the neighborhood, their children sometimes played in the public park, and it was all right with me. That is, I didn't play with them, but that really didn't matter. But at some point, I simply understood that the Arabs aren't . . . I don't know how to put it. It's like, Arabs, well, it isn't fitting, you know?"

"Definitely," I replied quickly, in total agreement. "I understand."

I knew right then that she liked me, and that if I invited her to the dance floor she would agree immediately. But because I wanted to be certain of the profound connection that had been forged between us, I wanted her to talk more—in other words, mainly I wanted her to notice that I was ready to keep listening. I was afraid a direct suggestion was likely to put me in another, different light; that suddenly I would become transformed in her eyes from a pleasant conversationalist to some drooling Arab.

"But," I continued slowly, weighing my words, thinking, being considerate, "how did all this begin? I mean, this hatred that you suddenly discovered?"

"I really don't know," she said, touching my shoulder like someone who had experienced a revelation at that very moment. "It was, like, natural. Suddenly I understood that I don't like Arabs: I don't like to see them in the street, I don't like the ones who work for my parents. I suddenly realized that they're not like us. For me they became, like, strange or different. And they really are different, and they just don't belong . . ."

I took a deep breath and took her hand to console her. "Everything will be all right," I told her, looking her straight in the eye. "I promise you that everything will be all right."

"I don't know," she said, in the tone of someone who seemed genuinely concerned about our future here. "Sometimes I lose hope that we'll have it good here someday."

"You'll see," I said to her in a gentle and authoritative voice. "All you have to do is just believe, and someday it will be a paradise here."

CRY ME A RIVER

February 26, 2010

At six in the morning last Thursday I wrapped up the last script. I returned the keys to the office where I'd spent the last five months, fourteen hours a day on average. We celebrated meeting the deadline, the production company sent me flowers and chocolates at home, and on Sunday of this week shooting began for the new series. But instead of feeling jubilant that the exhausting project is over, I find myself crying unstoppably, for no apparent reason.

"This week I want to be with the children as much as possible," I declared to my wife in a voice choking with tears.

"Gladly," she said. "So you'll drive them to school today?"

"Why do we worship God?" my little daughter declaimed in the backseat, prepping for a test on the religion of Islam. "Because he created us," she answered herself, "because he brought us into this world and commanded us to worship him and believe in him. Right, Daddy?"

"Right," I said, fighting back tears that threatened to start flowing by themselves.

My daughter continued with the question on the next page. "In what year was the prophet Muhammad born?"

My son stared out the window all the way to school. Occasionally I looked at him in the mirror and asked myself, forcing myself not to cry, whether they have it good, my children. When was the last time I drove them to school? How long has it been since I was really with them?

"Daddy," my son said when I parked the car next to the school, "please pick me up and hold me."

"Gladly," I said, and cried.

As I was driving home, the radio played the new song by Eran Tzur, and I cried. An elderly beggar woman wearing a kerchief knocked on the car window, and instead of giving her a coin I started to weep bitterly. The beggar woman took fright. "What happened? What happened? Crying over a shekel. You miser."

So it went the whole week, from one crying jag to the next, for no reason and uncontrollably. My mother calls, I just hear her voice and I start to cry. I discover that there's something called *Big Brother* on television—I watch for two seconds and start to bawl. I open the refrigerator, see the cultured milk product known as *leben*, which reminds me of my childhood, and I cry.

"Listen," I tried to tell my wife, "I feel like something inside me has broken."

"Probably the spleen," she said, and because I was crying she looked at me again. "What's wrong? Do you have an inflammation in your eyes?"

"No," I told her. "I don't know what's come over me. I feel a deep sadness that I don't understand."

"Are you looking for an excuse not to take the boy to his swimming class?"

It's been such a long time since I was with my son in his swimming class. I cried. "Are you the father?" the swimming instructor asked, and I nodded to indicate that I was, hoping he wouldn't notice that my body was shaking. "Look how he's already swimming," the instructor said, and my son, eager to show me, jumped into the water. "Like a fish," the instructor added, and I cried. I don't know, suddenly a fish makes me sad deep inside.

"I'm going through a really rough patch," I said to my wife, who was working in the kitchen.

"What's so rough? Your life is honey."

"On the surface," I whined, "on the surface. I despise the person I have become, really. I feel a deep need to ask for your forgiveness."

"That's it," she said, drawing the natural conclusion: "You don't want to take the girl to her music lesson?"

"Why are you talking to me like this?" I wailed. "Of course I want to take her to the music lesson. That's what I want to do most in the world."

"So what's your problem?"

"You understand," I tried.

"Come on, get to the point, the onion will soon be burned and I still have a load of wash to do."

"I'm talking about feelings."

"What about them?"

"Something inside, I tell you, something deep is pressing on me, hurting me. I feel . . ."

"Must be the liver. What did you think—that you'd drink like a fish and your liver would stay the way it was?"

"It's not the liver. I'm talking about me and you, I'm talking about my need for warmth, for love. Do you understand, I need you by my side, close . . ."

"Now?" she cried out. "It's not even evening yet. What, you just went on holiday and you can't control yourself?"

"Why do you humiliate me like this? Who's talking about that, anyway?"

"You know what?" she said, adding something to the pot that made smoke rise from it. "You're going to be late for the music lesson. Take the girl, try to control your basic needs, and in the evening I'll see if I have the strength to give you closeness, or whatever you've started to call it."

"You are humiliating me," I wept, and left with my daughter.

I saw the conservatory's sign and I cried, I saw mothers pushing strollers and I sobbed, pigeon droppings plopped onto my shoulder and I was moved to tears.

I waited outside while my daughter had her music lesson. I knew that if I heard her playing I wouldn't be able to hold back the tears. I tried to call my wife and share my feelings, but she didn't answer. When the lesson ended my daughter emerged with a big smile and my heart skipped a beat. Her teacher followed. "Oh, it's been such a long time since we saw you," she said, and I took a deep breath.

"Yes, I was busy."

"All right"—the teacher smiled—"so you're the one who will hear the news."

"News?" I said, hoping not to embarrass my daughter with my hyperemotionalism.

"I am going to play in the festival," my daughter said happily, and it took all the willpower I had not to burst into tears.

"That's right," the teacher said. "I chose her to play a new work in a serious festival."

"What festival is that?" I asked.

"It's a music festival in honor of Independence Day."

"Wow," I blurted out, bursting into tears immediately and giving my daughter a big hug. "I don't believe it. Independence Day?"

"Daddy," my daughter upbraided me, "what are you doing?"

"Excuse me," I said, wiping away the tears. "I'm so proud of you."

"What kind of proud?" my daughter said. "I didn't know it was for Independence Day, otherwise I would never have said yes. And," she added, turning to the teacher, "we call it Nakba."

Here I really did start to wail bitterly, and other parents gathered around to watch the show.

"Daddy," my daughter shouted, "can you calm down? What's the matter now?"

"Now," I managed to squeeze out between the tears, "now I am even more proud of you."

The people around, who didn't exactly know what was going on, were touched and applauded. My wife sent a text message of four words—"Eggs and soy sauce"—and I was so happy to discover that she was at last showing understanding for my feelings.

KASHUA'S COMPLAINT

March 26, 2010

It all started with Philip Roth and the new Hebrew translation of *Portnoy's Complaint*. Don't get me wrong, I really love the book and identify with the characters. So much so, in fact, that the descriptions of the constipation plaguing the narrator's father blocked up my own plumbing. And Roth just never lets up. Every few pages he elaborates on the agonies endured by Portnoy Senior each morning anew. And when I get into a book that I admire, I really get into it. Totally.

If only I could write the way Roth/Portnoy writes—about his family in particular and about the Jews in general. Not that I want to write about Jews; I want to write about Arabs. But it's hard, and writing about them this way, in the language of the enemy, is basically impossible. Until I actually learn how to write in Arabic, I wouldn't dare try to produce such hatred-filled portrayals suffused with an awareness of shared fate. Roth writes in English—his mother tongue and the language of the American Jews he depicts in his novel. And he writes to them about themselves, not about them to other people.

Anyway, ever since I began reading the book a few days ago, my life has been hell. Like Portnoy Senior—with his failed attempts to solve his chronic constipation using dried fruit, milk, and all sorts of remedies—I also tried to cure myself, but to no avail. "It's because of all that stuff you drink!" my mother shouted on the phone, after my wife told her about my latest affliction. "What did you think? That it wouldn't affect your health?!"

"What does that have to do with anything?" I replied, giving my wife a look that could be mustered only by someone extremely constipated. "I've been drinking for over twenty years and never had any problems—well, not this kind at least."

"Do you think you're getting any younger?" my mother scolded me. "Age takes its toll. You just refuse to accept that, that's your problem. Stop drinking and you'll see that everything in your life will flow smoothly."

"Did you tell him we're going to Mecca?" I heard my father's voice in the background.

"What? What is he talking about?"

"Yes," said my mother. "*Alhamdulillah*, we've signed up already and we're going on the pilgrimage, *insh'Allah*."

"What's with the *insh'Allah*?" I asked, letting out a squeal of pain that would pierce the heavens. "Since when are you so religious?"

"Here, talk to your father," my mother said, passing the phone to him.

"So what's going on exactly?" my father asked. "Constipation at your age is a sign from above."

"What does God have to do with my ass, Dad?"

"You should be ashamed of yourself," he chided me. "It's because of talk like that that you're being punished."

"But, Dad, you're a communist, remember?" I tried to figure out what was happening to my parents.

"And you know how long I suffered from constipation because of that communism? Not to mention hemorrhoids."

"Fine," I said, trying to end the conversation. "What can I tell you? Have a nice pilgrimage."

"Wait a minute—your mother wants to tell you something else."

My mother got on the line. "Hello," she said, and I heard my father correct her: "Say *Salaam alaikum*, not Hello."

"*Salaam alaikum*," my mother corrected herself, and then she asked: "Do you want anything special from the holy soil?"

"I don't know, um, no. Thanks."

"Okay, so I'll bring you a bottle of spring water from Mecca," she said. "If your problem isn't fixed by then, there's nothing like Mecca water to cure you."

"Fine, Mom. Bring me a bottle of water."

"Okay, and I'll buy some Playmobil toys for the children. God willing, they'll have Playmobil there, and *insh'Allah* it will be cheaper than Toys 'R' Us."

The Day of Wrath was the worst. It hurt so bad I thought I was on the verge of dying. And that evening I was supposed to take part in a panel on the future of Jerusalem. I knew that if my problem wasn't solved by then I wouldn't be able to stand on the stage at all, let alone give the lecture they'd invited me to deliver.

"Maybe you should go to the doctor?" suggested my wife, who could no longer handle the irate husband shuffling around the house.

"Are you out of your mind?" I protested. "You want the whole world to know that I, the acclaimed *Haaretz* columnist, am suffering from constipation?"

"What does that matter?" she asked innocently. "This is your health we're talking about."

"Oh, it matters," I replied angrily. "Constipation isn't something a serious writer should go to the doctor for."

"Fine," she said, and adding insult to injury, entered the bathroom while muttering—loud enough for me to hear—"As far as I'm concerned, you can just explode."

I tried to get out of appearing on the panel. Of course, I didn't tell the organizers what was really bothering me. Instead, I tried to come up with various excuses: "I don't know, it's just that it's the Day of Wrath and I think the Higher Arab Monitoring Committee has called a strike." It didn't help. Apparently, there was no strike. "My parents are leaving for Mecca, you see," I tried again, "and I have to go home to see them off."

"But people are coming to hear you," the event planners insisted. "We already printed the program and you're one of the main speakers."

I took the stage with tears in my eyes. The pain was unbearable. I cursed Philip Roth and his father and that goddamned Portnoy. Because of some perverted American Jew from the 1960s I need to suffer like this in twenty-first-century Jerusalem?

"Excuse me," I said to the audience in the middle of my talk, just when I'd started to speak about the lack of infrastructure in the Arab sector. I have no idea why I drifted onto this subject, but for some reason I had a sudden urge to talk about the problems with the sewer systems in Arab communities.

"Excuse me," I said to the audience when I could no longer stand up straight, knowing full well that if I didn't get to a bathroom in the next second, what followed could be considered a criminal offense. "I can't go on," I apologized to everyone, and started crying, so mortified I wanted to bury myself and disappear.

But instead of jeering or booing when I exited the stage, the audience members rose to their feet and gave me a long standing ovation. A few older women wiped away tears, their eyes glistening with heartfelt empathy. "Your words make me feel ashamed to be an Israeli," said one elegant woman in her sixties, who blocked my way and took me by the hand. "Your pain was just . . ." she began, as I tried to wriggle out of her powerful grasp and get to where I desperately needed to go, "so honest."

PART III

ANTIHERO

2010–2012

ANTIHERO

April 30, 2010

"We have to leave the country," I informed my wife as I went over the final proofs. "We won't be able to stay here after this book is published."

"Don't exaggerate," my wife said. "You're not the only one—there are a lot of bad writers and none of them is thinking about escaping from the country because of another embarrassing book."

"No, it's not that," I tried to explain. "The problem is the characters in the book."

"What, are you trying to tell me that this time you managed to use your imagination and created a character who isn't me?"

"Terrific, terrific, keep hounding me. You don't have a clue about how serious the situation is, and now that I think about it, I want you to know that it's all your fault."

"Me? You're blaming me? You know that without me you wouldn't manage to write one sentence."

"Because of that, it's too bad you're not a little different."

"What do you want from my life now?"

"Nothing, not a thing." I wanted to end the conversation, but I couldn't stop myself.

"Couldn't you be a little more militant?" I hurled at the main character, who was lying next to me. "Couldn't you be a little more activist? Go to demonstrations, go to marches, get arrested?"

"What?"

"Why not?" I snapped. "Yes, get arrested for nationalist motives. What's the problem? A nation under occupation, and you're
busy with twaddle like studies, work, home, and children?"

"Fine," she retorted, and turned her back on me. "Do me a
favor and let me get some sleep now. Unlike you, I have to get up
for work tomorrow."

Ya'allah, what I am going to do? That's it, the book is going
to press, there's nothing left to save. Where was I all these years?
Only now, six years after I wrote the first sentence, only now, just
before it goes to press, do I grasp the gravity of what I've done. What
exactly was I thinking when I started to write this thing? What am
I, an idiot? Where exactly did I think I was living? Switzerland?

"Tell me." I shook my wife.

"Do me a favor, let me sleep."

"Who do you vote for, anyway?"

"For whichever party promises to get you out of here," she
said, and went back to sleep.

Again I had come up with heroes . . . heroes, I call them—what
kind of heroes? Nothings, I came up with nonentities, afraid of their
own shadow. And I promised my father that my next book would
make me a national hero. Palestinian, I mean. With pathetic characters like these, every beginning Arab journalist will make mincemeat
out of me and become a national hero himself. Once more I had
fallen asleep on the watch, once more I had entered into my story
to the point where I forgot about the reaction of those around me.

But there's nothing that can be done now. It's too late. Only
to escape, just to pack my bags and hightail it out of here. To find
a place where a writer doesn't have to bear on his shoulders any
burden heavier than the story he's trying to tell, a place where writers don't feel a need to be national symbols.

Oy, how I would like to be like Mahmoud Darwish. And I'm
not talking here only about outward appearances. I know, I just
know that at this moment some readers are cursing inwardly and

saying, "How does this wretch who has no talent and, above all, has no values dare dream of even getting close to the shoes of the national poet?" They're right; Darwish didn't even write in Hebrew.

Only now, as I go over the proofs, am I starting to think about the Arab readers. Not that the Jews are a people apart in this area. If the Arab reader looks for a punching bag that will make him feel more congenial about his political impotence, the Jew will for sure look for a book that will give him an anthropological experience, a rare look into the mind of an Arab, or a book that is a journey into the very heart of Arab society. It's an undeniable fact that every time I am invited to an Israeli literary event I find myself sharing the stage with two belly dancers, an unemployed Arab academic, and a *darbuka* player.

Just this week I got a call inviting me to some cultural festival. "Have I reached Mr. Kashua?" asked the polite woman, and announced: "We are very proud to invite you to talk about your new book to an audience of readers."

"I would be delighted," I replied.

"Could you please just tell me in a few sentences what the book is about—for the program?"

"Of course. The book is about a Jerusalem lawyer who is married and has children. One day the lawyer goes into a used-book store . . ."

"Just a minute, excuse me," she said, interrupting. "It's not about the conflict?"

"No, not really."

"But it's a book about the condition of the Arab minority in the Land of Israel?"

"No, not exactly."

"About identity problems, maybe?"

"I wouldn't say that. It's a story about a lawyer."

"Then I—I'm sorry . . . I have to check with my supervisor . . . Because we thought . . ."

"Just a minute, just a minute," I shouted before she hung up. "The lawyer is an Arab."

"Ah, okay, go on."

"So the book is about an Arab lawyer with identity problems that have to do with the status of the Arab public in the shadow of the Israeli-Palestinian conflict."

"That sounds good," she said with an audible sigh of relief. "Please, go on."

"He has a wife, who is also an Arab, and she certainly has serious problems deriving from the status of Palestinian women within the Arab society in Israel."

"And how would you sum up the plot in one sentence?"

"In one sentence," I said, taking a moment to articulate my thoughts, "I would say that the book is undoubtedly a rare look into the very heart of Arab society."

CASTLES IN THE AIR

August 13, 2010

All right, I'm starting to feel like myself again. I can't remember the last time I woke up as I did today, enveloped in a feeling of domestic bliss, that familiar, pleasant sense of bitterness accompanied by guilt. Oy, how I missed that sense of misery, how I feared I was losing it, trading it in for a success story.

It happened last night. I can point to the exact moment when the change occurred. I was reading from my new book to a Jerusalem audience. The words got tangled, the lines got mixed up, and instead of concentrating on the text I began thinking about what I had been through in the past few months—the interviews, the bestseller lists, the television ratings charts, the reviews, events, compliments, and abuse. Look at me, I thought, choking up. Beads of perspiration appeared on my forehead, prompting a woman sitting a stride-length away to hand me some tissues. Look at me, trussed up in the outfit I just bought because the young saleswoman claimed—and I believed every word—that the "casual elegant" style suited me.

I looked down at the black belt and matching dress shoes, at the dress shirt and the Hugo Boss pants, more elegant than casual, and felt only disgust at myself. Nothing worked: not the text, not the standard jokes with the political barbs that the audience usually loves. Nothing worked. All I saw was a disappointed bunch of Jerusalemites who turned up their noses and regretted having left their air-conditioned caves on such a hot day to attend a literary event. That's it, it's over, I knew that clearly, something had gone wrong, it was a turning point. I'll have to struggle through another hour and a half and then it will all be behind me. Another hour and a half and I'll return home tired, beaten, a bottle of whiskey in my hand, class consciousness in my heart, and my self-confidence nowhere to be found.

I smiled to myself at the pleasant thought, leaving the audience to wonder at the foolish expression that crossed my face. I can still fix everything, I thought; two months lost to reality isn't the end of the world. I'll finish up here and rush home, rush to beg forgiveness.

A memory from last weekend caused me to grin incongruously, annoying the audience. "Yes, I am a knight," I had shouted to my wife, convinced beyond a doubt that no one merited the title more.

It began when some French organization asked me to send a curriculum vitae. "Tell me," I shouted from the study, "what year did we marry?"

"I don't remember," she replied impatiently from the living room. "Why?"

"Your husband is going to be a knight."

"What?" she said, and I heard her approaching the study.

"Just what you heard," I said with the permanent smile of the past few months, as she perused the document on the computer screen, "a knight, no more and no less."

"What is this?" she said, reading off the monitor. "'Knight of the Order of Arts and Letters'? What is this nonsense?"

"You never have a good word for me, do you? It's hard for you to give a compliment, isn't it? The whole world thinks I'm talented and only you refuse to admit it. Yes, a knight, yes, a decoration, and a knight of an order, not just any old knight."

"Good," she said, as usual. "I wonder if there's a helmet in France big enough for your head."

"You can laugh," I replied. Since I became successful her sarcastic remarks had ceased to bother me. "I know you're jealous and that deep down you're dying to be a duchess, but you, a girl from Tira, you're here and the aristocratic titles are way over there."

"Your problem is that you forget where you were born," she said, turning away and leaving me alone at the desk, which for a moment had become a round table.

I don't forget where I was born, I was thinking just a few days ago. I was born in Tira. And with a slight change in intonation and a shift of the accent from the first to the second syllable, it will turn into the Hebrew word for "castle," as befits a place where knights are born. I always knew there was something wrong; I always knew I wasn't getting the treatment I deserved. No more. The French are proving what I always felt deep inside, that I belong among kings and princes, not lice-infested commoners. Yes, a knight. And I will have a horse, any color as long as it's casually elegant. Yes, I want to be a knight, I thought, and lied on my CV: "born in a castle"—Tira, that's the truth, and my sword will be at the throat of anyone who questions it.

"Hello." I heard my father's amused voice on the phone. "I hear you have blue blood running through your veins." He laughed and then coughed at length.

"She told you already?" I said, furious to learn that the secrets of the kingdom were transmitted so blithely to enemy elements.

"Tell me, what's going on with you?" my father asked after catching his breath. "Lately you really have been acting as if your suit of armor is too small."

"You know what, Dad," I snapped, "it's time you two admitted that you kidnapped me, time to come out with the truth and tell me who I really am."

"What are you talking about, kidnapped you?" He called to my mother: "Come hear your son the baron. He thinks we brought him from Monaco. You look exactly like every other Kashua, down the generations."

I wanted to say it was well planned, that they had kidnapped others from the same family; I wanted to say it was an international conspiracy. But there was no point. In the end, a knight must know when to hold his tongue. But if he continues like this and leaves me no choice I will lead a charge of the elite cavalry at dawn.

"Why is he chuckling?" I heard someone in the audience ask. "It's not right."

"Excuse me," I said to the audience of readers. Soon, half an hour more, and it will all be behind me. My old life is returning, there's no doubt.

"Yes," said the embarrassed emcee, "and now it's time for questions from the audience. Does anyone have a question? Yes, please speak up."

A nice guy in the middle of the group stood up and spoke into the microphone being passed around for the purpose. "I wanted to ask you: You're always so critical of the place where you were born—what would your life be like if you hadn't been born here?"

THE WRITERS FESTIVAL

May 7, 2010

It all started with a phone conversation I had with my father. He told me he would be coming to the Jerusalem International Writers Festival that evening. "Your mother and I thought that we'd never forgive ourselves if we miss that event," he said.

"Wow, Dad, that's so exciting," I replied. "The only reason I didn't let you know about it is that I didn't want to bother you."

"It's no bother at all." My father shushed me. "What's the matter with you? It's an event that's once in so many years. Obviously we'll come."

"You have no idea how happy that makes me," I told him, trying to control the trembling of familial happiness in my voice.

"So is there a chance we'll see you after it's over?" my father asked.

"Of course," I said. "No question. As soon as I get off the stage I'll come over to you and maybe we'll go out for a bite afterward."

"What do you mean 'get off'? What stage?"

"What did you say?"

"What?" my father asked. "Do you also have an event at the festival?"

"I don't understand."

"*Wallah.*" My father guffawed. "I'm looking at the program now, and right, there's your name."

"What's so funny? I don't get it."

"Your event is scheduled at the same time as the discussion between David Grossman and Paul Auster," my father said, and chortled. "Don't worry, it's no contest." He was still laughing when he hung up.

How had I not noticed? My father was right. Going through the program, I discovered that in the whole International Writers Festival there are only two overlapping events, but exactly to the minute: me, and David Grossman and Paul Auster in a literary encounter. The first thought that went through my mind was: I won't show up. I won't let them exploit me. I won't let them use my name as the token Arab and then not even try to hide the traces of the attempts to make me disappear. I won't let this literary cleansing pass quietly. I'll call the festival director this minute and declare a unilateral disengagement. Who in the world is the director?

I did a Google search. Here we go: Tsila Hayun, creative director. As I was dialing the festival's office, I Googled her name to check out her literary background. I clicked on the first link that appeared and started to read: "On August 3, 2003, the Hayun family was returning from a vacation in Sinai to their home in Har Gilo, a settlement next to Jerusalem. On the road leading up to the settlement, they were ambushed by terrorists. The mother, Tsila Hayun, was struck by eight bullets. She was in critical condition . . ."

"International Writers Festival, hello," someone managed to say before I disconnected. There's nothing to be done. No scolding, no shouting, no canceling of any event. I will accept my punishment in silence.

Ya'allah, why does this happen to me? But all the time. Maybe it's better like this, I rationalized, this is preferable. After all, if people treat me with respect I might even start to develop self-confidence. What will I do if I discover one day that I am actually worth something? Probably I'll stop behaving like an Arab, and in the end I'll be likely to go bankrupt. It's all for the best, I told myself, and took a deep breath to collect my thoughts. Better that people should go on treating me as a foreign implant and remind me where I really belong.

But no one will come to my cruddy event tonight. Even I, given the choice, would go to see Grossman and Auster—what am I, an imbecile? And what will I tell my wife now? She's already bought a dress in honor of the launch of her husband's new book. An empty hall will give her cause to ridicule me for a whole year. And rightly so. I drove her crazy with my writing, with all that "I need quiet in order to create" stuff, and "I can't wash the floor, because it distracts me from fleshing out the characters," not to mention the claim that long hours of sleep help me to dream the plot.

I promised her that this year I would upgrade myself from an Arab author who writes in Hebrew to *the* Arab author who writes in Hebrew, which would add another NIS 2,000 to the gross wage. An empty hall will inflict ruin on my idleness-in-the-name-of-art luxury. An empty hall will be the picture my wife will frame for the living room. But what will I do? It's happening that evening. She'll soon get home from work, and then what? What will I tell her?

"Hello," I said, calling her at work. "Tell me, did things work out with the babysitter?"

"Yes," she replied. "I spoke to her, she can come today."

"It's twenty-five shekels an hour, no?"

"Yes."

"Expensive, no?"

"Like always."

"Why didn't you cook yesterday?" I asked her, trying to instigate a quarrel that might end with her getting angry and canceling her participation in tonight's event as a punitive act.

"What?" she replied, taken aback. "What are you talking about?"

"Yes. You didn't cook yesterday. I can't accept that. How do you expect me to write like a human being if you don't cook every day?"

"Have you flipped?"

"I haven't flipped," I replied in a high-pitched voice. "How do you think great writers become great writers? They eat well. Good food is cooked for them."

"Well, I made *fasulye* just yesterday."

"*Fasulye?*" I said, and remembered that we did actually have *fasulye* yesterday. "Do you think writers like Grossman eat *fasulye?*"

"What do you want from my life?"

"*Fasulye!* Paul Auster probably never even heard of that."

"Listen," she replied serenely. "No matter what you do, I'm coming to your event tonight."

"What are you laughing about? Did you see the program, too?"

"And I want you to know that I'm bringing a camera."

MEET THE AUTHOR

June 11, 2010

I'm sorry. You'll have to forgive me. I'm under a lot of pressure. Though I have never been considered a particularly calm person, during these past few days my anxiety level has reached new heights. Yes, it's all because of the book, the book. I've never felt as much of a merchant as I have this past week. I am prepared to do anything, even join the next voyage to Gaza, if a public relations person will promise me this means selling another few dozen copies. However, not all the marketing tricks have worked out well. For example, the television interview—to be broadcast soon—for which the interviewers insisted on meeting my parents, culminated in a mass disaster. At least two thousand potential sales were thrown into the trash as a result.

"Have you read the book?" the interviewer asked my father, who only nodded in a dissatisfied way.

"And what did you think of it?" continued the interviewer, and my father turned to look at me. Only because I was present and he did not want to hurt my delicate feelings, he made the effort of saying it was "an okay book," with the least believable "okay" one can imagine.

"Just okay?" wondered the interviewer.

And here my mother intervened in the conversation and said: "We told him a million times he should go study law but he insists on making problems."

"As a matter of fact, when he was little he wasn't problematic at all," said my father, annoyed. "He was a good boy, he never cursed, he never thought about girls. It's only because we made a mistake and sent him to study with Jews that he has a filthy mouth and cusses out everyone right and left."

"I don't know," said my mother. "I say, why should a person go looking for trouble as though there weren't enough."

It's not going well, I'm telling you. It is driving me out of my mind. One critic, about whom I couldn't tell whether he liked the book, wrote that I insist on writing about Arabs even though the characters could equally have been Jews from Sderot—that is, not really Jews, but poor, almost Arabs.

That same critic noted that writing about these characters could label me as an Arab writer. I was horrified. Me? An Arab? After all I have done. After I invested everything I have, heart and soul, they come along and write that I am an Arab, and for what? Only because of the characters? It is not good to be labeled an Arab, not good, not good at all. An Arab isn't recognized, an Arab is good for a clearance sale, not for a special deal at Steimatzky.

I decided to gird my loins and combat my reputation as an Arab, so when a nice researcher called from Army Radio and said the station was devoting one of its special Book Week programs to Arab writers, I immediately objected and told her I would not participate.

"I'm very sorry," I said to her, "but I don't want to be an Arab writer."

The researcher was stunned. She couldn't understand what had hit her and she sent her boss, apparently, to deal with it. She is called Tzipi Gon-Gross, the boss, and in a phone call I picked up that she is a leftist. She, too, did not understand why I did not want to be on a program of Arab writers and her tone of voice sent the message: "After all that we are prepared to do for you people, after we fought to bring Arabs into the special, too, in honor of Book

Week, instead of thanking us, you are telling us you don't want to participate in the program. How is there going to be peace this way? With whom is it going to be possible to talk at all?"

"You understand," I tried to explain to the boss, "I will of course be glad to talk about my book, but why with Arabs?"

She did not understand, and justifiably not. I don't blame her. Especially as she told me she had insisted the moderator would be an Arab. They had already confirmed with someone, she said, and mentioned the Arab moderator's name.

"I know him," I told her. "He's a friend of mine. He hasn't read a book since first grade."

"For your information," said Gon-Gross, "we have a special on literature and sport, and the moderator is a sports reporter and not a literary woman. We have a special on literature and psychology, and the moderator is a psychologist and not a man of letters."

"Yes," I tried to defend myself. "But Arab is not a profession."

And I don't know for whom this Gon-Gross voted, but I am telling you that at that moment she decided to swing to the right. Incidentally, in the end I agreed, despite the labeling and my fear I would get a reputation as an Arab.

Why does it seem to me that messing with the person who programs culture at Army Radio is an especially serious matter. On the day of the flotilla—and here allow me to note that I was for the naval commandos and against the Turks, because in the end Turks don't buy books in Hebrew, and if only for that reason I say they deserve to have a few thousand cut down—at any rate, on the day our heroic soldiers risked their lives to defend our sacred soil from our cruel enemies, I received a text message from Army Radio saying the special on Arab writers had been canceled, even though it had been scheduled for a week after the incident.

The worst was reporting to the book stand in Rabin Square in Tel Aviv and forcefully pushing the book on people. "I swear to you," I pleaded, "this is a good book. I wouldn't be recommending it to you if I didn't think it was simply brilliant. Especially as there aren't all that many Arab characters. It's a stigma."

This was so embarrassing. Oh my God. Fortunately, at the publisher's stand there was a keg of beer, which somewhat moderated the sense of affront and made the nightmare of selling tolerable. Every ten minutes I went over to the beer spigot to refresh my cup.

"Excuse me," a young man with designer glasses and a sackful of books addressed me. "Do you work here?"

"Yes. That is, I do have a— I'm Sayed Kashua," and I held out my hand to shake the hand of the reader of books.

"Swell, Sayed. Get me two glasses of Heineken," and he threw two shekels into my palm.

NIGHT CONVERSATION

June 18, 2010

"Do you love me?" she asked.

"Yes. Why?" he asked.

"No reason. You know—I missed you."

"Missed how? I'm home all day."

"So what? I'm not allowed to miss you?"

"Miss me, I won't do anything to you."

"And did you miss me?"

"When?"

"In general, I don't know, now?"

"But you're here. Opposite me."

"So what? Can't you miss me even if I'm here?"

"All right. Yes. I missed you. But my head is killing me, driving all day in the sun. I have to get some sleep."

"Don't worry, I don't want anything from you, calm down."

"No. That's not it. Do you understand? Why are you crying? You know I didn't mean it."

"Yes, I know. Since I stopped using contraception you just keep away."

"What can I do? You know, until you take care of it. Every day you say, 'I'll go to the doctor tomorrow.'"

"But you understand that it causes me hormonal problems?"

"Yes. I understand. Even though I think you're crying for no reason now. Really, well . . . enough."

"You're so dead set against having children?"

"What do you mean, against? We have children."

"Because you understand that my window of opportunity is closing."

"Never mind. We said two was terrific. Like Ashkenazim."

"Ah, that's it, two. Are you sure we won't regret it afterward?"

"I know I won't regret it. But listen, if you really, really want—I don't understand about these things, there's something biological in you women, *ana aref*, what do I know?—if you absolutely and definitely insist, that is. Maybe in another year or two, when we're economically stable, I can consider it. Why are you crying? Hey, *ya'allah*. You were calmer when you had the hormonal problems."

"You're so dense sometimes."

"Me? What did I do?"

"'What did I do?' You're not capable of thinking about anything except yourself. You're so wrapped up in yourself that no one else exists but you."

"What do you want from me now? *Ya'allah*, I really don't understand. All this because of the clothes dryer in the bedroom? I'll solve the problem, I promise, only it's complicated. But if it's so important to you I'll bring a renovations guy tomorrow and we'll see what we can do with the dryer's cruddy vent hose."

"Well, it really is about time to get the clothes dryer out of the bedroom. We need room."

"Good. The important thing is for you to be happy. I'll deal with the dryer tomorrow. Good night."

"What, are you fed up with talking to me? You can't stand me that much?"

"What's the matter with you? What not stand you? I adore you. I thought you were tired. Didn't you say before that you're tired and don't feel well? What, are you crying? Since when do you cry altogether? *Ya'allah*, but why?"

"What are you, an idiot? Why are you kissing me?"

"No kiss?"

"No, don't touch me. You don't love me."

"C'mon, what's the story. Since when do you talk about love?"

"So I don't talk about love? You know what, fine. You're right. It's what I deserve, I'm the one who doesn't talk about love. Why are you silent?"

"Ahh . . . Just like that, from love."

"Do you remember when we went out to Chakra with Shay and Einat?"

"Sure. We really have to do it again. We had a terrific time in that restaurant."

"Yes, ah."

"Yo, I drank so much. Unbelievable. And they pampered us, too—all those chasers on the house. Do you want us to try to make a reservation there for next Thursday?"

"I don't know."

"Ah, no. Whatever you feel like, I'll be happy. It's been a long time since we just chilled out with friends."

"Does it have to be with friends?"

"What? No. Of course not. We can go alone, too, if that's what you want. Whatever you say. What, are you crying? You're frightening me."

"You don't love me."

"Obviously I love you. Please, stop crying."

"Don't touch me."

"Sorry."

"You need to know that someone who loves someone has to accept her as she is."

"But I love you as you are. I don't even care that you're an Arab."

"Is something funny? What's funny?"

"Sorry. I take it back. Sorry. *Ya'allah*, a joke."

"I don't have the strength for your jokes."

"Fine. Enough. I swear to you that I love you as you are. Fine. As you are."

"Liar."

"Why do you say that? C'mon, what did I do to you?"

"Nothing. Nothing. But you don't mind saying things that you don't believe in the least."

"Hey, again you're crying? Are you sure you're all right?"

"I'm sorry. I love you. Hug me strong. It bothers me that you don't love me back."

"How can you say that? I adore you. Please, calm down."

"Liar."

"That's not true."

"So you love me?"

"No matter what."

"Swear it."

"I swear."

"Even if I tell you I'm pregnant?"

"Of course."

"Good night."

"Hello? Hold on, hold on, hold on. How? When?"

"What difference does it make, *neshama*, darling. The important thing is that now you know. *Ya'allah*, turn out the light, it's making me nauseated."

THE BYPASS

June 25, 2010

"Is there bleeding?" asked the doctor in the hospital emergency room as he perused the referral from the health maintenance organization. She just shook her head. "Good," he said, and continued to enter details on a stack of forms. "I will examine you now. Then you have to go to the patients' reception desk at the entrance to get stickers. You stick one of them on this form"—he waved a rectangular note—"and then go to ultrasound in the building opposite. Please," the doctor said, and gestured with his hand toward the examination bed. I managed to make a funny face at her before the physician pulled the curtain shut, but it didn't make her laugh.

The whole thing is my fault. I know. "It's all because of you," she cried, and hit me with trembling hands after the last routine checkup.

"You're right," I replied, hoping the blows would become stronger and hurt me. "I'm really sorry."

"I told you not to write anything about it."

"You're right. I'm really very sorry. I was a bit of an idiot."

"It's all your fault," I could hear her say, even though she didn't say it.

The clerk at the reception desk requested an ID, asked questions, and fingered the keyboard nonstop. Then she paused briefly, stretched out a hand to a bag on the floor, took out a headache pill from a metal container, and swallowed it. "Fine," she said, and

pushed a document into the fax machine. "Wait over there, please"—
she pointed—"and I'll call you when they fax the confirmation of
coverage."

"You don't have to wait with me," my wife said. "You can go
out for a smoke."

Patients, visitors, and hospital staff are taking refuge from the
sun, crowding onto the benches or huddling under a square lean-to,
and puffing on cigarettes at an insane pace. I tried to remember if I
was a smoker back then, when my wife and I first met, but couldn't.
If I was, it would have been the beginning and I smoked only one
or two cigarettes a day. I will have to stop, I thought in the Hadassah smoking area.

We spoke for the first time at Hadassah. She approached me
politely on the first morning of her studies at the university, as I
stood at the bus stop by the dorms on the Givat Ram campus. She
asked if I happened to know which bus went to Hadassah Hospital.
She was enrolled in nursing, but very quickly realized it wasn't for
her. On that day I decided that it wasn't enough to give directions
to a young female student who had just arrived in the big city from
the village. I decided to skip my classes, which were on the Mount
Scopus campus, and escort her to Hadassah. When we got there
she thanked me wholeheartedly for the sacrifice and went her way.
But I, concerned that she would not find her way back to the dorms,
decided to wait for her until after her classes, in order to show her
how to get back. The hell with philosophy classes, I thought then,
and still think so today.

"I need a green authorization from the blood bank," the hospital reception clerk said. "Then I will give you stickers for the
ultrasound. Turn right, all the way to the end," she explained with
tired motions of her hands.

"You have to get this stamped at reception," the courteous
ultrasound technician at the mother and child health center said.

"We can't wait such a long time in line," I said, ripping off a numbered piece of paper. Never had I bypassed a line; I also usually try to swallow my anger and say nothing when people bypass me. But now the situation was different. There was a long line of families, and I knew from experience that they were here to fill out lengthy forms for birth grants.

"Excuse me," I said to the clerk, who was sitting behind glass that was perforated with holes for communication. "It's a bit urgent," I said, offering an apologetic look at the waiting families, who seemed to be an understanding, unresentful lot. The clerk immediately took the rectangular form, stuck it in a machine, and handed it back to me in a second. "Thank you," I said, and we ran to the ultrasound technician.

"Sorry," I heard the technician say from behind the closed curtain. "You know, in cases like this I am always excited, waiting maybe to surprise people and, in contrast to the previous person, shout, 'Wow, there's a pulse, there's a pulse.'"

"Has that ever happened to you?" I heard my wife ask the technician as she dressed.

"To me, no," the technician, a religiously observant woman, said, "but it's happened to others who work here."

With the results of the ultrasound and a stack of forms, we followed instructions and went up to the gynecology unit in the main building of the hospital. A nurse greeted us and we followed her into a tiny examination room. She wrapped my wife's arm with the cuff of a blood pressure monitor and started to ask questions and write down details: "How many children do you have? Do you know of any sensitivity to medicines? Are you generally a healthy woman? Do you smoke? Is there bleeding? Regular menstruation? How many pregnancies have you had?" Then she undid the cuff and took my wife's temperature with an electronic thermometer that gave an accurate reading in a second.

"Are you fasting? How long have you been fasting? Can you read Hebrew? Please read this page. Now I need you to sign here on a consent form. Excellent," the nurse said at last, and tied a bracelet with details and a magnetic code to my wife's wrist. "Wait outside. I will call you when a room becomes available."

"Do you know," my wife asked as a cleaning woman wearing a kerchief pushed a floor-cleaning machine, "you once wrote in one of your columns that for political reasons the Central Bureau of Statistics fakes the data and does not tell the truth about the existence of a decisive Arab majority in the country."

"That's right." I laughed. "What brought that to mind now?"

"Look how many Arabs there are here," she said. "The patients, the cleaning people, some of the staff, the people who push the beds with the patients on them, the people who sell coffee, the visitors. Look how many Arabs there are here, and we aren't even talking about Hadassah on Mount Scopus."

"Kashua," the nurse in the waiting room called out, and she told us to follow her. "A room downstairs is now available, you are going into surgery immediately."

My wife slowed her steps for a moment.

"I'm sorry," the nurse said with embarrassment as she handed my wife the special robe. "It's the last one left in the department. It has no buttons. I'll close you up from behind," she said, pulling a strip of tape out of a white tube.

GOOD-BYE, DAD

September 17, 2010

"Could you drive a little faster, please?" she asked as I finished taking the car down the steep curves and the road began to straighten out at Sha'ar HaGai. I nodded, slid my hands over the steering wheel in an attempt to wipe off the flop sweat, and stepped on the gas a little more. I don't like driving at night, certainly not with the kids asleep in the backseat and definitely not on the highways.

"How are you?" I asked because I couldn't find the right words. She just kept on silently staring at her cell phone, checking that she hadn't missed a call. What is she thinking about now? I tried to guess what was going through her head. What would I be thinking if I were in her place, God forbid? I'd probably be flooded with memories, I thought. What memories does she have of him? They must be good ones, otherwise she wouldn't be crying. They must be childhood memories. At times like this, childhood memories are the only ones that are etched into the brain.

For some reason I picture her as a little girl with a huge smile and a genuine laugh, the kind only children have, and now I see how her father, much younger, is picking her up in his arms. This is the picture she must have in her mind now, I was sure, even though this image must have been shaped by those American movies where whenever a character misses a parent there is a flashback to an old home movie of happy, smiling children surrounded by their loving, protective parents.

What would I recall? And why won't any memories of my own father come to me right now? I've always been so certain of my prodigious memory, able to recite every little thing I experienced from age three through kindergarten, but now I find myself inventing memories that never happened. Is it the same for her? Maybe she doesn't have any memories of him, maybe she's trying at this very moment to insert him into childhood pictures that he was never a part of. Inserting him by force in the preschool birthday party that never was, making him build a sand castle on the beach with her.

And where the hell is my father in all those memories I know I should have? Why doesn't he appear before my eyes? Maybe I'm just anxious, I thought. Yes, I'm too nervous. I'll breathe a little more slowly. Ah, okay. I smile briefly as the childhood images return in full force. I wasn't mistaken, no. I'm almost happy for me, for her, for our parents. There he is in all his glory, the superhero, an inseparable part of the picture, coming to visit me in preschool. And here he is with the old Sussita in the garage. I wiped the smile off my face—this wasn't the time. She was crying softly now and looking at her cell phone again. "Please, a little faster," she repeated when we got on the Trans-Israel Highway.

I really wanted to floor it, but I couldn't. I hoped she could see it in my face. There was no chance of even getting up to the speed limit at that point. The car seemed to be sliding, first right and then left. Maybe it was the wind that wasn't blowing? Or maybe one of the tires needed air. I'm sorry, I wanted to say, but I can't go any faster. I have no control over the car, and with every little bend in the road I'm just praying we won't end up in a ditch. These French cars, I thought, I need a new car, something with more stability that gives a feeling of total confidence. And I know that the car is fine, so why do I feel as if I'm fording a raging river?

Once again she looks at her phone, and I take the blame onto myself. For a few days now she's been saying something's wrong with her phone and she's not getting all her calls and messages. I should have taken it in rather than just hoping it would somehow heal itself. Had she received the first phone call from the hospital, we surely would have been there by now. All I could do now was try to drive a little faster, and I couldn't even do that. I'm sweating again and the headlight beams from every oncoming car seem to shatter into a thousand pieces, sending me into a whirlwind of fear and mechanical taps on the brakes.

Something's wrong with the windshield, I thought. I'll replace it, no, I'll replace the car and it will have an antiglare windshield especially for night driving. Maybe if the kids weren't sleeping in the backseat I could drive a little faster. I give her an apologetic look and am relieved to see an expression on her face that contains no resentment. But it's an expression I've never seen before, and I don't know how to interpret it. A hollow look that might mean she is not having a single clear thought of any kind. Maybe this is the expression of someone who cannot herself identify this new feeling and is trying to cope with it, to label it, to understand its meaning for the first time.

"Faster," she said, and I knew it wasn't from anger, or because she could actually sense how fast I was driving, if at all. I could have stopped on the shoulder right then and I'm sure she still would have asked me to drive a little faster. Does it really matter if we make it in time? If it were me, I'd want to make it. But I don't know why. Curiosity, perhaps? A desire to give one last look that just says, despite it all, I love you very, very much. Or perhaps the expectation of a last look from him, a look that says, I hope you know that despite it all I always loved you. Is that it? A request for mutual forgiveness, a good-bye expressed in one last look?

As I turned right at the Kfar Sava exit I told her, "Soon I'll let you off and then I'll go on with the kids. Okay?"

She didn't answer and stared at the phone in her hand. She didn't say a word. Now she was crying, and her entire body shook uncontrollably.

"The kids," I scolded her shamelessly.

She took a deep breath, closed her eyes, and said, "Drive slow."

THAT BURNING FEELING

October 8, 2010

For some reason, Simhat Torah reminded me of Tira. "It doesn't even rhyme," my wife said as we drove late that morning to visit my parents. But I went on trying to work out what Torah and Tira have in common. The hourly radio news update began just as we drove past Qalqilyah on the Trans-Israel Highway. It's really lucky they planted trees along the fence there, so high that you can't see either the fence or the city it hides, because that's much more pleasant—far from the eye, far from the heart, as Grandma, may she rest in peace, used to say, and what a heart she had, a feast for the eyes. The newsreader said there had been five murders in the country on the eve of the holiday, and my wife and I immediately launched into our regular game. "Four to one, our advantage," I said; my wife bet 3–2, also in our favor. We listened closely: two from Kalansua, at a café in the village center; a married couple from a village in the north; and someone from the Negev. We were both wrong, it was 5–0 for us. I won because I was closer.

"What's that?" my wife asked, as she does every time we get to the Kochav Ya'ir junction, pointing to a large neighborhood that grows bigger with every visit to Tira. "Is it the Jews'?"

"I don't know," I replied, as always, reminding myself that this time I must ask my parents about the huge development going up between Tira and Taibeh, and why it's called Tzur Yitzhak. "Remind me to ask my dad," I said to my wife, as always. I don't know why,

but that monstrous neighborhood, which sends a pang through my
heart every time I visit Tira, is forgotten when we reach my parents'.
"There's no way it can be a new Jewish neighborhood, no way, not
between Tira and Taibeh. It's like giving the finger to the Triangle,
there's no way, remind me to ask."

My father was frying the tastiest falafel in the world and my
mother was washing tomatoes for a salad. "Tomatoes?" I heard my
father ask as we came in. "When tomatoes were a shekel a kilo you
didn't make salads, but now when one tomato costs ten, you're
throwing them into the salad?"

"Well, what do you want me to do?" my mother responded
defensively. "You want people to eat falafel without salad?"

"Yes, without salad," my father snapped. "Pickles and tahini
will do. Hide the tomatoes for really hard times."

"All right, all right," my mother said, and began drying the
tomatoes. "We don't need tomatoes, I'll make a cabbage salad."

"Cabbage?" my father replied even more angrily. "Do you know
that a crate cost me one hundred shekels? One hundred shekels!"

"Then why did you buy it? I don't understand."

"I don't know," my father said. "I have no idea why."

"Hello," I said, disturbing my parents' domestic tranquility.

"*Ahlan*"—they had only now noticed our presence—"*ahlan wa
sahlan*," my mother said. She dried her hands and came to us. My father
only tried to smile and continued to monitor the frying falafel balls.

"What's wrong with Dad?" I asked her. "Political depression
again?"

"As you see," she said with evident sorrow. "The political situation is destroying him."

"How are you, Dad?" I said, raising my voice as I walked over
to him.

"You listen," he replied without preliminaries. "Next week
write this: the Palestinian nation is no longer interested in an in-
dependent state."

"What?"

"What you heard," he said as he shook a perforated spoon holding a few perfect falafel balls. "Write that we want everyone to get an ID card, that we no longer want a state, not in the West Bank and not in Gaza, and that if Abu Mazen weren't ashamed he would give Israel the keys back and say, 'Here, please, take it, it's yours, do what you want.'"

"Just don't tell me you put in your hot pepper again."

"Don't worry," he said. "I made a special batch for you, with no pepper at all. So you'll write it?"

"Write what?"

"That since in any case they do as they please, what's the point of this charade of there being a leadership?" Turning to my mother, he said: "Where's the salad? The falafel is ready and you haven't even started chopping the tomatoes?"

"You see how it is?" my mother whispered in my ear. "Since the start of the negotiations he never leaves the kitchen."

My father had once again put black pepper into the special falafel he had made for me. I said nothing. I know he hasn't come to terms with having a son who can't eat anything even remotely spicy. He always cheats and sticks in a little, hoping I'll get used to it. He watches my face and I try to ignore the burning feeling raging in my mouth from the first bite. "Very tasty," I said, nodding, and tears came to my eyes as my younger brother told me that at a meeting with parents his son's first-grade teachers had requested that the children bring toilet paper from home because there was no budget for it this year. My father scolded my brother and said that his son, like his father, like us, his four children, had to learn that an outstanding student must never use the bathroom in the Arab schools. Dad was right. I remembered how when I was sent to my Jerusalem boarding school it took me months to grasp that I could use the toilets. When that thought crossed my mind just then, I realized that that was where my identity crisis had begun.

There, in those extraordinarily clean bathrooms, was where I began to doubt everything my parents had taught me.

"It's not too hot, right?" my father asked.

"No," I said.

My older brother's wife rescued me by saying that the cars of five of her fellow teachers from Tira had been torched that week. "You see?" my brother said. "Now do you understand why you mustn't trade in the 1990 Lancer?"

"What do they want from us?" my father said as he helped himself to salad. "Didn't I tell you no tomatoes?" he said to my mother. "What do they want? But really, I want them to say what they want, offer a solution, say it out loud, and we will accept every solution of theirs, let them just say what the solution is already and I swear to God we will accept it.

"Separation? Accepted. Citizenship? Accepted. They want us to convert? To scram? To be surrounded by fences? Let them just say it—write to them in the paper that they should only say what they want."

"I want tahini," my daughter said to her grandfather.

We left Tira that evening, at the end of the holiday. The radio reported two murders in Lod.

"Two–nothing for us," my wife said immediately, and she was right.

"That doesn't count. He said Lod."

"What's that?" my wife said, pointing to a huge neighborhood going up between Tira and Taibeh.

A FRIEND IN NEED

January 7, 2011

"Tell me," I asked my wife on another boring Friday evening at home, "how did we run out of Ashkenazi friends?"

"You really don't know?" she replied.

I tried to think for a minute about why the number of our white friends had constantly fallen off since we moved to the new building, to the point where now there were none. It wasn't like that in the past. We were always invited, or we had people over for dinner on every weekend that we stayed in Jerusalem. And now, nothing. Every Friday I wait for the phone to ring and some friend to invite us over, like in the good times. At first I myself made a few calls to invite friends over, but for some reason they were always at their parents' for the Sabbath-eve meal.

Something in our friends' family ties with their parents had strengthened since we moved to a Jewish neighborhood. Don't get me wrong—I greatly respect tradition. In fact, it's the Sabbath-eve tradition that has been getting us down lately. Every Friday evening I see the building's parking lot start to fill up as the neighbors' guests arrive. Through the peephole I watch the visitors going up the stairs—children, friends, smiling relatives, happy, sometimes carrying pots or trays that give off good smells. Then the clinking of cutlery and dishes, occasional bursts of laughter, singing, table talk. We are the only ones who are stuck here, not talking, watching the weekly newsmagazine.

"No," I said to my wife, "I don't know what has changed."

"It's because of you," she said in a calm, confident, authoritative tone of voice.

"Me?" I cried from the sofa. "Why? Did I change in some way? What?"

"No," she continued in that laid-back tone, trying not to remove her gaze from Amnon Abramovich, "you haven't changed. You are still the same crummy person I met fifteen years ago."

"So what's the problem?"

"You don't barbecue anymore," she said. "That's why."

What? What is she talking about? What does that have to do with abandonment by the Ashkenazim? It's true that once upon a time, in the village, when we had a yard, I would always, but always, make a barbecue when friends came over, and that since we moved here more than two years ago I haven't come close to a fire, but that could hardly be the reason that friends were ostracizing us. But my wife, she was always like that; it's hard for her to be complimentary, she thinks everything in life is a vested interest. But she's wrong, she's always wrong, and she is wrong again now with this absurd claim about grilled meat.

"You're at liberty to believe whatever you want," she said, "but now be quiet, I can't hear what the head of the Police Investigations Branch is saying."

"*Lehayim*," I heard from the neighbors' place, and, hurt and friendless, I felt alone in Jerusalem and took Hans Fallada to bed with me. I don't accept what she says; there's no way it contains even a grain of truth. My friends, the ones I once had, were never like that. My friends like me because of what I represent, not because of the meat I barbecued. Then the thought crossed my mind: What do I actually represent? But I immediately got rid of it with a vigorous shake of the head—I mustn't even think about that.

I tried to bring to mind those wonderful times when I was surrounded by friends, but the only thing I conjured up was the groans of pleasure with every bite my friends, their wives, and their children took of the grilled meat. "Mmm, Sayed, this is just wonderful," I kept hearing. "What is it, mutton? Wow, Meni, it's mutton, just taste that rib. Where do you buy mutton, anyway?" And, like an idiot, I would boast about the local butcher shop, explain to them how I chose the cuts from the refrigerator there and how I asked the butcher to mix lamb with the mutton and add mint when he ground the meat into kebabs. Like an idiot, now I see myself smiling at them with all my heart when they visited us at home, even as I slaved and sweated over the barbecue I had prepared in advance. With a towel draped over one shoulder, tongs in hand, and smoke in my eyes, I spiced the meat, turned it over, and served it in a pot at the table, then ran back to turn over the skewers, chase away the cats, and make sure the guests had everything they needed at the table. It was always a barbecue.

But after we moved, what did I make friends when they visited? Goulash. That's the only thing I know how to make—goulash. They must have grown tired of it, they probably know how to make it themselves. Sure, there's no lack of shoulder cuts at the Tiv Taam chain. But no, no, no. It's not true, I know it, that's not the reason that Roni, Asaf, and Shira don't come here anymore. They are going through a rough time, or maybe a good time, with their families. Friday is sacred to them, I know. I tried to escape into Fallada's Berlin, to focus on the text and concentrate on the doings of the German couple who wanted to topple Hitler by means of protest postcards.

"Your phone is flashing," my wife shouted over the TV.

"Can you see what it says on the screen?" I shouted back.

"'Asaf,'" she said, and I jumped out of the bed.

"Asaf," I answered with a smile that reminded me of the barbecue era and made my wife sneer in contempt. "What, you're at your parents' place? Ah? I knew it. How are they?"

"Tomorrow?" I said when Asaf asked me what we were doing the next day, and I looked straight into my wife's eyes as I said to her, "Asaf wants to know if we're busy tomorrow, because they are inviting us over to their place for lunch."

"We're not busy," she said, shaking her head.

"We'll be delighted to see you tomorrow," I told him. "*Wallah*, we missed you, too," I echoed my friend's comment, all the time hurling accusatory looks at my wife, looks that said: "You have a problem, you have a problem of inferiority, you think you're smarter than everyone else, with people like you there's no way to make peace here, because of people like you there is no trust between the two nations. Please, here is a true friend who is inviting me to his place tomorrow, and no, it's not because of the barbecues that he likes me."

"Great, one o'clock is excellent," I answered happily. "Do you want us to bring anything?" I asked out of courtesy before hanging up.

"If you wouldn't mind going through Beit Safafa, to your butcher shop," Asaf said, while my wife gave me inquisitive looks, wondering why I was nodding and not hanging up. "I could buy here, you know, but I have the feeling that it's better at your guy's, and if he has mutton that would be great." He went on: "There's bread here, but maybe you could bring a package of pitas. Do they also have good hummus there? Or would you rather go through Abu Ghosh? I just bought a barbecue this morning and put it in the garden, and I bought this American coal that's self-igniting—is that good? Okay, I'm relying on you to lend a hand with that."

"No, sorry, I can't, no," I replied, trying to ensure that the expression on my face did not give away the character of the conversation. "Yes, too bad. I have something tomorrow, too, at—work. Never mind. Another time. Bye."

"What nerve," I informed my wife immediately, as she looked at me with curiosity and waited for an explanation of the surprising cancellation. "Where am I supposed to get him apple strudel now?"

PILGRIMS' PROGRESS

December 17, 2010

My mother decided she was going to become religiously observant. She was always afraid of God, so she started to pray, and a few months ago she started to cover her head with a kind of colorful kerchief. At first she tied it in some ridiculous way, but with time she got the hang of it, and since then she never leaves the house without a kerchief. She now even goes to the gym, which she insists on calling the Homeless Place, in Nike shoes and a kerchief. The truth is that nothing has changed in the house since my mother found religion. She is still hooked on Egyptian TV series, massive furniture, and paintings of birds, preferably black swans, on Swiss lakes.

The blow landed a few months ago, when Mom decided that the time had come to go on pilgrimage to Mecca. Pilgrimage is one of the five basic precepts in Islam, and Mom was determined to fulfill it. "You are going on pilgrimage with me to Mecca," she said to Dad, who at first was reluctant, because of his illness, and suggested a weekend in Bulgaria instead.

My father lost his faith in God at some point in 1967. "Not only because of the defeat," he told me once. "You have to understand: when I was a boy, I was told that there is a rock in Jerusalem that floats in the air and on which you can see the footprint of the prophet Muhammad, who ascended to heaven from there. After the occupation I went there and didn't see any rock floating in the air. On the spot I became a communist."

But Mom persisted. At first she tried to persuade him by gentle means. It's a spiritual revelation, she said; they would both go through the process together, slowly, without complications. She spoke of the blessing the pilgrimage would bring to their lives and to the lives of their children. But Dad wasn't persuaded, so Mom had no choice but to move to the contingency plan: "Do you want people to remember you as a communist infidel? Who will come to your funeral? And I haven't even gotten to the part about the torments of the grave and the fire in which you will roast in hell."

She instilled fear in Dad's heart. He started to pray and registered with Mom for the hajj. I did all I could to talk them out of it. I talked about the crowding, his illness, and what would happen if, heaven forbid, he should need treatment there. I have to say that I myself was very frightened, mainly because of the familiar stories about pilgrims who are trampled to death from time to time for unclear reasons. Mom said it's a blessing to die there, because you are ensured a direct entry into paradise. Dad said that the ones who get trampled in Mecca are mainly Indonesians, Pakistanis, and Indians, who, if they did not die because of the crowding in Mecca, would certainly drown in some mudslide or other natural disaster. My father claims it's a curse they suffer from, and has nothing to do with the ordeals of the hajj.

They went a few weeks ago and left me by myself for the longest period I have ever known: they were gone for twenty-five whole days. Back when I was a boy, I really hated it when my parents went on a trip; I was worried, I got uptight, I was sure they would never come back. Since growing up I was sure I had overcome this, but their trip to Mecca showed me that I am not yet ready, I still need them, and I still don't know how I will be able to cope if something should happen to them, heaven forbid.

The peak came at the Feast of the Sacrifice. It was the first time I had come home for the holiday without my parents being in the house. We didn't know what to do; my brothers and I were at a loss. Usually our parents see to everything, but here we were, four brothers on the Feast of the Sacrifice with no idea of what to do. "Maybe we'll just have a barbecue?" my younger brother suggested as a compromise. But it was too late, because everyone buys the meat before the holiday and not on the day itself, when all the butcher shops are closed. Finally we bought frozen hot dogs and hamburgers from some supermarket in Kfar Sava.

During the holiday, the Arab TV networks broadcast live from Mecca. We followed the ceremonies closely, trying to spot our parents amid the incomprehensible crowd of four million pilgrims all dressed in white and all performing the same rites.

"What will we do about decorations?" my older brother asked two days before my parents were expected back.

"That's right," we all replied. "Everyone decorates ahead of the pilgrims' return."

"What will we do?" my younger brother asked.

"We will do nothing," I suggested.

"But what if they're disappointed?" my older brother asked.

"Why should they be disappointed?" I asked.

"Maybe they underwent substantial changes, I don't know, what if something happened to them there and they want to be true pilgrims?"

The thought that my parents might have changed in some substantial way frightened me very much. In my mind's eye I saw my father kneeling opposite the Black Stone in Mecca, weeping bitterly and seeing the light. He probably already has a beard, I thought, and Mom has probably changed the colorful kerchief for a hijab—maybe she's already walking around with her eyes covered, like the most pious women.

"Why do you say things like that?" I scolded my brother, trying to chase out these thoughts.

"Well," he replied, "things like that happen. You never know. Besides, our parents were always extreme."

In the end we pasted up huge banners on the walls of the house, and my brother went to Ra'anana to buy balloons with hearts on them and ribbons saying "Welcome Home" in Hebrew.

We didn't know exactly when our parents would get back from Saudi Arabia. After the holiday I had to get back to Jerusalem with my family for work and school. I continued to follow the news and called home to Tira every few hours to check if my parents had happened to return already, primed for whatever changes the journey might have caused, to find out if they were still the same. Sometimes, when I held the receiver waiting for an answer, I was afraid my father would answer with *salaam alaikum* and declare that he was not going to let me into the house again if I continued to drink.

And then it came. Another routine ring and my mother answered.

"Hallo."

"Mom?"

"Hi, how are you all?"

"Fine. How are you? How's Dad? How was it?"

"Excellent. We bought the children an Xbox."

"Really?"

"Yes. Just a minute, I'll put Dad on."

"Dad?"

"How are you?"

"Fine. How are you and Mom?"

"We bought the children an Xbox in Mecca."

"Really?"

"Yes, it plays burned DVDs, too."

DISHING IT OUT

February 4, 2011

I decided at the beginning of the week that I just had to get a Facebook page. I've refrained because of my tendency to develop addictions, but now I realized I had no choice. No way was I going to miss the next revolution. Not that I really understood how revolutions are made on Facebook, but I figured I ought to be on there, just to be on the safe side.

For more than a week now, I haven't been able to tear myself away from the news. All the television and radio stations, newspapers, and websites. I feel a need to be up to date at any given moment about what's happening in Egypt. I'm pleased and worried by the news and hoping it all turns out well.

This week I discovered that I love revolutions, at least on television. They have a way of making most existential concerns disappear. When there's a revolution in Egypt, you can't really get depressed about not knowing what happens after you die. When there are millions out on the streets, that's not the time to start panicking about contracting swine flu.

"Quiet!" I shouted at my daughter when she asked me to give her a ride to her music class earlier in the week. "Music? They're bringing down Mubarak and you want to talk to me about music? Do you know what it means to get Mubarak out?"

"Hey, maybe you could get the dishes out of the sink," suggested my wife.

"What's wrong with you?" I barely turned my head away from the screen when I responded. "You want me to miss the event that's about to change the face of the region just because of a few dirty dishes? People are dying in the streets and you want me to take care of some dishes."

"Fine," she said. "I'll take her to her class and you keep on starting revolutions from the sofa. Just watch where you spit out the sunflower seeds."

That's it, everything's about to change here. Not that I understand how or why, but that's the general feeling. Otherwise, how do you explain the fact that the authorities in Israel are so fearful of change? Ah yes, they're afraid of the Muslim Brotherhood and another Iran on the border. After all, most of our analysts have already decided that contrary to what the demonstrators in Cairo's streets are demanding, there is no chance for democracy in the Islamic world.

"That's not right," argued Dr. Uriya Shavit on Reshet's morning program. "Indonesia is the largest Muslim country in the world, and it has a real democracy."

"Yes," countered Eli Shaked, "but Indonesia is not an Arab country. And there's a difference." According to the former Israeli ambassador to Cairo, whose employment history proves he must know Egypt like the back of his hand, Arabness is the problem that's preventing democracy.

And it's not racist, he explains to the host. They just don't have the good old Judeo-Christian values, says the ambassador. In other words, it's not a matter of education or poverty or long years of oppression; it's the lousy Arab character that's prevented us from reaching the status of Christians and Jews, who tout acceptance of others as their supreme slogan.

I used to think one of the troubles with this place, where people are always buzzing about humanism and accepting others, was the lack of knowledge of Arabic. After listening to our Arab affairs analysts, I reached the conclusion that it would be better not to teach Arabic at all here. In fact, Yisrael Beiteinu should get a law passed banning Jews from learning Arabic, if the result is going to be analysts like Guy Bechor.

"Women?!" he said, laughing, when the host asked about the role of women in events happening in Egypt, and he cited a completely true story about how Saddam once mocked the Americans for sending a woman representative to warn him of the consequences of invading Kuwait. Bechor ignored all the television images from the demonstrations showing women taking a substantial part in the events in the Arab street. But as Bechor himself said, "I've come here to explain to you how the Egyptian mind works." The Israeli media can't manage to be consistent. At the start of the demonstrations, our analysts all decided that what was happening in Tunisia would not happen in Cairo. Afterward, they went back and forth between declaring that these were Mubarak's final days and insisting that what happened to Ben Ali would not happen to Mubarak, instead of providing the plain facts, showing some respect, and telling the simple truth, which is: "We have absolutely no clue what's going to happen."

There's a lot of hypocrisy and condescension in Israel's institutionalized support for Mubarak's tyrannical rule, in its backing of a corrupt leader who established a brutal secret police state to suppress his citizens and keep their mouths shut. Sometimes it seems that what really worries the Israeli government, even more than the Muslim Brotherhood, is the real Egypt. It has always been more comfortable for Israel to fight the Muslims, as evidenced by the WikiLeaks documents that revealed how pleased the former IDF military intelligence chief Amos Yadlin was about the Hamas takeover in Gaza. The real problem is that, unlike Mubarak, an Arab democracy will not accept and will at least issue a voice of protest against Israel's policies in Gaza and the territories. It will make relations with its neighbor contingent upon the existence of a real democratic regime that is not based on intolerance and the trampling of the other. "One thing is certain," President Shimon Peres said this week, "Mubarak knew how to keep peace in the Middle East." That's precisely the problem, Mr. President: *There is no peace in the Middle East.*

One of the Israeli tourists who hastened to cut short his Cairo vacation and was interviewed upon landing in Israel gave a good description of what Israelis are feeling: "We were in a taxi and suddenly we saw thousands of people with sticks and stones coming toward us. It was terrifying." I know it's hard for us to conceive that the whole world isn't circling around us, but I have the strong impression, contrary to what many Israelis think, that the demonstrations in Egypt are not against Israel, and that whether or not the revolution succeeds, it is aimed at toppling not the government in Israel but rather the one in Cairo.

"How do you get on Facebook?" I asked my wife when she brought the kids home from their activities.

"If you do the dishes, I'll show you and I'll add you to my friends list."

"Don't bother just yet," I said, as I went back to staring at the live pictures from Tahrir Square. "A lot of water still has to flow in the Nile before revolution arrives here."

A LESSON IN ARABIC

March 4, 2011

We left the house together that afternoon. My wife took the car and drove our daughter to her music class at the conservatory, and I, seeing that it wasn't too cold, decided to walk with my son to the swimming pool. Moments like this fill me with a sense of triumph: my girl is on the way to the conservatory, my boy is heading for a swimming lesson. These are the kind of statements that I like to describe as "sayings you don't hear in Tira." Things that reassure me that it was a smart decision to move to a Jewish neighborhood—difficult, but right. A heated swimming pool next to the house, a conservatory ten minutes away by car—these definitely make a persuasive response to all the critics, Arabs and Jews alike, who attributed political, cultural, and national motives to an act that was driven mainly by the search for a better quality of life.

My son and I cross the neighborhood park, and he pulls his hand out of mine and runs across the green grass, stretching his arms to the sides like the wings of a plane and tilting his body right and left in turn. He runs in circles—sometimes returning to me, smiling, and then away again running as hard as he can. "Look how fast I can run," he says, and I, walking slowly, almost asked him to stop running so he could preserve his energy for swimming. I had momentarily forgotten the ability of small children to run and cavort all day long.

This is the second year of swimming lessons for my son. I remember how scared he was of the water two years ago and how the elderly Russian teacher gave him a smile and immediately called him a hero, how at the start the teacher persuaded him just to sit on the edge of the pool and splash his feet in the water, then quickly gave him the confidence to join him in the water, "just to stand." Already in the first lesson my son was diving and learning how to make bubbles, trusting his smiling teacher.

This will be the last lesson with the Russian teacher. "The work conditions here are bad," he said a month ago, when he announced he would be leaving. "They don't pay me overtime." My son was very sorry about this. The first thing he said was that he would not go on with the swimming lessons if his teacher left. The other children in his group had already been assigned to other teachers; only my child refused to enter another group and insisted on staying with his teacher until the last minute. The elderly teacher was delighted. "I knew," he said, and the two of them entered the pool for a private farewell lesson.

The pool was filled with children of all ages. In one corner, girls were practicing synchronized swimming, the bigger children who had already taken part in competitions were swimming quickly in two lanes, and the younger ones were practicing first strokes with their teachers in smaller groups. My son knew that this would be the last lesson—more like a hotel pool than being strict about the right strokes. The pool was very noisy, and from my seat among the parents I couldn't hear the conversation between the teacher and my son, though from time to time I saw that they were both smiling, diving, and coming back up, laughing. There were also moments when the teacher talked and my son listened sorrowfully, nodding his head and dipping under the water to wash away a feeling of unease or to deepen some fine thought.

"You are a hero," the elderly teacher told my son at the end of the lesson, and ran his hand through the boy's wet hair. "You will be a great swimmer," he said before the two parted for the last time. I shook the teacher's hand and then he held my son's hand in a long grip before turning to go.

"He loves you very much," I said to my son as I rubbed him down with a towel.

"What will he do?" he asked.

"He will probably teach swimming somewhere else," I replied.

"So can I go somewhere else?" my son asked.

I had no answer. A little boy approached us and shifted the conversation to a different place. The boy came up to us in the way children have, with a hesitant gaze, keeping a safe distance. Seeing him, my son bent his head in embarrassment as he always does, occasionally stealing a glance at the boy.

"He wants to be your friend," I said to my son, who now plucked up the courage to look the new boy in the eye.

"What language are you speaking?" the boy asked with a smile.

My son looked at me as though requesting permission to embark on a new relationship, already forgetting his former teacher, and I nodded, permitting him to take matters into his own hands.

"Arabic," my son told the boy, smiling.

"*Ichsa*," the boy said in response, and went on staring at my son for a moment before returning to his mother's arms.

I will never forget the look that passed across my son's face. It was a look that gave me the chills and made my hands shake as I went on drying his wet body. It was a look that passed rapidly from smile to stunned gaze, affront, and finally accusation. A look that I heard telling me, "Why did you lie to me, why didn't you do something, it's all your fault."

What did I do? That was the question that resonated in my mind all the way home and wouldn't let go of me. Because of me and my caprices, my son has to cope with situations like this, and at his age, too. I lied to my children when I taught them that everyone is equal; I lied when I said there are no differences between Muslims, Jews, and Christians. I cheated them when I surrounded them with protective hothouses of mixed kindergartens and pleasant neighborhoods.

"You know," I said, breaking the silence and aware that I was about to utter another lie, "that boy is really dumb." I tried to chuckle, to laugh off the whole incident, to paint it as anomalous, unnatural. He didn't reply.

What is he thinking about now, the little boy? How much does he really hate me? What does he understand from the other boy's *ichsa*? And what will it do to him? Will he now stop talking to me in Arabic if there are strangers around? Will it make him more cautious? Make him ashamed of what he is? Oy, what I wouldn't do for God to tell me what my son is feeling now.

"Please," I said in the most caressing tone of voice I could muster at that moment, "what do you say, eh?"

"Dad," he said, "I don't want to go to the pool anymore."

"Why?" I asked, trying to conceal my sorrow. "You like swimming very much."

He said nothing for a moment and then replied, "I don't want another teacher."

HOLY WORK

March 11, 2011

We had no choice, we had to have a housemaid. I was again immersed in a sea of work, and my wife, the social worker, had declared a strike. At first I managed to overcome the piles of laundry, keep the dishes under control, drive the children to school and to enrichment groups, order pizza or stop on the way home to buy something in a pita so the children wouldn't be considered hardship cases—at least not now, with the social welfare bureaus on strike.

Occasionally I gave the children a shower; once in a while I vacuumed. But in the past weeks, what with franchisees, deadlines, and nervous producers breathing down my neck, even the little housework I did became a huge burden. "You have to get a maid," said almost every friend who had risked a visit to our place recently.

It took more than two months after making the decision until we managed to find a maid who was both legal and available. An affluent Jewish friend who's always complaining about a lack of money recommended his own maid. "Tikva is absolutely amazing," he said, "and I persuaded her to make an effort and save a good friend who's in distress."

"Thanks a lot," I replied. "You have no idea how hard it is to find someone with references."

"Yes," the friend said, "I know, and it's not easy for me to share her, either. But you have to pick her up from her home and take her back afterward."

"No problem," I said, ready to fulfill almost any condition.

"She's also a bit expensive," the friend added.

"Money is no longer a problem" was my reply.

"She doesn't know that you're Arabs."

"What?"

"Listen, Sayed," the friend said, placing a hand on my right shoulder, "I want to tell you that I've known Tikva for more than twenty years already. There's no way she would have agreed to work in the home of Arabs."

"I don't understand," I stammered, "so how exactly . . ."

"She doesn't have to know," the friend replied firmly. "Listen to what I'm telling you: for her to work in an Arab's house is almost like denying God."

"She also believes in God?"

"Let's put it like this," he said with a sigh. "She spends everything she earns on flights to Uman."

"I don't want to hear about it" was my wife's initial reaction. "Have you lost your mind?"

"You know what?" I shouted, losing my patience. "Then you clean the house. I don't care anymore. I have no time. I'm going to get fired from my job soon because of all this housework. It's not my problem. You don't want Tikva? Then clean the place yourself, and you know what? Start cooking, too. It's about time."

"Fine, fine," she said after a moment's thought. "Okay, the children are in school during those hours."

I understood that she had agreed to an act of deceit.

"Shalom, Tikva," I said on the phone after taking a deep breath. "Shalom, I am the friend of—"

"Shalom," she replied jovially. "Yes, you're Israel?"

Israel? That's the name he gave her, the nutcase. "Yes," I replied. "I wanted to know where I should pick you up tomorrow . . ."

This is it. It's happening. Our first housemaid will arrive on International Women's Day. Our first Jewish housemaid, our first

Jewish employee. When all is said and done, I wonder how many Arabs have been in a position to pay a Jew for work.

I arranged to pick her up at eight. At seven thirty I would send the kids off to school, take my wife to a friend's house, and then get Tikva. It doesn't have to be complicated; there's no sign with our name at the entrance to the building. Afterward I will leave her on her own—my friend said she's very reliable—and when she's done I will return to drive her home. At which time I will also pay her. I will actually take money out of my wallet and pay the Jewish woman. Okay, my wife really let me have it, but I still think it's a type of revolution.

Now I have to hide every telltale Arab sign in the house. First I disconnected the telephone, in case my mother should phone, heaven forbid, and frighten our Tikva. Then I started to take the family photos off the walls.

"What are you doing?" my wife shouted.

"With all due respect, and you are very beautiful," I told her as I went on taking down the photos, "but still, it's sometimes pretty obvious that you are an Arab."

I hid the family photos together with a stack of children's books and a few books of poetry in the storeroom. I made a final tour of the house to ensure that no scrap of paper, workbook, or other sign of Arabic remained visible. A few paintings we had received as gifts that I was afraid suffered from "Arab taste" were also thrown into the storeroom, which I then locked. To be on the safe side, I threw out a bag of squash and a package of pitas that announced in Arabic, "Beit Safafa Bakery." "That's that," I asserted when my labors were done, my gaze scanning the empty walls. "This is what a Jewish home looks like."

Everything went according to plan. I sweated a little in the car, but that didn't bother Tikva. When we got to the apartment, she immediately turned on the Hebrew music channel at high volume. She took a quick look at the apartment, turned her head left and right, and said she worked seven hours a day, tops, and in her opinion would not manage to do half the work our place needed. I nodded in agreement, said I would collect her at three and then pay her, and left for work.

I wasn't able to write a word. I stared at the blank computer screen, consumed with worry, upset, wondering whether I had left something that might give away the secret after all. A huge surprise awaited me when I got home at three. I didn't believe the apartment could look like this. It was so clean I almost slipped on the floor. "What, it's glass?" I asked in amazement when I looked at the door of the oven and discovered that it was transparent. "All I can say is thank you," I said, almost in tears when I saw that the window could let light into the apartment. As I took out my wallet my emotion reached a peak, like at a historic moment, and I was sorry I had no camera to capture the event.

"Listen, Israel," Tikva said, curbing my excitement, "if that's really your name."

"Did something happen?" I started to shake.

"I found textbooks in a cupboard and I saw that you tried to hide them."

"What textbooks?"

"Honey," she said with a malicious smile, "I am half Iraqi, you know, and letters in Arabic, believe me, are something I can recognize."

"I apologize deeply," I said, starting to stutter. "I really don't know what to say, but I just couldn't tell you, I couldn't expose myself."

"Sweetie," she said with a smile, "you have nothing to worry about, my soul."

"I don't understand."

"Listen to me, you people are doing holy work," she said, leaving me with my mouth agape, not least because I had never told her my occupation. "It's a great honor to work for someone like you," she said, as she at last took the money I was holding in my hand and whispered to me with a wink, "My father was in the Shin Bet, too."

CAR NOIR

April 8, 2011

I got a new car this week. Not just any car: an "executive" car. I've never had one like it—and I've never been an executive, either. It's a whole different world, the world of executives. You have to experience it in order to understand what I'm talking about.

Suddenly, from a small car with a small engine, I have this huge company vehicle and have no idea how to park it. Lucky for me I have those reverse-parking sensors—not that I can calculate the distances behind me according to the beeps, but I am still very happy to have those sensors. If the government weren't so racist it would install those sensors in the back of every Arab car, at its expense. Arab kids are always playing behind cars, and it's the duty of the state to safeguard them. It's also a lot simpler than building playgrounds for them.

Anyway, I got this fancy car. And it's black. With a turbo engine that knows how to generate 156 horsepower at 6,000 rpm. A car with black leather seats and buttons on the steering wheel that have names like "cruise control" and "telephone activation." Every click of a button changes the image on a screen, and there are a lot of screens in the new car. I can also control the audio system via the buttons on the steering wheel. What an incredible system. I've never heard Israel Radio so clearly.

"Listen up, listen up," I instructed my wife and children on the way to Tira immediately after getting the new car. "Do you hear this?" I shouted, turning up the volume and changing stations with a gentle press of the buttons.

"Amazing," the kids said, and asked me to turn it up higher.

"It's awful," my wife said.

I immediately castigated her for not knowing how to pay a compliment: "Instead of enjoying such excellent sound quality as this, you say it's awful?"

"I was referring to the story on the radio about the Palestinians who were accused of raping that boy."

"Why do you have to spoil things?" I scolded her, and changed the station.

I had to go to Tira, to drive through the streets slowly, as slowly as possible, and look around so people would recognize me and know it was me driving that luxury automobile. And see that I, too, in the end, am some kind of success story. And that yes, it's possible to make a living, even to get rich, from writing. Even though that's not true, but no one has to know how I got a gorgeous car like this.

It started with shouting. That morning, I arrived for a meeting with the executive producer of the company I work for. He asked how the script was coming along and became furious when he understood that because of me, the company might not meet the deadline it had promised the broadcasting bodies, which would delay the shooting schedule and cause economic damage. The producer, noticing that I was suffering from a hangover, started to shout at me like no one has shouted at me since primary school. And I, hypersensitive in the wake of another night of drinking and surprised at the yelling, simply started to cry.

The producer had not expected that a respected author like me, who on the day before had been at the Sapir Prize ceremony, would howl like a small child. He gave me a hug, asked the secretary to bring me a glass of water, brought me tissues to wipe away the tears, and patted me gently on the back, saying, "There, there, I'm sorry." But the crying wouldn't stop.

"I'm so sorry," the producer went on, "I didn't mean it, I just wanted you to work. Stop already, you're tearing me apart. What can I do to calm you down? Enough, I'm crazy about you, you know I love you. You know what: I'll get you a new car. Not just any car, an executive car. What do you say?"

My parents were taken aback when they came out upon hearing the honking of the horn. What a honk this car has: a honk with character, a honk you have to pay attention to.

"Use it well," my parents said.

"How much did it cost?" my father asked with pride, and I, wanting very much for him to think I had bought the vehicle, said casually, "Two hundred," with a questioning tone in my voice.

"That's all?" he asked, surprised.

"The rest in installments," I added, all of us still sitting in the car.

"Well, aren't you coming out?"

"No, we have to go."

It's so nerve-racking, the streets of Tira. How do they expect me to drive a car like this on these bumpy streets with all the potholes? I've never seen such inconsiderate behavior toward executives. With all due respect to respect, I thought, I'll have to visit my parents less often.

It's amazing the effect a car like this has on your inner self. I drive and I know I am holding the steering wheel differently, with a kind of self-confidence. I look differently at the other drivers waiting with me at the red light, as though I have more control over my life, as though I have cracked the secret of success, and from now on I'll get through rough patches and difficult stretches with pulsating pistons and fabulous suspension.

Now, as my wife sits beside me with her legs stretched out full length, I know she feels she made the right choice. The children are sleeping in the back with a smile on their lips, knowing that I will always be there for them. What pride fills my heart when I return to the parking lot next to the building, knowing that this is the most expensive car there. I am the kid who made it all the way from Tira to a black executive car. I am the one who will prove to everyone that it's possible, really possible—you just have to believe.

"Ya know what," my neighbor, the one with the PhD in art, said to me the next morning when we met in the stairwell, "this building is going to the dogs. Really scary."

"What happened?" I asked, frightened.

"It looks like some serious goons have moved in here," he said. "Didn't you see the black car parked next to the building?"

THE BIGGER PICTURE

May 20, 2011

I don't know how to explain this, but something happened to me recently. A kind of nationalism that I never knew was in me suddenly emerged and began to rule me. Maybe it's the influence of Israeli discourse, which is dripping with chauvinism; maybe it's the "Nakba Law" passed by the Knesset; or maybe it's actually the revolutions all around us that filled me with a desire to commemorate Nakba Day this year, together with my children.

As opposed to the superficial and predictable speeches of the prime minister, who bases his entire philosophy on scare tactics and describing an enemy whose goal is to exterminate us, for me commemorating Nakba Day doesn't include any desire to destroy Israel and has nothing to do with hatred of Israel. On the morning of Nakba Day I was set to take a trip with my children to one of the Arab villages in the Jerusalem area, and I said to myself: As long as the school system, the government, and the media sell themselves a noble story about the pioneers who returned to the land of their forefathers, there will be no chance of understanding who here is really prepared for painful concessions.

"Acknowledgment," I declared to my children as we stood in the doorway, "acknowledgment that Grandpa, who was killed in 1948, also has a share in the story of this place."

I was already outside the house when the phone rang. "Hello, have I reached Mr. Sayed Kashua?" asked the charming voice on the other end of the line.

"Yes," I replied proudly ("Mr." does that to me), and the speaker identified herself as the representative of the cable company to which we subscribe. In a very affectionate tone she told me she was happy to inform me that they had decided to let me join their VIP department. The VIP department, she added, would provide various benefits, including a direct phone number to the service manager, which would preclude my having to wait ages for a recorded response like ordinary people.

"Wow," I said to her, "thank you very much, I'm very happy about the acknowledgment."

"Dad," asked my daughter, pulling on my shirtsleeve, "have they acknowledged the Nakba?"

"No," I whispered, "more important. VIP department."

"We're very proud to have you join our department. Is there anything I can do for you, sir?" asked the woman with angelic politeness. And I, being a VIP, couldn't refuse. After all, she so much wanted to help, and I was also embarrassed by the fact that I didn't have an HD connection and that I still hadn't asked them to install a VOD converter, which can record or order a speech by the prime minister and stop it in the middle. I had a feeling that I was the only one in the department of influential people who still made do with a basic package and a pre-1948 converter.

"Yes," I heard myself saying in a strange voice, which came in the package with the title VIP, "yes, to tell you the truth, I've been wanting for a long time to ask for your new sophisticated converter, but I didn't have time. I was simply . . ."

"Yes, sir," she replied, "of course you're a very busy man, that's why we're here. It's an amazing converter and I'm sure you'll enjoy it, you and your entire family. With your permission, I'm writing down the order."

"Dad," chirped the two children, who were standing next to me with hats on their heads and knapsacks on their backs. "Nakba Day, Dad."

"Just a minute," I whispered to them, "I'm arranging VOD for you, and with a discount yet."

"Sir." The representative of the beautiful people returned to me. "I see that I can send you an installer today. Are you busy?"

"No," I told her, "I actually took the day off," and immediately regretted it, hoping she wouldn't think that—God forbid—it was because of the Nakba or something strange of that sort. "You know, I do that sometimes for the inspiration."

"Our technician will be at your house within two hours," she said. "Is that suitable, sir?"

"Of course it's suitable," I replied, and she said, "Have a nice day, sir."

"All right, so we'll go to the Nakba in two hours, so what? What's the hurry? As though the Nakba will run away if we postpone it a little," I said to the children.

"So where did you take the children?" asked my wife, calling from work.

"Uh, we're at home," I stammered, telling her about the technician who was on the way.

"You took a day off! You didn't send the children to school because of your VIP package?" she shouted angrily.

"All right, I'll take them later," I promised. "Meanwhile I'm having a Nakba activity for them at home. Do you know how much they're suffering? There's knocking at the door, it's the technician. Don't worry, in fifteen minutes I'll take their picture in an abandoned village."

The technician brought the converter, but he was unable to connect it. "The converter is too far from the Internet, it's not me. Because you're in the VIP department there will be a technician coming who knows what to do." About two hours later another technician came, who said it would be really ugly but he would have to install a seven-meter external cable from the Internet to the converter. But there may be another solution, for which they would send another technician. The third technician claimed that the specific Internet connection I had in the house wasn't compatible with the specific converter that the previous technician had brought.

"Dad," said my daughter when it was almost three o'clock, "the Nakba!"

"All right," I shouted, "don't you see that I'm stuck here without VOD and without television? A bit of understanding is all I'm asking for."

"Dad," she continued, "soon Mom will be coming back, and if she finds out you didn't do a Nakba Day with us, you'll turn into a refugee."

"You're right," I said, loading the children into the car. On the way I spoke to my brother, who knows a little about wires and technology, and he explained how to solve the problem the three VIP technicians had been unable to solve.

"So where are you?" asked my wife, just as I was standing in line at the Bezeq store in Romema (this time she was calling from home).

"We're just hiking between the villages of Sheikh Badr and Lifta."

"Very good." I heard my wife calming down.

I exchanged the wireless router for the model my brother had told me to get, and I dashed to Office Depot in the mall to purchase two outline network connections.

"We're hungry," said the children when I had the equipment in hand.

"I'm a little worried," said my wife over the phone. "There's a lot of tension and chaos because of the Nakba, are you watching over the children?"

"You have nothing to worry about, right now we're eating on the lands of Malha village," I said as I paid for two children's meals at McDonald's and got a balloon as a gift.

My wife was really emotional when we returned home. She hugged the children and gave me a kiss. "I don't know how you suddenly became so brave."

"We wanted to inform you that we're taking care of the problem, the senior echelons in the company are also involved," said the VIP representative, updating me over the phone.

"There's no need," I informed her, smiling in front of the amazing picture on the screen. Palestinians from the refugee camps were climbing the fence. "Look," I said to my wife proudly, pointing to the television, "look how well you can see the Golan Heights."

AND THEN THE POLICE ARRIVED

July 1, 2011

The bedside clock showed 1 A.M. when I woke up. A group of noisy teenagers had chosen to hang out by a fence beneath my window. They sang, screamed, and shouted fragments of sentences in their adolescent voices, not realizing how irritating they were being. I got up to check on the children, looked at the exultant teenagers, and hated them with all my heart: if they only knew what I'd gone through today, if they only understood how much I needed these hours of sleep! Honest to God, if I were strong and courageous enough, I would go down and hit them, kick their young asses, shut them up, and force them to collect the fragments of glass and apologize for their laughter while they were smashing bottles.

I drank some water and went back to bed after closing the windows and turning on the air conditioner—the usual effective method of shutting out the noise of summer vacation. But I hate turning on the air conditioner when the children are sleeping. I'm afraid of a gas leak, although I installed detectors. I'm afraid of a blown fuse that could cause a fire, and that's why I don't turn on electrical appliances at night. Everything will be all right, I told myself, trying in vain to get myself to fall back asleep. So I'll stay awake, I'll wait for the terrible gang to leave so it will be quiet again, and then I'll turn off the air conditioner and open the windows wide.

I went downstairs to the study, where the windows are always open because of cigarette fumes, and the youthful noise again accosted my ears. As soon as all the pressure is over, I vowed, I'll stop smoking. I'm no longer young and the cigarettes are wearing me out, I thought, as I coughed and lit up.

Contrary to all logic, I felt alert and thought for a moment that maybe I'd turn on the computer and do some work. After all, I didn't write a single word today. I could go back to work on the series and try to finish an episode that I was supposed to submit a few weeks ago. Or I could also write the column for the paper instead of waiting till the last moment.

I deliberated for a long time as to what to do first, until I decided to forget it. I'll soon get tired again, I figured. I'll just finish this cigarette and those annoying kids under the window will leave and I'll go back to bed. I must sleep, after all; I have an exhausting day ahead of me tomorrow, too.

The scream of one of the girls outside reminded me of my wife's scream when she woke me up twenty-four hours earlier.

"I'm bleeding," she shouted, and got up in a panic, holding her stomach and running to the shower. "It's heavy bleeding," she shouted, as I threw on a shirt and flip-flops.

The children were still sleeping and I didn't know how I could leave them alone in the apartment. I called an ambulance and immediately regretted it. How would I send her alone to the hospital in an ambulance? And the children? I've never left them alone. If my little boy wakes up and doesn't find me at home he's liable to . . . I don't even want to think about it.

"Sweetie," I whispered as I gently woke up my daughter, and smiled as though about to inform her that she had won some sort of gift. "Listen, sweetie," I said to her when she opened her eyes,

"Mommy's fine, but I have to take her to the hospital for a checkup."
She nodded her head, promising me that she understood every
word. "I'm leaving you in charge of your brother because I know
I can count on you."

"Of course," she said, getting out of bed to see Mommy before
we left.

The security people at the hospital let us through quickly,
opening gates whose existence I hadn't been aware of until now.
Again the hospital, again the same terrible elevator that announces
the names of the departments in the Mother and Child Pavilion
at Hadassah in Ein Karem. "Pediatric intensive care," "neonatal
intensive care," "at-risk pregnancy," "pediatric surgery," "emergency
room and delivery rooms . . ."

"I don't feel any movement," my wife told the nurse who received her, and the nurse immediately connected her to a monitor.

"There's a pulse," said the nurse, and I saw my wife breathe
a sigh of relief.

Things were already beginning to look different. The young
doctor who had arrived quickly determined that the bleeding had
abated, did a few tests, and said that to be on the safe side they
would prepare her for surgery, but he was optimistic that everything
would be all right.

"Daddy," asked my daughter, who hadn't gone back to sleep,
over the phone, "how's Mommy?"

"Everything's all right," I answered her. "I'll be coming back
home right away. Go back to sleep, sweetie."

"Can I speak to her?"

The sun blinded me as I went back home. I felt around in my
pockets for a cigarette I knew I wouldn't find. The moment this
thing is over, I have to stop smoking.

The children were asleep when I arrived, and soon I'll wake
them up for school. First I'll change the stained sheet, I'll turn over

the mattress so they won't see what happened, I'll wash the floor, I'll clean the toilet, and then I'll wake them up with a big smile, so they'll know that life is a wonderful thing.

I finished the cigarette to the noise of a vehicle with a diesel engine entering the neighborhood slowly. I crushed the cigarette in the ashtray and looked out the window of the study. A police van was dispersing the cheerful gang of teens. One of them shouted at the police as he tottered off.

"What have we done, really?" he yelled, adding a curse word in Arabic. "Let us enjoy life a little!"

And for some reason I thought for a moment that he was right.

WHAT'S IN A NAME?

July 29, 2011

"You have to take the kids on vacation," my wife said in the morning.

"What, and leave you alone?"

"Yes," she replied. "The day camps will soon be finished, and the poor dears went through a few hard months and haven't been on a trip for a long time."

"You're right," I said, knowing that the two older children had been a bit neglected in the difficult months of pregnancy, and definitely deserved a pampering holiday before going back to school. "I'll try to find something for August," I told her before going out with the children. "In the meantime, do us a favor and try to find a name for the baby."

Finding a name for an Arab child is hard work. We browse websites that suggest names, pore through Arab dictionaries and books of poetry—we even looked for appropriate names in the Koran, but all in vain. Every name was disqualified, one after the other. You have to make sure the name doesn't rhyme with a curse, which is almost impossible, because every name in Arabic has a rhyming curse, and even if it doesn't, that won't prevent other children from inventing curses without bothering about whether they rhyme. In the end, strong and threatening children are the only ones whose names don't rhyme with demeaning words and humiliating phrases.

We can't take a chance with this child, because he was born a preemie. It's likely the new child, like his brother, will enter a mixed

education system, so we have to make sure to find an Arabic name
that won't make things too hard for the teachers and the Jewish
schoolchildren. It's not pleasant when your name gets mangled. Still,
whatever you do, in the end they'll always call you Said.

In general, experience shows it's best to give an Arab child
a universal name, one that doesn't sound like a suspicious object,
won't make security guards jump, or cause raised eyebrows when
it's called out in an Aroma Espresso Bar. Most of the children who
are in school with my kids were given Arab names such as Adam,
Adi, Ram, Dani, Sami, Noor, and Amir, and I'm talking here about
the Muslims, because the Christians can also go for George, Peter,
Michel, Chris, and Michael.

On the one hand, we don't want to be thought of as making
special efforts to be accepted, to assimilate, to integrate into the
Israeli crowd. A little dignity, please; we'd like an Arab name with
meaning that will undoubtedly affect his identity. But hey—am I
really going to name my child Mustafa, Muhammad, or Ibrahim?
Won't that be an impediment on his path to finding a job, getting
accepted to school, or just going for a walk on the beach with pals?

After despairing, I entrusted the task to my wife. Let her
choose a name, and if he complains when he's older, I will point
out the one to blame.

"Well?" the redheaded director asked when we met in the
parking lot of the production offices. "Have you decided on a
name yet?"

"Not yet," I replied. "It's getting to be a bit much, eh?"

"Yeah. It's not pleasant," he said. "And is that why you're so
down?"

"No," I replied, "there's no one reason. It's everything—the
pressure in life, at work, being late in handing in stuff. And I still
have to find time for a vacation with the older ones."

"Maybe you'd like to join us?" he suggested as we walked up
the stairs. "It'll be really nice. My wife says it's a charming place—she

reserved a weekend in the middle of August. The question is if they have any more rooms there."

The resort was called Maagan Eden, the director said, and I entered the name in the search engine. Really charming. "Just two hours from the center of the country," the website said, "and you're in a different world—on a real Israeli vacation that is relaxing and enjoyable."

I called the number that appeared on the website and got through to reservations.

"Shalom," I said to the fellow who answered. "I want to ask, please, if you have rooms . . ." I mentioned the dates on which the director and his family would be there.

"What type of room do you want?" the fellow from reservations asked.

"A room suitable for one parent—me—and two children."

"I'm sorry," the fellow said. "I don't have rooms on those dates."

"Too bad," I said. "Any other dates in August?"

"No," he replied immediately. "I don't have rooms available in August at all. Everything is taken."

"All right," I said, "thanks." I hung up.

"I told you," the redheaded director said. "In August, everything is taken."

I don't know why, but I had an uneasy feeling. "Iris," I asked the tough producer, "could you please call this number and ask if they have rooms available on these dates?"

"What?" the redheaded director exclaimed with a cynical smile. "Don't you think you're being paranoid?"

"I know I'm paranoid," I said as Iris started to dial the number. "Tell him it's for one parent and two children," I told her, and she nodded her head.

Yes, she was told by reservations, there were rooms, and yes, they were suitable for a parent and two children. Yes, they had rooms on the exact dates in August that she asked about. She could even choose among several types of rooms that Maagan Eden had to offer.

"I don't believe it," said the redheaded director, who had been a witness to the conversation. "I just don't believe it."

"Enough," I scolded the wimp, who had started to cry. "Where are we living? Where are we living?"

I dialed again and got the same fellow. "Yes," he said, "but I told you a second ago that there are no rooms available."

"Fine," I replied. "I know there are rooms. Transfer me to the manager, please."

"My name is Sayed Kashua and I write for *Haaretz*," I told the manager. I told her what had just happened and asked for a response.

"It's like the stock market," she said. "One minute there are rooms, and the next minute there are none. People come to us from all sectors."

"Wonderful. And what is the situation of the stock market now? Are there rooms?"

"Yes," she said, "now we have rooms. Would you like to make a reservation?"

"Sure," I replied, and gave her my credit card number.

"I don't believe it," the redheaded director said, shaking and wiping away the tears as the tough producer laughed in his face.

"Hello," I said to my wife on the phone. "I organized a holiday for the kids. Did you find a name yet?"

"I'm still looking," she said. "Did you reserve at a good hotel?"

"A terrific hotel," I replied. "They don't allow Arabs."

LOVING ONE'S SON JUST AS NATURE MADE HIM—UNCIRCUMCISED

September 2, 2011

"No," I told my wife firmly. "Absolutely not. I refuse. No is no. End of discussion. Have I made myself clear?"

"So you want our son to be different?"

"You mean to tell me that circumcision is what's going to keep him from being different? He's an Arab, for God's sake."

I was absolutely certain that I was not going to have my baby boy circumcised. Certainly not after the trauma we went through exactly six years ago, when his older brother was circumcised. I remember that we called upon a pediatrician from Hadassah who was recommended by neighbors and friends, a pediatrician who had taken a mohel training course and who showed up equipped with an impressive medical case and gave us a sense of confidence. After all, it's a procedure everybody goes through—the baby cries a little, makes a little peepee, and then he's over it.

But then everything went wrong. Fifteen minutes after the doctor left the boy was still screaming and a check of his diaper revealed some notable bleeding. "Bleeding is natural," the doctor said on the phone, and I decided to wait a little longer and then check that everything was okay. But nothing was okay, and the baby kept on bleeding and screaming. Half an hour after the barbaric ceremony, we were in the pediatric emergency room at Shaare Zedek with the baby bandaged, hooked up to IV fluids, and having to endure all kinds of uncomfortable tests, and a mother who had to give blood in the event the baby would need a transfusion. We were discharged from the hospital after four difficult and exhausting days, and ever since I'd known for sure that there was no way I would ever want to have more children, and that if my wife somehow imposed her will on me, and if we had another boy, there was no way I would take the risk and have him circumcised.

"So you want him to be the only one of his friends who's uncircumcised?" My wife persisted in her persuasion campaign for her lost cause.

To be honest, I don't know where this theory actually comes from. Why should anyone ever see my son naked? Why do people always think that boys have to be on a soccer team where the players shower together after the game, waving their things all around? Is that really the way it is? Is that what soccer players do? Is that what boys do?

From family experience I know that he has a much better chance of being on a chess team than on a soccer team, and in chess, I know, you don't shower with the rest of the team, even after an especially exhausting game.

"Okay, not soccer," she went on. "But what about in the pool locker room?"

"You should know," I told her, "that you're just giving me more good reasons not to have him circumcised. I don't understand men who insist on walking around naked in the swimming pool locker room. I mean, put a towel on or something, get dressed in one of the stalls. If the foreskin is what's going to prevent my son from being one of these public undressers, then I say let's leave it on. Let's supersize it, even."

I honestly don't know what Islamic law has to say about circumcision. Unlike Israelis or Jews, who for some reason seem to have plenty of knowledge of religious law, I grew up in a not very religious home and I'm not always aware of what's allowed and what's not, of what we're commanded to do or not to do. I know that Muslims circumcise their sons, and I know that contrary to what Israelis think, they do this when the baby is a week old, or two weeks old, and not at age thirteen as the common notion has it.

"It's written in the Koran," argued my mother, having been recruited by my wife in the war of attrition against the foreskin. "It's a divine order," she stated with authority, although I certainly wouldn't rely on my mother when it comes to matters of Islamic law.

"Even if you're right," I told her on the phone, "I don't care what it says in the Koran. I'm not circumcising my son and that's it."

"But it's haram," she insisted in vain.

"I don't care," I insisted right back. "I'm not letting them cut my son and that's the end of it."

"Hang on, your father wants to speak to you."

"Hello, Dad," I growled into the phone, so he would know he had no chance.

"So . . . ," he went right ahead, "I understand that your son came out like you."

"What do you mean?"

"With you, too, every millimeter was critical, and your mother and I thought long and hard before we decided to have you circumcised."

"Nice, Dad," I replied. "That's not funny."

"So what is funny?" he asked, knowing exactly how to get to me. "For your son to get infections and diseases, God forbid?"

"What are you saying?"

"What am I saying?" he went on. "You don't know that having a foreskin is a surefire recipe for medical problems?"

"Uh, no," I started to stutter. "I really didn't know. Who told you that? That's rubbish . . . I mean, come on—all Christians aren't circumcised and I don't see that they're any less healthy."

When my father began ticking off examples of babies whose parents delayed the circumcision for one reason or another, elaborating on all the troubles they suffered, everything from urinary tract infections to heart attacks and terrible seizures, I started to retreat a bit from my firm stance against circumcision. My parents even gave me phone numbers to call that would prove them right about the whole issue of health and circumcision.

"Fine," I said to my wife after enduring my parents' scare campaign. "What should we do? Last time we used a doctor and look what happened!"

"A doctor? You think I'd take a chance like that again?" she said, full of self-confidence.

"I don't understand. Then who?"

"Rabbi Yishai," she said. "He's been recommended by absolutely everyone. He's cut half of Jerusalem without a problem."

"Rabbi Yishai? And just where am I going to find him?"

"He'll be here tomorrow afternoon," she said, proving once again that, just like with the pregnancy, she wants to hear my opinion only after the fact. "What's most important with these things is experience, and what are you going to do? A rabbi has more experience than anyone else."

"But a rabbi?" I was still trying to understand her decision. "Are you sure?"

"Hey, if we have to live in a Jewish state, then why not take advantage of what it offers?"

STILL SMALL VOICES IN THE NIGHT

January 6, 2012

Since the baby was born I've been sleeping in the living room. My little son hasn't yet learned to properly appreciate sleep, especially at night. I find this rather unsettling, for I come from a family that excels at sleep more than anything else. I myself love to sleep, I always have. When I was little I would go to sleep at seven, and when I got older I started getting into bed at nine.

Contrary to the popular belief that retirees become embittered folks who resent feeling useless, my parents eagerly looked forward to the day when the two of them could stop working so they could take a snooze whenever they felt like it.

And I once heard my wife chatting with my sister-in-law about my older brother's contemptible sleep habits. His wife said that he believes in the saying "I sleep, therefore I am."

In recent months, sleep has become a lofty goal for me. To the point that sometimes I feel like if I had to choose between ending the occupation and getting a few more hours of shut-eye, I'd go for the latter. Plus "excluding" my wife in the master bedroom with the baby hasn't particularly helped the quality of my sleep, either.

At first I put a mattress on the floor of my older son's room, but soon he started waking up at night and complaining about my snoring. I tried to persuade him with a profit-and-loss analysis: he ought to let me sleep in his room since I'm a grown-up who can protect him at night from the pirates and terrible monsters that could burst into his room at any moment. But my intimidation tactics didn't faze him much; he insisted he wanted me out so he could have quiet.

My daughter categorically refused to allow me to settle in her room, and my wife agreed with her: "She's a big girl already, almost a teenager—how could you think you could sleep in her room?"

I had no choice but to try to sleep next to my wife, who claims to have come to terms with her bitter fate and maintains that my snoring is one of my more bearable faults. But this attempt soon proved to be counterproductive, since the insomniac baby began to think that Daddy's snoring was a kind of game, and instead of waking up every hour he just tended to stay up all night.

As a last resort, I decided to put a mattress on the living room floor. Now, every night, I wait for everyone else in the household to get into bed, and only then do I take the mattress down from on top of the cupboard, lay it down next to the sofa, put the sheets and blanket on, and try in vain to fall asleep. Problem is I'm in the habit of reading a book before bed and there's nowhere to plug in a reading lamp here. So when I finally feel I'm too tired to go on reading, I can't just stick out my hand and flick a switch to turn off the light before sinking into a pleasant slumber.

"So buy an extension cord," said my wife, having identified the source of the problem.

"Sure," I answered for weeks on end. "Tomorrow, after work, after I pick up the kids, I'll go and buy an extension cord that will solve my sleep problem."

But what always happens is that after work, after I pick up the kids, after I drive them to their after-school activities, after I help them with their homework—all I want to do is just get into bed. It's just a thin mattress with no reading lamp beside it, but for me it's still a bed.

"Why don't you at least buy a real mattress?" my wife suggested, when she noticed that I'd started walking all hunched over from back pain. "That one will kill you."

But the idea of buying a real, good-quality mattress to lay on the living room floor seems too extreme, because even after all the months I've spent in the living room, I still prefer to believe that this is just a temporary glitch that will soon be set right. So meanwhile I'll suffer a little insomnia and back pain as I stand guard over my family: from the living room I can monitor all the noises they make, and every so often I get up to check on them. If my infant son doesn't wake up crying every hour on the hour, I jump up from the mattress to make sure everything's okay.

This baby worries me. My wife says I was just as worried with the other two kids, but that I'm more sensitive this time around because he was born prematurely. I closely observe his development.

"Why isn't he turning over?" I ask sometimes after perusing websites about babies.

"Because he doesn't lift his head up high enough yet," my wife replies.

"Why doesn't he lift up his head?" I ask.

"It's fine," she reassures me. "You're thirty-six, and you still haven't learned to lift yours up."

At night I sometimes wonder why they don't have development calculators for older ages, too. Why isn't it written somewhere what the normative or desirable behavior is for someone in his 432nd month? What should I have learned to do by now? How is a man my age supposed to react to political and economic changes? Where do I stand on the development chart?

"You're losing it," said my wife, troubled by the direction my thoughts were taking and by the dark bags under my eyes. This week she finally decided not to wait any longer and went to buy me an extension cord. "Maybe you'll read a little and finally be able to get a little sleep," she said.

That night I put the sheets on the mattress, unfurled the extension cord, placed the reading lamp within reach, and, at long last,
started reading *Comedy in a Minor Key* by Hans Keilson. The book
opens with an airstrike, with a refugee, with the body of a refugee.
Soon I'll nod off, I'll just read one more chapter about this refugee
who's hiding with a Dutch couple. I have to know what happens to
him, even though I already know that he dies eventually. Very soon
I'll get tired and fall asleep; very soon my life will get back to normal.

When I discover that I've already read more than half the book
I leap up in a fright and rush to the bedroom. My son hasn't cried
for more than five hours. I stand over his crib, pick him up with
both hands and gently shake him. Only when he wakes up with a
loud wail do I breathe a sigh of relief.

"Are you out of your mind?!" shouts my wife. "He finally
sleeps more than one hour in a row and you have to wake him?!"

HOMEWORK

May 4, 2012

I smiled fleetingly as the plane landed in Los Angeles, my last stop on a two-week trip: tomorrow I would already be heading home. The smile gave way to prolonged gloom when I thought about the flights that awaited me the next day, first to New York City and then to Tel Aviv.

The driver, who I had first thought was an Arab but later, when he spoke, I guessed might be Russian, was waiting for me with a sign bearing my name. I love it when that happens to me, and I waved my hand to signal that the sign was in my honor. Then I looked back to see whether any of the passengers who sat near me on the flight now realized I was not just another drunk with a weird accent who managed to order two Jack Daniel's and two beers on the short flight from Seattle, but probably some important personality. But no one paid attention to me or the waiting driver. That's how it is in the United States—a different nation whose citizens don't care about other people.

After we left the terminal, I moved a few meters away from the gate and lit a cigarette. There are tough smoking laws in the United States, which are different from one state to the next. At first I felt like a leper whenever I walked out of a hotel to have a smoke, and on two occasions guests came up to me and asked if I was their taxi driver.

A smoke after a long flight has an effect that evokes the memory of the first cigarette; I tried to keep stable and fight the dizziness. One more event, one more night, and this nightmare would be over.

"Nice weather," I said to the taxi driver, who was quietly pushing the cart with my big suitcase.

"Yes." He nodded and stopped in front of the entrance to the covered parking area. "Finish the cigarette," he said in an accent that recalled the character of an immigrant from *The Sopranos*. "There's no smoking inside," he added, gesturing with his head toward the parking area and taking out of his coat pocket a metal cigarette box, from which he pulled out a long cigarette with a gilded filter.

The weather really was good—warm and pleasant. Too bad I'd be in this city for only twelve hours. In Seattle it had rained nonstop. The day before that, in Ottawa, there was a heavy snowfall, big machines had raced across the runways to clear them, and I was seized by panic when vans with cranes started to defrost the small passenger plane I was sitting in.

"Bentley?" I shouted as the driver pressed a button on the remote and the car lights blinked before he opened the trunk. "Bentley?" I asked again, and the driver smiled at me and nodded. I handed him my cell and asked him to take a few pictures of me leaning on the car. Afterward, he let me sit in the driver's seat.

During the trip to the university guesthouse, I looked out the window of the Bentley and tried to catch the surprised looks of drivers in other cars who would glance my way and wonder who the guy sitting in the backseat of a Bentley with a private chauffeur might be. No one looked my way; all the drivers—white, black, Asian, Latino—ignored me systematically. That's how it is in the States—no one cares about anyone else.

According to my crowded schedule, I had two hours in the room before someone would pick me up for the first meeting at the university. I switched on the computer and made a video call home. "Daddy," my little boy exclaimed, "I haven't touched you for two weeks." He stretched out a hand toward the screen, and I tried to smile and remind myself that all would be well and that tomorrow I would start the trip home. My wife held the baby in her arms, pointed at the screen, and prompted the baby to say "Daddy," but in vain.

"Where are you now?" my wife asked. "I've stopped following your flights."

"I'm in L.A. now," I told them. "The weather here is fine."

"Did you buy me a harmonica?" my little son asked.

"Yes," I told him, "in an amazing music store in Seattle."

"Show me," he said, and I immediately went over to open the suitcase, taking advantage of the opportunity to move away from the computer and wipe away a tear.

"Daddy," came the voice of my older daughter.

"Go back to your room and don't come out until you finish the essay," my wife said to her, and reminded me that everything was normal at home.

"But Daddy," my daughter insisted. "Just a minute, I'll ask him."

"Listen to your mother," I told her when I got back to the computer screen.

"But I don't know," she said. She held a sheet of paper with her homework. "What is a nation?"

"What do you mean?" I asked her.

"Homework," my daughter said, reading from the sheet of paper. "It says here: 'What nation do you belong to, and why?'"

"To the Palestinian nation," I told her.

She wrote it down on the sheet of paper and continued: "And why?"

How many times had I heard that question on my book tour? Relentless questions about identity, culture, and belonging. I met Israeli students who already missed home; I was a guest of Palestinian students who wanted to go home already. I met Lebanese,

Egyptians, Arabs, and Jews who could barely speak Arabic or Hebrew, and whose English was appallingly American, but nevertheless
longed for home, even if they had no intention of forsaking Boston,
Canada, or New York City. A former Israeli professor told me how
important it is for him that his children will know Hebrew, and I
wondered why. Why is it so important for him if they live in the
United States? He replied that it's important to him culturally and
asked me if I didn't care whether my children would know Arabic.

"Of course," I found myself replying without hesitation.

"Why?" he asked, and I replied, after thinking about it, that it
was because of the war, because of the conflict, because of the separation and the uncertain future. Afterward I wondered out loud how
sacred Arabic would be if we lived in a country where the citizens
were equal, at least under the law. I didn't find a convincing answer,
but I said nevertheless, "In that case, preserving the language would
be my selfish desire, the desire for the children to know another
language and be familiar with another culture."

"Well, Daddy?" my daughter pressed me, and moved her
brother away from the screen. "I wrote 'Palestinian.' Why?"

"Because of Israel," I wanted to reply, but then I insisted that
she read material on the computer and in books and think for herself.
"We'll talk later," I promised her.

"Oyvayvayyuf," she said, and moved away from the screen.

"Straight to your room," my wife urged her. "So tell me, is the
offer from the university serious?"

"Yes," I replied, already regretting that I had told her about
the offer to spend a year with the family as their guest.

"But I know you," she said testily. "You will never accept."

"I don't know anymore," I said. "I'm starting to like the idea
that no one cares about anyone else here."

"Daddy," my son said, jumping in front of the camera, "show
me the harmonica."

DUTCH TREAT. OR NOT.

May 10, 2012

I arrived in Amsterdam that evening in a jet-lagged stupor that I acquired in Los Angeles. I couldn't allow myself to sleep on the plane despite the vast quantities of alcohol that were surging through my bloodstream. Still, I clutched the armrests of my seat with all my might, knowing I had to be prepared, because otherwise who would save the plane if, heaven forbid, something went wrong up there.

"Welcome," a tall, flaxen-haired Dutchwoman, who was holding a sign bearing my name, said to me in the arrivals hall.

"Thank you very much," I replied to the woman, my editor. I shook her hand and followed her to the parking area.

"How was the flight?" she asked.

I told her it was fine and that I was happy to be here in Amsterdam, and thanked her and the Dutch people for the translation of my book, "even though the cover was a little odd for my taste," I noted politely. I then asked, "Why do you think they chose a cover like that in Holland?"

"I don't know," she said, taking the car keys out of her suit pocket. "I haven't seen your book, sir."

The answer baffled me—until that same tall, flaxen-haired young woman opened the trunk of her taxi and asked if I needed help with the suitcase.

I arrived at the hotel late at night. According to the timetable I received at the reception desk, representatives of the publisher would

be waiting for me in the lobby at 9 A.M. From there I would be taken
to be interviewed for a culture program at a local television station.

I couldn't get to sleep in the hotel room: my body was behaving
as if it was early afternoon in Los Angeles. I stared at a Dutch TV
channel for hours and my eyes remained as wide open as an owl's.
The clock showed five A.M. when I woke up, and I knew there
was no chance I would get back to sleep. At six I went out for a walk
in chilly Amsterdam. I wandered around the city center, strolled
along the canals, and observed the beautiful buildings, making sure I
looked down occasionally to avoid stepping into the piles of garbage
that littered the sidewalks. Endless quantities of Heineken beer
cans, cigarette butts, paper cups and dishes, and remainders of food
accompanied me throughout the walk. I started to wonder where
the rumor that Europe is a clean continent originated.

"I apologize for the condition of the city," a PR man for the
publisher said after we had exchanged the usual polite greetings.
"Yesterday we celebrated the queen's birthday," he added, explaining that everyone had been drunk in the streets from the morning
until the wee hours.

"Too bad you didn't invite me a day earlier," I replied with
genuine regret at having missed the debauchery. "I've always wanted
to celebrate something related to a queen."

I thought I saw Paul Auster sitting in the hotel lobby, but
didn't dare say a word to my host. What if I was wrong? What if
it wasn't the writer but just another tall European in sunglasses?
After all, the night before I had mistaken a taxi driver for a serious
editor. I kept mum and followed the PR man to the taxi that was
waiting outside the hotel.

Tall, flaxen-haired Dutch people greeted me at the TV station. The moderator of the program shook my hand, praised my
book, and promised a relaxed, cordial conversation. A polite makeup
woman worked a long time to erase the black bags from under my

eyes and to obscure the signs of sleeplessness as well as she could.
When she was done she smiled and wished me good luck.

In the waiting room my host told me there was a large minority
of Moroccans in Holland. He also mentioned the names of some important, first-rate Moroccan writers who wrote in Dutch and whose
books sold well in the country. What a country, I thought, immediately starting to consider Holland as an immigration option instead
of the United States. The Dutch have Moroccans who are considered good writers and are also probably considered full-fledged
citizens. It must be great to be a Moroccan citizen of Holland.

A smile crossed my face as the man with the sunglasses from
the hotel lobby entered the waiting room together with the moderator of the culture show.

"Mr. Auster," the host said, "I want to introduce you to Mr.
Kashua, who is also a guest on our program today."

"I like your work very much," I found myself telling Paul Auster,
and hoping that the makeup was hiding the flush that spread across
my cheeks. Paul and me on the same program—I can't believe it.
In Israel they would have probably brought me David Grossman at
most. Holland, that's the place! I will integrate beautifully; I will be a
highly regarded author without any connection to my origin. There
you go: I've been here only one day, the book hasn't yet reached the
stores, yet Paul and I are already having coffee together and the two
of us are completely equal, being interviewed about our new books.

Auster was asked about his latest book, which is about memory.
His replies were intelligent and filled with inspiration. "Writing
is actually remembering," the charming moderator intoned, and
Auster shot back, "Actually, it's remembering mostly things that
never happened."

I nodded in assent, impressed by his brilliant comments and
promising myself that I would read the memoir as soon as it appears in Israel.

It would soon be my turn. I tried to take in some air, focus on my book, and prepare for the moderator's questions; he seemed to have read the books thoroughly.

"Mr. Kashua," the moderator asked in English, after an introduction in Dutch, which I didn't understand, of course. "Tell us where you were born." The question took me by surprise—he hadn't asked Auster where he'd been born. "In Tira," I replied, and the moderator insisted that I describe my childhood in the village. How hard were things there? he asked. What kind of childhood did you have? Did you have a library in the village when you were little? When did you start reading? When did you start writing? What's it like to be a foreign minority?

I almost choked. I felt bad for Auster, who sat there listening to the moderator's questions, which had nothing to do with the book but were aimed most of all at showing that a wretched Arab kid had learned how to read and write a book pretty well. It was an interview that recalled interviews in Israel from twenty years ago. Nothing about literature, no questions of the kind Auster had been asked, which might begin with "Writing is the music of the body," but only anthropological stuff derived from the finest colonial tradition.

"Thank you very much," the moderator said, shaking my hand warmly at the conclusion of the interview, his flaxen hair waving on his head, and a tear of solidarity with the downtrodden almost cascading down his cheek.

"It was a good interview," the PR man from the publishing house said in the taxi on the way back to the hotel.

Sanitation workers had been deployed in droves on the streets to clean up. I looked at them and tried to find one worker, just one, who was tall and flaxen haired. No such luck. Some were black, others looked a little more like me, but all of them, I could swear, had black bags under their eyes.

PART IV

THE STORIES THAT
I DON'T DARE TELL

2012–2014

THE STORIES THAT
I DON'T DARE TELL

May 18, 2012

On Nakba Day I can't stop thinking about my grandmother. If only she were still alive; if only she were the way I like to remember her: strong, sharp witted, always waiting for me after another day of school, sitting on her lamb's wool prayer rug. I would shrug off my heavy book bag and run to her, bury my head in her bosom, and silently weep.

"Why are you crying again, my child?" She could sense my body trembling.

"They keep picking on me," I would tell her. "They keep picking on me and won't let me breathe."

"Who?" she would ask. "Tell me who and I'll show them what's what."

"Everybody," I'd answer her. "And my friends are worse than the others."

"That's how it is"—I'd like to hear her say that now, just like then, as she stroked my head—"because you're a smart boy, the smartest, and they all want to be like you but they can't."

If I'm so smart, Grandma, then how do you explain the fact that I still haven't figured out how to get along in life? If I'm so smart, how do you explain the terrible fears? And, yes, I'm sorry: I no longer sleep with a small Koran under my pillow, as you taught me to do when I was young. I want to tell you that it never helped, Grandma—I was always afraid at night, and now more than ever. Except I no longer have anywhere to escape to, there's nowhere to hide. And you know, I'm a father now and I have children who get scared at night and come to me to hide. Three children, Grandma. Sometimes I tell them the same bedtime stories you used to tell me.

I told them how you used to have these huge watermelons that you would load on the backs of a convoy of camels to take to the sea to be loaded on boats. I told them about the cows, the donkeys, and the horses. About how on holidays you would dress up in a man's clothes, put on an abaya and a kaffiyeh, and gallop on the horse together with Grandpa all the way to Jaffa. About the café in Jaffa and how you always told us about the city women who sat there shamelessly smoking narghiles just like the men.

"But so did you!" I would always say, laughing, and you would answer: "Yes, but no one knew I was a woman, not like those wanton Jaffa women. You should have seen them, coming into the theater after us and sitting next to us, those loose women, may God roast them in the fires of hell."

But the other stories, Grandma, the ones that made you emotional, that made you cry when you told them—those I haven't yet dared to tell. Sometimes I think I wouldn't want my kids to have to bear that burden, maybe because I want to give them the illusion that a home is a permanent thing, strong, protective, so they wouldn't fear, as I do, a disaster lurking just beyond the doorstep. So I haven't yet told them that Grandpa was killed in the '48 war and I haven't told them how you became a young widow. I haven't told them about your lands, which were all lost. Or about the bullets that whistled all around and the shells that fell right and left.

I haven't told them about how you hunched over your baby son, my father, in the wheat fields, using your own body to protect him from the fire, and how you always used to say at that point, "As if my body would have really protected him—if the fire had caught me it would have taken him, too, but at least I would have died before my son."

So I don't tell them that one, or the most terrible of all your stories, about that moment when the shelling ceased and silence suddenly descended, that moment when you tried to go and bring food from the field for your children and you saw that nothing was the same anymore. I remember that look, Grandma, that same look on your face each one of the thousands of times you described that awful day, always the same look, with eyes glazed over with tears in just the same way. And I remember you always pulling out your handkerchief with that same delicate motion, and saying, "In that one moment I understood that everything I had was lost."

How hard it is to live with this feeling, with the constant fear of the future, the idea that I must always be prepared for the worst. The feeling that at any moment everything I have could be lost. That a house is never a certainty and that refugee-hood is a sword hanging over me.

Meanwhile, I've become a storyteller myself. In a language you wouldn't understand, but don't worry: not that many people who speak it really understand. Sometimes I feel I'm basically telling all the same stories I heard from you, and just as you used to do, I repeat them time after time in all different ways and all different forms, to no avail. People here aren't ready to believe your stories, Grandma, or mine. If only you were here now, on this Nakba Day, I would get on a horse and gallop all the way home, ask your forgiveness for having run away from you in your final days, and bury my head in your bosom for more silent weeping.

"Why are you crying, my child?"

If you only knew what I go through, if you only knew how hard it is to tell stories.

"Who's picking you up? Tell me and I'll show them what's what."

"Everybody, Grandma, and what really makes it hurt is I thought they were my friends."

"That's how it is," I know you would have said, as you stroked my head until the trembling stopped. And then you'd say: "So, are you hungry?"

PRIDE AND PREJUDICE

July 6, 2012

I know, I brought this on myself and I brought it on my children. My sweet children, my smart children. The two older ones brought home excellent report cards on Thursday, and I decided we would go to the mall to celebrate. "You can buy whatever you want," I promised them joyfully. "A present."

"I don't want a present," said my daughter, looking down at the ground.

"You always do this!" shouted my son, thinking he was about to lose the promised gift and readying to pounce on his sister.

"Whoa, cool it!" I said, grabbing him before he reached her.

"She always does this!" he repeated, tears already welling in his eyes.

"Don't worry," I reassured him. "We're going to the mall and buying you a present. You can just get something to eat with us," I said to my daughter with a smile, trying to dispel some of her anger, which has been growing more incomprehensible by the day.

"I don't want to eat anything," she said in that same insidious, preteen tone of voice.

"What's the matter?" I asked, hugging her, having learned that at this age a hug is more effective than anger or punishment.

"Nothing's the matter," she said, wriggling out of my grip and dashing the hugging theory I'd so recently adopted.

For order's sake, I had my big girl sit in the front seat and fastened her brother, who just finished first grade, into the backseat. She didn't say a word the whole trip. Her expression was unreadable and she kept her eyes cast down. I thought maybe it was because it was her last day at her old school—maybe she was a little sad and nervous about the new school she'd be attending in the fall. But when I asked, she didn't answer, except to shake her head impatiently.

As we approached the security guard at the entrance to the car park, I turned up 88FM, as I always do, and put on my biggest smile.

"Hello," said the guard, peering in the car window. "Everything okay?"

"Everything's good," I replied as my daughter glared at me for a second.

"Go right ahead," said the guard.

"Yes!" shouted my son as we started to move forward, because again we'd won our little game and the guard hadn't asked to look inside the glove compartment or the trunk. "We did it!" exulted my son.

"What's wrong?" I asked my daughter, who said nothing, her expression continuing to darken.

My son spent a long time wandering the aisles of the big toy store. He tried out all kinds of things, sometimes getting excited and sometimes being disappointed, not knowing what to choose and getting totally confused.

"Maybe you want to get something, too?" I said to my daughter, venturing another hug.

"I'm not a little girl anymore," she said, removing my hand from her shoulder.

"Can you please tell me what's the matter?" I tried again. "You know that you don't have to switch schools."

"I know," she said. "But I want to."

"So what's the problem?" I was starting to lose my patience, next to a Power Rangers display.

"This one boy in my after-school class . . ." She started crying without warning. "I was just playing there and I accidentally bumped into him . . ."

"And what happened?" I hugged her again, and this time she let me. "What happened? Tell me already."

"Then he said . . ." She tried to hold back her tears. " . . . 'Oh, gross, the Arab touched me!'"

"And what did you do?" I said, my blood starting to boil.

"Nothing. I acted like I didn't hear him. I even smiled." Now she broke into sobs.

"Hey, I don't get it," I said, annoyed. "Why didn't you tell me right away when it happened?"

"And what would you have done?" Now she changed her tone of voice, became rebellious again, and pushed away from me. "What do you always do? You're afraid, too, and you smile at them all the time."

My son was enjoying his McDonald's kids' meal with his new Lego motorcycle kit on the table in front of him. My daughter sat there quietly, gazing around the food court at the Malha Mall. I wanted to ask her what she was thinking—was she thinking about the janitors there, the way I do whenever we go there? I wanted to tell her that she was wrong about me, that in the mall I see only the lowly workers, the simple salespeople, and it really pains me. I wanted her to know that deep down I'm still a revolutionary, that every day I think about how the world could be saved, about how to put a new gleam in the eyes of the poor, and about how a laborer should make just as much money as a contractor.

But my daughter is right, I don't do a thing. And I don't know exactly when hope gave way to despair, and courage to cowardliness. She's absolutely right. What would I have done?

I wanted to tell her that I fight with words, but she's smart enough to know that's a lie. I wanted to tell her that I wasn't always this way, that at her age I, too, wanted to blow up the whole world.

That at her age I believed in justice and went out to protest against injustice, but I know that won't do any good right now. I wanted to say, yes, I may seem like a coward, it may seem that I avoid confrontation, that I don't tussle with security guards, that I ignore racists. But I wanted her to know that fear is one thing and pride is another. I wanted her to know that I have never felt inferior to anyone—quite the opposite—and that I never let anyone step on me. But I didn't know how.

"Hey, listen," I somehow blurted out.

"What?" she replied without looking at me.

"I'm not what you think I am . . ." I tried to explain, but her gaze suddenly met mine and silenced me.

"I'm sorry," I said as we were walking out. "When you grow up . . ." I began, but then realized there was no point.

On the way out I stopped the car near the security guard whom I just smiled at on the way in. I opened the glove compartment and started looking for a CD with Arabic songs. Then I searched the pockets in the door and even in the trunk. I couldn't look my kids in the eye when I came up empty.

SPLASH BACK

July 20, 2012

"Daddy," my son said from the swimming pool as I sat on the edge and watched over him. "Do you want to see how I can do a somersault in the water?"

"You bet," I replied, and as he dived I looked for my daughter, who preferred to swim far from my watchful eye and check out the deep end of the pool.

"Excellent," I said to my son as he completed the somersault. "Way to go."

"Daddy." He smiled, pleased with himself and adjusting his goggles. "Now I'll do three in a row. Want to see?"

"For sure." I smiled as he filled his lungs with air.

It was very hot on Saturday, and that morning I had tried to enlist the heat index promised by the weatherman to back out of my pledge to take the kids to the pool in such sweltering weather.

"You're right about the heat," my wife said that morning, "but they will swim in the shade and drink a lot, and it will be all right. We already promised them."

She left me no choice. Anyway, she knew perfectly well that the heat was only an excuse and that I had a serious problem when it came to swimming pools. Maybe it was newspaper articles I read or movies I saw, but mostly it's childhood experience that raises my level of rejection anxiety whenever I have to take my kids to the swimming pool.

I loved pools when I was little. They were a type of dream, an aspiration. I saw them mostly on television and in the movies, and at the time I was convinced that someone like me would never get to splash around in one. Every so often, my father would come home from the coffee shop in the center of the village and tell Mom about another local family that had been refused entry to pools in the nearby communities.

We never tried to get into the Jews' pools when we were little. Dad said we had to preserve at least a modicum of pride. The kids at school talked about some families from Tira, my village, who had memberships at a pool in Kfar Sava or Beit Berl, and about other local kids—not from our elementary school but from other schools—who actually went to a pool and enjoyed themselves there like everyone else.

I wasn't sure if these stories were true, but the kids at school always mentioned the names of children with rich and educated parents, or of others who, according to my father, were allowed into the pool at Beit Berl because their parents were the minions of the Labor Party.

I think I cried on the day the municipal swimming pool in Tira was dedicated—one of the first and only ones in any Arab village. I must have been in the fifth or sixth grade. My father was so proud. He said the head of the village had refused to back down, had organized demonstrations at the Jews' pools in the area, and had shouted at the interior minister, "They won't let our children swim in Kfar Sava? Then they will swim in Tira."

I loved the pool. It was exactly as I had imagined it would be, just like in the movies. In the summer we had season tickets and went every day.

One day, a pretty girl with curly hair whom I had never seen before came to the pool, though apparently she was the only girl who did occasionally come for a swim there. I watched shyly as she spoke to the lifeguard and afterward to the manager, who was called over.

"There is no law against it," I heard her tell them, and when they turned away she jumped into the water and swam to the deep end without so much as glancing at the boys. The boys said nasty things about her. I so much wanted to shut them up, to yell at them that they were wrong, that they didn't have a clue. But I said nothing: I was afraid people would know I was in love.

There were no fixed days on which she came to the pool, so I waited for her every day. I was the first one there, and sometimes I waited on the stairs until they finished cleaning and opened the entry gate. And I stayed until closing, because maybe she would come for a short swim at the end of the day. I knew I had no chance, not with someone like her, who knew how to swim—a girl who for sure had been allowed into the pools of Kfar Sava and Beit Berl. Her parents must be important people, certainly rich. I really hoped she was not a minion of the Labor Party.

A few weeks later, a poster at the pool announced that one day a week would be reserved for women, and that boys and girls were not allowed to be in the pool together then. The young males cursed the females for depriving us of a day at the pool and said it was all the fault of that bossy girl, who had insisted on it.

I never saw her after that and never found out her name. I enjoyed the pool less after she disappeared, but still went every day during summer vacation because there was nothing else to do. Until one day when three kids we didn't know showed up, smiling and looking happy. Suddenly I saw the man in charge run toward the pool and gesture to them as they were taking off their shirts. A few of the boys climbed out of the water and went over to listen to the conversation.

I stared as the manager spoke to them. I remember the look on the boys' faces. I remember one of them lowering his gaze for a moment and then looking toward the water, straight at me. I wanted to avert my eyes, but couldn't. Then they dressed and left. The boys who had listened to the conversation jumped back into the water and laughed: "*Wallah*, great—they're from Qalqilyah and wanted to swim here."

"Daddy," my son shouted, catching me off guard. "Did you see? A triple somersault."

THE HEAVENS WILL WEEP

October 5, 2012

On Friday morning I was again seized by the need to escape from Jerusalem to a place of shelter, to abandon what I had made of myself for a moment and go back to being the good boy I probably never was. On Friday I wanted to hide at my parents' place, to feel protected and secure in my element. To get into my childhood bed, bury my head in the pillow, and maybe Mom will come in, notice that my body is shaking, and ask if I'm crying, and I will deny it without leaving the pillow, and she will pull the blanket tighter, caress my head, and promise that everything will be fine and there's nothing for me to be afraid of.

Early Friday evening we drove to Tira. The way to my parents' house was blocked because of a wedding in the neighborhood, and I had to find an alternative route to get there.

"It's from the wedding," my father said when I tensed up at the sound of shooting. "Everything is fine," he said as he shook my hand.

"Maybe we won't eat outside?" my mother said, looking at the surprising clouds in the sky.

"There's nothing to worry about," my father said. "It won't rain until Sukkot. Trust God."

My three brothers, with their wives and children, gathered around the table in the yard of my parents' house.

"Is everything all right?" Dad asked.

"Yes," I lied, "everything is just fine."

"You look a bit pale," my mother said, concerned.

"A little pressure at work." I replied with the answer she liked to hear.

"He got drunk yesterday," my wife said. I couldn't figure out whether she was trying to get help or only humiliate me. "He got back close to dawn and threw up his guts."

"Why?" Dad said angrily, his hands tightening on the arms of the chair. "A million times I told you. Why? If not for yourself, think of the children."

And I thought of the children, who ate at top speed so they wouldn't lose any of the little time they had to play with their cousins.

"The liver, the lungs," my mother said. "How much longer will you go on drinking and smoking? You're not a child anymore."

I'm not a child anymore, I know. It's been a long time since I left the primary school where my nephews and nieces now go, and which my father also attended.

"The ceiling in the school is crumbling," my brother said worriedly. "Pieces of ceiling are falling on the children."

"Didn't a wall collapse there last year?" my father asked.

"Yes," my brother replied. "Lucky it happened when the school was closed. It's a real hazard."

"And the principal?"

"She cries," my brother said.

The plates were collected from the table and replaced with cups of tea, bowls of fruit, and sweets. "Come and have cake," the mothers called to the children, who replied with "In a bit" and went on chasing one another in the yard, laughing and perspiring. Sounds of gunfire froze people's expressions and sharpened the senses. The children stopped their game and waited, as I did, for a reassuring word, such as "wedding" or "fireworks," from the Tira veterans.

"Go inside," Dad asserted, standing next to the table.

"Hurry," I yelled, "everyone inside."

In a timeworn drill, my parents and my brother went into the living room. My father held the phone, my brother the laptop. "Anyone hurt?" my father asked on the phone. "Who? *Ya'allah.*"

" 'Three wounded in Tira gunfire,' " my brother read on the local news site.

"Just yesterday the neighbor was shot," my mother said. "They went into her house and shot her in the legs."

"She's the family," my father said. "*Ya'allah* for this village."

On the Friday evening of our visit, a young man shot three people in the center of the village, one of them a boy of eleven. On the local news site I read about a toddler in Kafr Kara who was shot and killed on Friday, about people wounded by shooting in Kafr Kassem, Jisr a-Zarka, and other places.

A call for Dad, and another one. The young man is from the family, twenty-one years old, according to the report from the hospital. "They say he won't make it," my father said, summing up the calls. "His poor parents—his father is a good man, simple—may God help them."

"May God help us all," my mother said.

The children went into one of the rooms and played a lot more quietly. Another call from the hospital: the *diwan* next to my parents' house should be prepared. "A *diwan* can be a happy place, too," I remember my father saying when he agreed to donate the structure to be used as a *diwan* by neighboring families. "It can be used for family meetings, for a wedding, for an engagement party. Who said it's only for a mourners' tent?"

Afterward we talked very sadly about Tira, refusing to believe that it had come to this. Refusing to let go of the childhood illusion of a warm, protective village. We cursed the police, the government's policies, the courts, the neglect, and the local residents who were raising ruthless monsters.

"I have whiskey at home," my younger brother said, looking at me. Dad nodded his head in quiet assent.

"Maybe we'll go back to Jerusalem after all?" my wife suggested.

"No," I told her, knowing very well that I didn't want to let go yet, didn't yet want to forgo the reason for which I'd come to Tira for the weekend. "We promised the children we'd stay overnight."

One sip of the whiskey made me feel nauseated. I managed not to throw up. After the children fell asleep on the mattresses, I took a shower, brushed my teeth, and got into my childhood bed. I buried my head in the pillow and waited.

"Are you all right?" my wife asked, letting a hand rest on my head.

"Yes," I lied, my body cringing. I tried with all my might to cry as I once did, when I was a boy in Tira, in the same bed, but I couldn't.

WITHOUT PARENTS

October 19, 2012

"Daddy," my daughter called to me as she emerged from her room with a work sheet. She started to read it aloud: "What does my name mean?"

"What are you talking about?" I replied impatiently, like always when I am asked for help with homework or any sort of help at all. "You know it's a musical instrument."

After jotting down a short answer, she continued with the next item. "Was I named for someone? And is she dead or alive, and how does that make me feel?"

"No," I told her, "you are not named for anyone. It's just a lovely name that your mother chose."

"Why did you choose to give me that name?" she went on, clearly beginning to lose her patience.

"Uhh," I said, dredging up the depths of nostalgia, "it's a name that was in a poem by Kahlil Gibran—a poem I love very much."

"And that's it?" she said testily, writing down the answer.

"No," I said proudly, "it's also a song that the legendary singer Fairuz performed wonderfully. You should have heard the way she emphasized your name in the song."

"Does my name appear in the Bible?" she went on in an irritated tone of voice.

"Why would your name appear in the Bible?" I shot back, just as irritated. "Not in the Bible, not in the Koran, and not in any

other religious book. Musical instrument, Gibran, Fairuz, no Bible. I
already told you. It's a lovely name. What's your problem, anyway?"

"What's my problem?" she shouted. "My problem is that you
and Mom decided to amuse yourselves, to listen to love songs and
to give me any old name because you felt like it, and now I don't
have any roots."

She went back into her room, slamming the door behind her.

"What kind of roots?" I shouted back at her as I opened the
door to her room. "Have you freaked out?"

"No," she said, sitting on her bed with tears in her eyes. "It's
our project this year—roots—and I already see on my first assign-
ment that I have nothing. Just a plain old name."

"Roots?" I took the work sheet from her and started to read
it carefully. "What is this, homework?" I asked.

"It's a project," she said. "The roots project, our most important one this year. We also have to make a newspaper in the end."

"All right," I said in a conciliatory tone before leaving her
room with the work sheet. "Sorry, I didn't know. I apologize if I
hurt your roots. Wait here."

"You know what?" I said to my wife as I entered our bedroom,
closing the door behind me.

"Shh!" She shushed me with a look of murder in her eyes and
whispered, "For an hour I've been trying to get the baby to go to
sleep. What's all the fuss between you two?"

"Roots," I told her, trying to stay calm. "The junior high has
a roots project."

"So what's the problem?"

"What's the problem?" I snapped back in quiet agitation. "If
it were an Arab school, all right—roots here, roots there—and if it
were a mixed school I would also get by. But this is Leyada! Do you
have any idea what Leyada is? Bibi's son goes there."

"I still don't understand," she said. "What's it got to do with
Leyada? Roots are roots."

"It's war," I said to my wife. "Believe me, they don't do a roots project just like that. It's part of the war of narratives; it's a battle for ownership of the land and someone here has to fire back, I tell you. And remember, she is the only Arab in her whole grade."

"Aren't you exaggerating a little?"

"Exaggerating?!" I said, flabbergasted at my wife's serenity. "You'll see tomorrow: if we don't prepare for the roots project properly, then we, we of all people—who are so stuck here that we never bothered to find out our origins—will come out lacking roots. You'll see. I know them: for them, roots are to die for. In the end, it'll turn out that we came from some desert tribe and they were here since before the creation of the world."

"You're right," she said. "I barely know the name of my great-grandfather."

"What did I tell you?" I said.

I tried to work back a few generations. "There's my father, there's my grandfather Ahmed, his father was Mohammed . . . and that's it. I don't know what comes next."

"I have the feeling it was another Ahmed," she said. "But the story of the two of us is good. We'll give them a fight."

Yes, she's right. Both my wife's parents were born in the village of Miska and became refugees in 1948. My grandfather was killed in the war. That's fine for a narrative, but it's not enough for a myth.

"We have to go way back," I said to my wife. "We have to go a lot deeper with the roots—three thousand years deeper. You know them—they go all the way back to the burial plot the patriarch Abraham bought in Hebron, or wherever it was."

Suddenly it hit me. "I've got it!" I shouted. The baby started to cry.

"I'll kill you," I heard my wife say as I hurtled out of the bedroom.

"Write this down," I said to my daughter, who was sitting on her bed waiting for her roots. She was holding a notebook and a pencil and started to write what I dictated.

"My name, which was given to me by my parents . . . are you writing?"

"Yes," she said impatiently. "Go on."

". . . is a musical instrument that was especially beloved by the Canaanites."

"Is that with a C or a K?"

"With a 'C,'" I shouted, "and watch your step with me! We're talking about your forefathers here, goddamn it!"

LOVE THERAPIST

December 7, 2012

"Is it you?" the young woman sitting to my left at the bar asked.

"Yes." I nodded uneasily, because that evening I had wanted to drink in a place where I'd never been before, where no one would recognize me, and where none of the regulars would be hurt if I was not communicative and sociable.

"I admire your work," she said, reminding me how much I hated my work at that moment and how little I aspired to or deserved admiration. "It's just a job," I wanted to tell her, but decided not to, "a horrible, hard job."

"What are you so disturbed about?" she asked, surprising me.

"I'm not disturbed about anything," I lied to her. "You seem to be projecting."

She lowered her gaze and examined her smartphone, grimaced, and threw it back onto the counter.

"You're right," she said, tears welling up in her eyes. "The political situation is disturbing, no?"

"Yes." I nodded again. "The best thing is to observe and not take it to heart."

"And do you manage to observe?" She smiled.

"Not really," I replied, "I take everything to heart."

"Ah, the heart." She sighed and took a long swig from her beer. "You're a guy, a writer—you must understand other guys."

"Not really"—I told her the truth this time—"I was never very good at understanding people."

"What?" she retorted, chuckling. "I read you. You build up excellent characters."

"Thanks," I replied, but stuck with the truth. "I don't have a clue about human behavior. I only try, unsuccessfully, to decipher it. I think my characters are also only looking for understanding, and in fact if you read closely, you discover that they don't know anything about their feelings or about the feelings of those around them. Not a thing. They don't have the slightest idea how they are supposed to feel, or where or when."

"Want a chaser?" she asked.

"Only if I pay."

"Right on," she said, and ordered two shots of Bushmills after I told her I didn't care what. "You see, that's the problem with guys. You want control."

"You see," I replied, "and until now I was sure that women are the ones who pursue power and achieve it."

"Us?" she replied, and raised her glass. "*Lehayim!*"

"*Lehayim,*" chugalug, burning sensation, shaking of the head. "Yes. Anyhow, that's how it always seems to me. That you girls are a lot stronger than us, can control your feelings better and stick to something like plans of a certain kind."

"Plans?" she said scornfully. The flickering of the cell phone made her tense up with hope about the incoming call. But the hope morphed quickly into a contortion of pain.

"Are you also waiting to hear something good about the political situation?"

"That isn't really what's disturbing me," she said sorrowfully. "It's a guy. Oy, what an idiot I am, you know? And I was sure that everything was good, that everything would at least . . . I mean, there was no sign. And I don't understand why. I have no idea why.

If there's something I want to shout out, it's 'But why?' Sorry I'm telling you all this, I don't know why I got on your case."

"It's all right," I told her. "I'm happy to listen, but you should know that I might write about you this week."

"Are you that desperate?"

"A lot more than you can imagine."

"Do you believe in love?" she asked.

"Why? Don't you?"

"I don't know anymore. Suddenly it looks to me like a cheap swindle." She sighed and the tears started again. "And like an imbecile, I thought I was the one who was ending the relationship, if you can believe it. I wrote to him, 'That's it, I'm not going to take it any longer.'

"I was sure he would apologize, beg, and I would have forgiven him right away, you know, and he also knows that very well, I'm sure. But suddenly he's totally gone, like he was waiting for this, like he was waiting for one small remark to end it. I thought the angry remark would only make him feel sorry, and now I imagine him cackling like the Wicked Witch of the West, and I, look at me, I am the one who's crying and waiting. Sorry."

"It's all right," I told her, by now wanting her to stop telling her story, because I had to hold myself back from crying.

"He disappeared on me four days ago, in the middle of a conversation. 'I'll get back to you in five minutes,' he said, and I didn't hear from him for three days. Don't I have the right to get angry, to tell him that I want nothing to do with him? Do you know what suffering I went through in those three days of waiting? I, like, died. I couldn't take in the lectures at university, couldn't write papers. Nothing. All I did was sit and wait for the sound of e-mail, Facebook, and bloody messages. And in the end I completely fill up with happiness because after three days he writes me 'Hi,' as though nothing happened, and I scolded him lightly. It's my right to be angry, isn't it?"

"Yes"—I nodded—"it's your right."

"And there was no sign, nothing. If he wanted to break up, why didn't he say so? You understand?" she said, and blew her nose. "Sorry." She giggled. "And I don't know whether I should be angry or scared or be hopeful or what. I have no explanation for his behavior and I have no explanation for my feelings at all. All because of a cruddy guy, you understand?"

"Would you like another Bushmills?"

"Yes," she said. "Thanks. Even though you should know that I hate whiskey." She laughed loudly.

"It'll be all right, you'll see," I lied to her and to myself. "*Lehayim!*"

"*Lehayim!*"

BIBI DOES

January 11, 2013

I should have canceled the meeting at the Baka al-Garbiyeh college, I thought last Tuesday morning when I got onto the Trans-Israel Highway, heading north. It was raining hard and the fog generously provided me with a field of vision of a few meters. I chose the right lane and drove slowly, straining hard to see what the car in front was doing. Why don't drivers here know how to use their fog lights, damn it? I cursed quietly, trying to breathe calmly.

I shouldn't have left the house, I should have stayed with the children. We kept them home from school because of the rain, the winds, and the freezing cold. In the house it isn't cold, and the car is also quite warm. I haven't been cold for a long time, I thought, with a twinge in my heart when I recalled how cold I used to feel. I remembered the freezing cold winters in Tira, although it's much warmer there than in Jerusalem. I remembered the pain of the contact with the mattress, the frosty blanket in the children's room, and the time it took until my bed warmed up a little.

I also remembered the mornings at the bus stop by the dormitories of the Givat Ram campus at the Hebrew University of Jerusalem, the heavy student's coat, the long underwear I wore under my jeans, and the woolen socks my mother bought for me. My mother was, and still is, a big believer in good socks. "Keep your feet warm," I remember her saying, "and your whole body will stay warm." I was also cold in my apartment in the Nahlaot neighborhood. My roommates and I used to cover ourselves with heavy blankets in the evening and try to warm ourselves next to a pathetic electric heater.

I was cold when I got married and moved to a one-room apartment in Beit Safafa, and I was cold when my wife got pregnant. It was prior to our first winter as parents of an infant when we realized that there was no choice: we had to find an apartment with central heating. "She won't survive the winter without heating," said my wife, and I agreed with her.

On the radio they were discussing the damage from the storm, the closed highways, and the terrible traffic jams. A large truck drove in front of me, and the trail of water it sprayed on my windshield left me no choice but to give up on the right lane and to carefully pass the terrible truck.

On the radio they were reporting on the flooding in south Tel Aviv, Nahariya, Jaffa, Bat Yam, and Hadera. They reported on flooded neighborhoods and residents who couldn't stay in their homes. The presenters of the programs after the news were concerned primarily with the traffic jams in Tel Aviv, which, according to them, were the main problem.

I realized that cold is related to poverty. The more money you have, the warmer you will be in the winter. Flooding is usually the fate of the poor. Why is that so? I wondered. After all, I'm convinced beyond any doubt that well-to-do people don't choose to live on mountaintops, yet the first to suffer from disasters, including natural ones, are the weaker elements in society.

How frightening it is to be one of the weak. And how frightening is the knowledge that very soon I may return to the days of being cold, although I didn't suffer that much during those periods. Perhaps the opposite was the case: sometimes it seems that it was even more pleasant back then.

But there's a realization that you can't blink for even a moment, a realization that I'm sure is common to all those who have nothing to rely on except their work, who weren't born wealthy, who cannot rely on help from their parents and know that everything can be destroyed overnight.

I'm warm now, and hope that my family is also warm, but deep inside I feel that this is an act of deception, an illusion that could be shattered with one irresponsible decision. Decisions like starting to give up lectures because of a storm, or discontinuing this column, because at least when it comes to writing, I'm not good at whitewashing acts of betrayal.

"Tira is really flooded," said Dad over the phone. I had to answer his call, for fear that there had been an accident, God forbid, although I had promised myself not to answer the cell phone and to focus on my mission of reaching the college in Baka. "Cars are underwater," he said. "The Tira-Taibeh highway is completely closed; there's a river there."

Not only Tira, but also Taibeh, Kalansua, and many Arab communities looked like one big swamp in the pictures on local websites. I hope the situation in Baka is different, I prayed silently, wishing the rain would let up, at least a little. I shouldn't have left the house, I should have listened to my wife and stayed with the family.

On the radio they started talking about the election, and that was the first moment I actually grasped that there's going to be an election. I mean, I knew there was one, but didn't know how close it was and somehow wasn't at all bothered by it. Once my friends and I, Arabs and Jews, used to talk about the election; it would preoccupy us, make us angry, engender hope or frustration. Only now do I realize the depth of my indifference toward the election.

Even during visits to Tira they didn't talk about the approaching election, and I remember that once there used to be a real uproar about it.

"Here we're busy with the floods for now," said my father. "When the rain lets up, everyone will talk about who shot whom. Who has time to talk about politics?"

On the radio they said the rain would only become stronger and that the prime minister would remain the prime minister. And I thought that I should have stayed home and laughed when I thought about my little son, the baby who speaks only Hebrew because of his playgroup. The one whose first word was "iPod," and who says "Papa" instead of *abba*, and is afraid of an Arabic accent.

I laughed when I remembered how, before I left the house, he declared for the first time that he had done "bibi." "What?" I asked him, not believing my ears.

"Bibi," he repeated, pointing to his dirty diaper.

And I drove slowly and checked the instructions on the signs, hoping against hope that I wouldn't get lost.

OLD MAN

January 18, 2013

I began to feel it only recently. Suddenly the image staring back at me from the bathroom mirror seemed slightly different.

As I usually do in such cases, I blamed the mirror. But the same thing happened in all the mirrors where I checked my reflection. I always knew my hair was turning gray, but I've started to notice it clearly only now. My reflection had changed, and all at once I began seeing an older man—much older—without understanding how this had occurred.

The worrisome telltale signs continued to appear one after another. Thus I discovered this week, upon getting into bed and eagerly picking up my bedtime book, that for the past few days I have been reading a novel by Jane Austen. And we're not talking plain reading, but reading I looked forward to with great anticipation.

I found myself being wholly drawn into the story of the delicate maiden Anne Elliot in *Persuasion*: waiting for some admiral to arrive at the family estate in Somersetshire, and praying that this ship's captain will fall desperately in love with that same kind and good-tempered Anne, who suffered greatly at the hands of her hurtful relatives, primarily her father and elder sister, who is all haughty arrogance.

The situation was so grave that even though I understood why I was behaving this way, I was incapable of abandoning the book for

a moment, and went on to the next page, cursing all the members
of the Royal Navy for their callous hearts and their indifference.
This was also the week I understood in an instant that I am
not funny anymore. In a lightning flash I realized that what I had for
years considered a sense of humor that only lent me greater charm
had become tedious, bordering on the pathetic. I saw myself on one
of the channels telling a joke at the television awards ceremony,
and I was filled with pity at the sight of an older man who insists
on playing the clown. My kids are right, I just realized, I really do
embarrass them.

I told a joke to one of the teachers when I picked up my little
boy at school, and he stared at me furiously, gritted his teeth, and,
when the teacher wasn't looking, gave me a kick in the leg that left
a mark. "So long as you sit quietly," my daughter said when she
realized I would be the one coming to a parents' meeting in class.
"Just don't try to be funny, Dad," she said. "You only embarrass me
and yourself."

When did all this happen, I thought as I drove from Jerusalem to the library in Kiryat Motzkin, and how is it that I am only
now realizing that I graduated from high school a very long time
ago? Heavy concerns accompanied me on the way to a lecture at
the library.

The image of a witty, funny, hurting man faded away and was
replaced by a miserable wretch who constantly repeats himself as
he attempts to wring laughs and sometimes also a few tears from
an audience that mainly pities him. Oh God, I thought, I should
have canceled the lecture; it will end badly.

"What are you talking about?" my wife said when she answered
the phone. "You look exactly the same and you sound exactly the
same."

"But I'm telling you," I said, trying to make clear to her how
serious I was, "I feel different. I know that something major has
happened and I don't know why."

"Cut out your nonsense," she persisted. "Do your usual show, exactly like a week ago, and everything will be fine."

"Nothing will be fine," I said, trying to clarify the gravity of the situation. "This week is not last week anymore. I feel different. I feel old."

"Right," she said, as she usually does when inclined to wrap up a conversation, "leave me alone, I need to get the kids in the shower."

My body trembled as I mounted the stage at the library. I remained silent for a long stretch and gazed at the audience, which had begun to suspect it had fallen prey to an act of deception. Whisperings and looks of dissatisfaction pierced my flesh. I don't have a choice; I have to act automatically, stick to the usual lecture, and hope the evening will pass quickly.

"Good evening," I began, "I am very glad to be here this evening, and I will start from the beginning." A mere five minutes had gone by since I opened my mouth and I realized that everything was fine, that the lecture was working and the audience was having a good time. When I wanted them to cry, they shed a tear; when I wanted them to laugh, they fell on the floor. Everything's all right, my wife was right, nothing has changed; but still, I know that everything has changed. Everything was going according to plan, and right on time I allowed, as I do toward the end of such events, questions from the audience.

I have good, wise, funny answers to the questions, which are always the same: "Why do you write in Hebrew?" and the follow-up question "What language do you dream in?" And after that someone will ask, "How is your writing received in the Arab community?" And I always begin my reply to this question with "As always, with celebratory gunfire." I leave the audience a few moments' laughter and then provide a smart and reasoned answer regarding the perception of satire amid a public that feels persecuted and threatened.

Likewise the question addressed to me by a lady who raised her hand politely was among the familiar ones: "Where do you get your optimism?" And as usual I began replying with a standard joke, "Oh, I get my optimism from whiskey," and as always the audience laughed, and then I launched into the regular and correct response, which begins with there, in fact, not being much cause for optimism, and we really are in a dark period, but that somewhere deep inside I know that the situation has to change. I am a great believer in the goodness of pe-o-ple . . . I began stuttering because I realized what was going on with me: I felt I was starting to lie, mainly to myself.

I stopped giving the answer I had been providing wholeheart-edly until a week ago about optimism, and came to understand precisely why it was that old age had attacked with all its might. "I don't know," I found myself saying onstage, my body trembling. The library director saved me when she stood up and announced that we had gone well over time; the audience applauded and I stood there and realized for the first time that I had lost hope.

QUEST FOR
ANOTHER HOMELAND

March 8, 2013

It was cold in London, and on the news they said the queen was slightly indisposed and they weren't sure whether she would cancel her planned trip to Italy. "People have probably already gotten ready," said the correspondent who covers the royal family. "They've bought flowers and dresses for the queen's visit."

In Washington it was a little colder, and on television they said a serious snowstorm was approaching the city, perhaps the worst of the season. They also said that McDonald's was offering a new children's meal at a discount.

Now I'm in Chicago, and the taxi driver who picked me up this morning from the airport said that this was definitely the last flight to land at O'Hare International Airport. Chicago is covered in white, and on the news they promised that during the course of the day the snowfall would only intensify and that this really was the biggest snowstorm of the year. The meteorologist promised ten inches. I tried to calculate that in centimeters, unsuccessfully.

I'm still at the beginning of my trip, and I really miss home—or to be more precise, my wife and children. I mark every mission accomplished with an X, every city in which I land, every flight, and every day that passes. Fortunately, I'm too busy to become mired in a profound depression, and I meet interesting people everywhere

I go. Most of them are academics, many Israelis, and quite a few
Arabs. Somehow I already had the feeling that only immigrants
would attend my readings.

After those events there's always a meal or a reception. People
ask how things are in Israel now, and I answer, *"Alhamdulillah"*—
praise God. People are always telling me about the time that has
passed since they left their homeland, about longings and difficul-
ties, as well as success and the simpler life they have subsequently
found. The phrase "I can't go back to that crazy place anymore" was
repeated incessantly, immediately followed by comments about the
children, the language, and the idea that maybe they will go back
someday after all.

There are Israelis who say that only after leaving the country
did they realize how illogical life is there, how stressed they were,
and how all of a sudden there are different concerns now. Concerns
related to work, to everyday life, to the weather, and mainly to the
family.

I know I would like to leave. Not to emigrate, just to leave
for a year, two years at most. To take time out from the war, and to
work seriously on my new book. Although I don't spend more than
twenty-four hours in each place I visit, immediately upon landing
I begin to imagine myself there, to calculate the rent for a year,
to ask about the education system, to find out about the weather,
transportation, and the crime rate.

I have to get away a little, I have to calm down; I have to find
a refuge, for myself and mainly for the family, the children. I was
always taught that I have no place else to go. My parents have always opposed the idea of emigration or studies abroad. "You have
no place except Tira," my father used to say, and he still says, "You
have nowhere to go."

I would like to teach my children otherwise. I know that if
they want to leave one day to study or live in a distant country, I'll
be heartbroken, but I feel an obligation to provide them with an

"exit ticket." I feel I have to present that as a real possibility. I have a lot of guilty feelings when I think about my children, on whom I forced the lifestyle that was forced on me.

Sometimes I feel guilty about the so-called mixed education system—or, actually, the exclusively Israeli one—in which I've enrolled them, "for the sake of a better education," as I tend to convince myself. Sometimes I'm scared by the very fact that I have forced them to live in a Jewish neighborhood. "It's not your natural place, nor theirs" is another thing my father says regularly. Sometimes I worry about their reaction to the situation, about the confusion that they're liable to suffer, the illusions that are probably in store for them.

I must help my children understand that Israel is not the end of the world—that if, God forbid, they don't succeed there and they feel ostracized, different, or suspect, or when reality blows up in their faces, they'll know that there are other options. It's true that they'll be different, but in a different way. They'll be immigrants, and maybe they'll have an accent, and they'll feel a little strange. But they'll be strangers in a strange land, and not in their homeland.

I'm so worried about the day when they grow up and understand the depth of their distress, and accuse me of destroying their lives because of my whims. I'm afraid that one day, because of my children, I'll realize that my father was right, that I have no place other than Tira, and that there is such a thing as a natural place for raising people.

"Hello," I said to my wife, calling home via the computer after calculating the time difference.

"What do you want?" she answered, the way a woman abandoned on her own in a strange city with three children answers. "I'm in the middle of making supper."

"Nothing," I answered. "I have to leave here soon and I wanted to talk to the children."

"All right," she said, beginning to calm down. "How are you?"

I told her the truth: "Tired. I'm on my way to Minneapolis soon."

"Did you find a place?" she asked.

"I'm working hard on it," I told her.

"I know you." She snickered. "You'll never leave here," she managed to say before the two boys were already in front of the computer camera and joyfully shouting, "Daddy, Daddy."

"Hi." I smiled at them and waved at the screen, trying to stop the tears of longing that threatened to well up of their own volition.

"Would you like to see the snow?" I asked as I lifted the computer up to the window of the hotel room, directing it toward white Chicago.

They were excited. They didn't believe that snow could fall anywhere except in Jerusalem the capital.

THE COURT!

March 22, 2013

My suitcase is packed. My ride to the airport will be here soon and I'll start the journey home. I'm standing by the window in the hotel room and looking out at snowy Montreal. "This is one of the most significant snowstorms of the year," said the Canadian weatherman, and joked with the anchorman about how it was happening at the end of March, just when the city was eager to welcome spring.

I stand and stare at the snow, which has been coming down hard since the early morning, and pray that my flight won't be canceled. It's been twenty-one days since I left Israel. I've given more than twenty talks and I'm as ready as I'll ever be to get home.

Three weeks have gone by and I'm exhausted and badly missing my family. I've cried a lot during this trip, not always for a clear reason—the waves of sadness hit without warning, leaving me helpless to stop the tears from flowing. Twice it happened when I was standing onstage in front of an audience.

Three weeks have gone by, and in these three weeks I've been drinking like never before. I drank to calm myself before the talks. I drank to forget the talks as soon as I finished delivering them. I drank before and during flights. I drank when I remembered, I drank when I forgot. Mostly, I drank in order to cope with the relentless pressure and the powerful feeling that I was constantly on trial, required to justify every word, every joke, every statement.

Sometimes it seemed that I was making a terrible mistake by agreeing to speak to an audience. I ought to have just let my work speak for itself. I would rather my writing be judged, not my speeches, because I've always believed that I truly think about things, weigh them and feel their meaning, only when I'm trying to put them in writing.

The court was the audience. Granted, for the most part the members were nice and polite, but there were times when my remarks got on the nerves of an American Jew who probably has been to Israel only twice in his life but still considers himself the proud owner of the place—so much so that he's sure he cares more about the future of the country than I, who actually live there. "You said you don't understand why there aren't any mosques in Tel Aviv," said one fellow from Vancouver. "Did you ever think about what happened to the synagogues in Hebron?"

"You talk about '48 and about your tragedy," said a Jewish Canadian woman of Egyptian descent. "Did you ever think about the Jews who were forced to leave Egypt?"

"How dare you use the Hebrew language," said a female Palestinian refugee who was born in Jaffa. "The language in which your people are oppressed."

"You should be grateful you live in a place that gives you the freedom to write," said another American. "What exactly would you be writing about if you were born in Syria?"

A young Palestinian woman doing her doctorate at Berkeley came up to me after one lecture. "You know," she said, "you only used the word 'Nakba' twice, and you mentioned the occupation only once." She spoke very calmly, despite the whiff of rebuke in her words. Then she said: "And you didn't use the word 'colonialism' at all."

Then an Israeli who left Israel thirty years ago took me by the arm. "I know it's hard for you, but between us, Kashua," he said with a wink, "wouldn't you rather live with Abu Mazen?"

Everyone wanted to talk about identity, about nationality and foreignness, about detachment, self-determination. They wanted to hear about language, about humor and fears, and the future. And I drank a lot and thought about myself and this thing called a "Palestinian citizen of Israel."

I thought about Israelis who are searching for a kind of understanding (in the best case) and words of thanks (in the extreme case), and about the Arabs who are seeking an apology and clarification. And at first I really did feel a powerful desire to apologize to every side, because I've always been the self-protective type, one of the skeptics, with a lack of self-confidence—at least when it comes to national pride. But for some reason I didn't give in, and I wasn't prepared to tolerate the criticisms of the Israelis and Arabs.

I thought about my grandmother, who had nothing left after the war and yet still did everything for the sake of her son's education. I thought about my father and mother, who worked hard all their lives for the sake of their children's future. I thought about Tira, about the Triangle, the Negev, and the Galilee. About us, who, without anyone asking what we thought, became Israeli citizens.

I thought about that weak population of the villages who lost their land and were orphaned overnight, about those fellahs cut off from the wider Arab world and trampled by the Zionist vision.

I thought about us for a moment, and realized that I didn't want to apologize to anyone—not to an Israeli Jew when I talk about the rape and oppression, and not to the Arab and Palestinian who accuse me of exploiting my citizenship and castigate me for using the Hebrew language.

Just before I was about to apologize, I realized that what I really wanted to do was shout at them all to go to hell, that I can say whatever I want and blame whomever I want. I've earned it. I wanted to shout that nothing good will come from the Israelis who hurl accusations of betrayal and disloyalty, just as nothing good will come from those Arabs who hurl accusations of betrayal and segregation.

It's okay, I thought as I stood by the window in Montreal and thought about the critics—Jews and Arabs—who live in Western democracies. It's okay. We're okay. I can be confused. We can be inconsistent when we talk about identity, about language, and about nationality. It's okay, we've earned it honestly. "Somehow," I mumbled to myself by the window that was fogging up, as I checked for the passport in my coat pocket once again, "somehow we'll be okay in the end."

ELECTRICITY IN THE AIR

May 24, 2013

On Nakba Day, which this year fell on Shavuot, we had a power outage in the apartment. There was no school that day, and the children wanted to make popcorn. Instead of two minutes, they set the timer for two hours, and within three minutes I smelled something burning. Smoke poured out of the microwave, the popcorn bag was on fire, the sides of the microwave melted, and the power in the apartment went. I cursed the children, doused the burning popcorn in the sink, and unplugged the microwave, which wasn't easy. I couldn't get my hand into the round hole in the back of the cupboard. I had to unscrew the oven from the cupboard; that was the only way I could reach the microwave plug. I unplugged the microwave and then went to the fuse box, outside the front door of the apartment. I tried to lift the fallen fuse. The whole house was blacked out. A few attempts to flip some of the fuses up and down had no effect.

"Where am I going to find an electrician now?" I grumbled. I called a friend, who gave me the number of someone he said was excellent.

"I'll be there within half an hour," the electrician, an Arab, told me. He took my address.

"It's got nothing to do with the microwave," he said after checking the fuse box.

"But the microwave burned out," I told him. "It just melted."

"I understand," he said, playing around with his screwdriver, unscrewing some fuses and moving others. "That might be the case, but your problem is the bridge. It wasn't installed properly."

"The bridge?" I asked. I'd never heard of a bridge in electricity. "Is that complicated?"

"Look," he said, sighing and pulling another piece out of the panel, "it's no problem to give you your power back"—it came back on as he spoke—"but the whole fuse box needs to be reset."

"Coffee?"

"Sure," he said, still fiddling with the panel. "Thanks."

"With milk?"

"Don't you have any Arab coffee?"

"No," I replied, embarrassed.

"Whatever you have, then," the electrician said in a tone of condolence.

I made the coffee. The voices of the children could be heard from a room inside. They were speaking Hebrew. I asked them to lower their voices. "And if possible," I whispered, "please speak in Arabic, okay?"

"Thanks," the electrician said as he removed another fuse, explaining that it was unnecessary, and went on pulling wires through the fuse box. "Excuse the question," he said, "but I take it you're Arab?"

"Yes," I replied, "of course."

"I'm really sorry to say this to you," he said between sips of coffee, "but a tree without strong roots will not bear fruit."

"Could be," I replied, feeling abashed as the children went back to speaking in Hebrew.

"Don't be angry with me for saying this," he said, "but I don't like people who try to imitate others."

"Of course," I said, starting to stutter, "neither do I."

"Look at your kids," he continued, knowing very well that he had the upper hand. "*Lo haram?* Isn't it a pity?" he asked as my son came into the living room and asked—in Arabic, happily—whether he could watch TV already.

I don't know how it happened, but I found myself apologizing and feeling embarrassed, being accused by an electrician from East Jerusalem who had come to fix a fuse. My eyes were downcast as he spoke, and I nodded my head, agreeing with every word he said, feeling like a little boy being scolded by his parents after being caught doing something naughty.

"What is a person without his history, without his roots, without his natural condition? Nothing, right?"

"Right," I replied.

"What will your children be raised on? Tell me."

"You're a million percent right."

"I'm only telling you this," he went on, "because you look like a good person. Believe me, I don't say this to everyone. A pity, a real pity. Look at your son." He pointed the screwdriver in the direction of my son, who was contentedly watching SpongeBob on television. "What values will he be raised on?"

My son heard the conversation and lifted his head. Our eyes met.

"All right," the electrician said, "it's all hunky-dory now. If you decide to stay here after all, I recommend that you get a new fuse box with proper settings. But as a brother, my advice to you is to just sell and move to a place where you can raise your children."

"Fine," I said. "What do I owe you?"

"*Wallah*, whatever you want."

"What do you mean? How much do you take for this kind of job?"

"*Wallah*," he said with some sort of embarrassment. "What can I tell you? This is why I don't like doing work for Arabs."

"Why not?" I asked. "Did they do something bad to you?"

"No. But, you know, they make problems with the price. Just give me whatever you like."

"How do I know what electric repairs cost? *Nu*, tell me how much."

"*Ana aref*, I don't have a clue." He scratched his head and was silent for a bit. "A hundred and fifty is good."

"Fine." I opened my wallet and took out money.

"All right, then," he said, "make it a hundred twenty."

"Are you sure?"

"Yes," he replied, his eyes downcast again.

"Do you know what day this is?" my son said, taking the electrician—and me especially—by surprise.

"It's Wednesday," the electrician answered him with a smile. "What grade are you in?"

"Second grade," my usually shy son replied. "I know it's Wednesday, but what special day is it?"

"What, Shavuot?" the electrician shot back and gave me a smile.

"No," my son said. "Shavuot is a Jewish holiday—yesterday we had cheese and quiche at the neighbors'. But what day is it for the Arabs?"

The electrician had no idea what my son was getting at.

"Today is Nakba Day," I said, coming to the electrician's aid.

"Really?" he said. "*Wallah!* A guy has so much work that he . . ."

"Do you know what the Nakba is?" my son said in such an insistent tone that I gave him a hard look.

"You know what?" the electrician said. "A hundred's enough," and he handed me back the twenty.

IS THERE A FUTURE?

June 7, 2013

I was so tired that morning, I was afraid I would fall asleep at the wheel. It was just a short drive in town, but I had to shake my head every so often and open the window. We'd had a rough night with the baby: his fever hasn't gone down for four days, even though he's on antibiotics. The evening before, the pediatrician told us to take him to the ER. We went to Hadassah University Hospital, Ein Karem, and it was hard, very hard.

I have to stay awake, I reminded myself, and turned on the radio. Jews originally from Arab countries were talking about the moment they left, the expulsion, their flight, and what they'd left behind. Mizrahi voices, tormented and lamenting, told about the trauma, the fear. Then followed the resonant voice of well-known storyteller Yossi Alfi. He declared, in the name of some government ministry, a project called "And You Shall Tell Your Son," and then talked about two thousand years of Jewish tradition in Arab lands.

Expulsion and flight? Despite everything, I managed to muster the strength to be irritated by yet another wretched public-service broadcast. This is the Jewish tradition in the Arab lands? This is what you will tell your child? Expulsion and flight? Maybe I really have to leave, I thought. Leave everything behind and get out of here.

A security guard with a tag bearing an Arab name politely asked me to turn off the engine and open the hood and trunk; another guard checked under the car using a pole with a mirror attached. They then wished me luck and showed me how to get to the parking lot.

I checked twice to make sure I had everything: passport, two photos, payment voucher, request form, confirmation from the American immigration service, and other documents and authorizations that the American employer had asked me to bring to the interview in the consulate, just to be sure.

"How is he?" I asked my wife by phone, before joining the line.

"His temperature is 39.5 degrees," she said. "I gave him Nurofen, don't worry."

I worried, and I worried even more because I had to hand in my cell phone at the entrance to the consulate. I was afraid of being cut off from the world, from my family, and from my little son for a few hours. A short security check and I was sent to the hall of visa applicants for the United States.

"What type of visa?" the clerk asked.

"Immigration," I replied, and the clerk punched a machine, which ejected a piece of paper with a number.

"Wait your turn."

Numbers flipped by on the digital board and sent people to the right window. There were Jews, secular and religious, in the hall, but mostly there were Arabs—quite a few Arabs wanted a visa that day. The Arabs looked different from the Israelis in the hall. The men were immaculately shaved and were dressed for a public event; the women looked as though they were going to a wedding. Self-confident Israelis allowed themselves to show up for a visa interview in short pants and flip-flops. I had shaved in honor of the event.

"This is a crap place," a man in his forties sitting next to me whispered in an East Jerusalem accent. "There's no future here. Your first time?" he asked, and I shook my head.

I thought about my little son and I was scared. It was the first time I had ever left an emergency ward at my initiative. And if something should happen to him? I thought at that moment, as I had thought through that whole sleepless night. I'd had no choice but to leave the hospital, I tried to convince myself. After all, I never would have abandoned an emergency room without a doctor's discharge unless I was convinced it was better for my son to get out of there.

That evening, the children's emergency ward had been packed like I'd never seen it before. Not only were all the beds occupied, so were all the sofas and chairs. Many of the parents, me included, had to stand and hold our little children in our arms.

The doctors and nurses scurried among the patients and their parents: those behind curtains, those sitting on chairs, and those who were standing. After some time a nurse came to us, checked the crying baby's pulse and temperature, rubbed an anesthetic on his arm, and said, "We have to wait an hour and then we'll do a blood test. You can wander around in the meantime."

We wandered around, the baby burning with fever. We took turns holding him and trying to calm his crying. We tried to give him a Popsicle, which he usually loves, but nothing helped. We walked for an hour and came back. The ward was still overcrowded with sick children and irritable parents. "Come back in half an hour," the overworked nurse said. We left with the baby and somehow got through another half hour in the hospital corridors.

"Please," I found myself begging the nurse when we returned at the end of the thirty minutes. "You see how he's screaming. There isn't even a chair to sit on."

"I know," she said. "Right away."

We waited, still standing, and finally our turn for a blood test arrived. The baby screamed on the bed, my wife held him down, and I helped the nurse steady his arm when she stuck in the syringe. The baby twisted, howled, and looked at me accusingly. The nurse played with the syringe, turning it left and right, and announced that she could not draw a blood sample.

"Shall we go home?" I asked my wife after three hours in the packed ward, when it occurred to me that leaving would be best for my son's health.

"Yes." She nodded quietly, the baby squirming in her lap.

"I am so sorry," a young doctor said when she heard about our decision to leave before the baby had been examined by a physician. She apologized and said that, according to the rules, anyone who refuses the treatment that is offered has to pay NIS 850.

"What treatment was offered, exactly?" my wife hurled at the tired doctor. "We weren't even offered a chair, and you want eight hundred fifty? We won't sign, you can do what you want."

"I am very sorry," the doctor said, lowering her eyes. The ward was still astir with sick children, agitated parents, and restless, choiceless doctors. The numbers on the digital board changed, and an automatic voice referred people seeking treatment to different windows.

"This is a crap place," the Arab man sitting next to me in the consulate said to a young man who had sat down in front of him. "First time here?"

"Yes," the young man said, holding the visa documents tightly in his hands. "First time. I am here for travel, to see the world."

"Don't come back," the older man told him. "There is no future here."

"But how?" the young man asked in a whisper, and moved next to the man.

"I will tell you exactly what to do," the man of experience replied, and the young man looked left and right to make sure no one was listening.

AN OPEN LETTER FROM THE PIECE OF SHRAPNEL IN THE REAR END OF AN IDF SOLDIER

June 21, 2013

Hey, Yoav. Yes, yes, you—the soldier from Golani—why didn't you tell me you were a friend of Bennett's? Man, I would've given you props. Yes, it's me talking—the piece of shrapnel in your bottom, close to the spine. I know it's surprising that a bit of metal can talk, and in Hebrew for that matter. But hey, that's what happened—I've been stuck in your ass and been a part of your body for so long that I ended up learning your language. Forgive the accent, but my mother tongue is a bit more guttural. By the way, man, I'm sorry that it's agony for you every time you go to the bathroom, but, believe me, I'm even worse off. No offense, but God do you stink. I can hardly breathe.

I have to be honest, I felt a little surge of pride when Naftali Bennett mentioned you in his speech. His voice sounded kind of familiar, though I can't see anything up front, you know. Where Bennett's concerned, you're doing me a favor, I grant you, but couldn't you have turned your back to the screen for a little bit during Peres's ninetieth-birthday celebration? I'm dying to see how the guy looks now. They say that he's got the hottest piece in the neighborhood stuck in his ass.

Anyway, you should know that it's not easy for me to have this conversation with you. Ever since I found out you're close to Bennett, I've been wondering what to do. I even consulted with some other bits of shrapnel I met yesterday when you went to Beit Hachayal. They actually told me to keep quiet, that it wouldn't help, but still I told myself—I'm different. I've known you since '48, and even if you do whatever you can to forget I exist, I'm there in the back all the time, and somehow I've started to feel I'm a part of you. I know you don't like it, but that's just how it is, man. Believe it or not, I even worry about you a little.

Listen to me, Yoav. Don't listen to your friend. Don't listen to Bennett. Remember that he's mostly looking out for his own ass. He doesn't know how much you suffer and how it keeps getting harder as time goes on. You're not young anymore, Yoav, and you still haven't found love. You fought hard, I can attest to that myself, and you deserve a healthier life. Yoav, I know that it's hard for you to sleep at night, I know how hard it is for you to look in the mirror and lie to those around you. If you haven't noticed, you're not going to parties as much as you used to, and who better than me can understand. Remember that I'm stuck in your behind and hear everything people say about you the minute you turn your back.

This isn't easy for me to tell you, Yoav, but yes, people say you walk crooked; some even say you're ugly. Even people who you think love you, who keep coming to your birthday parties, who smile at you, see a pathetic man who won't be able to go on keeping it together. For now they're afraid of you because of your power, they smile at you because of the hardships of the past, but they despise you, Yoav. Not because you were born this way, but because of your actions, because of your attitude toward me.

I know it's hard to be alone. Look at me. Aside from you I have nothing. I, who exploded into a thousand pieces, was left here alone. You think I don't want to reunite with all the other bits of shrapnel? You think I don't dream of returning home, to the land?

Have the operation. Save me and save yourself. I'm taking a risk here too, you know. We also have a saying—better the ass you know than the ass you don't. I often think that maybe I've just grown too accustomed to your smell. Often I'm afraid life will be harder on the outside. As you know, pieces of shrapnel can sometimes be very fragile beings, and sometimes just the thought that I'll have to go around in the world as one who came out of a Jew's ass makes me want to curl up and not move. I know, it must hurt you—again, my apologies.

Know your body's limits, Yoav, and stop telling yourself lies, don't bequeath them to your children. We both know you have no idea what the Jewish people is, where it begins or ends. We both know you don't know exactly what the Land of Israel is, where it begins or ends. Not to mention me, whose maneuvering room stretches from your intestines to your anus. Although there are times, I swear, when it's quiet and peaceful, that I can actually hear your heart beating—and that gives me a few moments of tranquillity, even hope.

Your time is running out, Yoav, and as the years go by, you're just getting uglier. How long do you think you can go on living exclusively amid people like you? How long do you think you can survive without love and without the ability to hold your head up and walk erect?

Sometimes, when you get together with your few friends, practically the only ones who are still willing to talk to you—those friends who all, without exception, suffer from a piece of shrapnel or two here and there—I am filled with pity and truly touched. When you meet to encourage one another, when you vow to trample all the bits of shrapnel to dust, precisely in those moments when you're filled with self-confidence and talking about pain relievers that will suppress the shrapnel, or about laser surgery to make it disappear, I'm talking with my little metal friends that have gathered along with you. I admit that it's pretty scary sometimes, but we all know that if you continue in this way you're doomed to become extinct and decompose, and only then to set us free.

A REVOLUTIONARY PEACE PLAN

January 10, 2014

I have thought long and hard how to respond to the proposal to annex the Israeli Arab communities in Wadi Ara and the Triangle to the West Bank, under Palestinian sovereignty. I decided that instead of raging out, as is custom for us Arabs to react to government plans, I would be a pioneer and proactively initiate my own peace plan, the main points of which are listed below.

1. Whoever lives between the sea and the river and holds a document of residency/citizenship papers/driver's license and wants to be a citizen of the new state will be entitled by law to be a citizen.
2. Everyone who entered Israel after January 1, 2014, and was granted citizenship only because his mother is Jewish is not a legitimate citizen of the state and should be considered a remnant of the old colonialism, until he proves otherwise.
3. The new state will be a haven for every Jew from around the world, who must go before a committee and prove that he is being persecuted and discriminated against because of his Jewishness.
4. The new state will be a haven for every Palestinian from around the world, who must go before a committee and

prove that he is being persecuted and discriminated against because of his Palestinian-ness.

5. The wealthy, whether Jewish or Palestinian, will get breaks from the admissions committee.
6. The Triangle will be replaced by a Square.
7. The Jews will ask for forgiveness wholeheartedly.
8. The Arabs will forgive wholeheartedly.
9. The Arabs will ask for forgiveness, mainly from one another.
10. Playing *matkot* (paddleball) will be prohibited on all the beaches in the country.
11. The high school students in the new country will have to complete a matriculation course on "how to stand in line."
12. Wadi Ara will be expanded into a full-fledged river.
13. There will be zero tolerance for every manifestation of racism.
14. Belief is permitted.
15. Heresy is permitted.
16. The state will not have a religion.
17. It will be forbidden to establish Jewish parties.
18. It will be forbidden to establish Arab parties.
19. Arabs and Jews will live wherever they want.
20. The admissions committees for private communities will be abolished.
21 Arabs and Jews will be permitted to love.
22. Citizens will be able to marry persons of either sex.
23. Arabic and Hebrew will be compulsory languages in all the education systems, until they merge into one language.
24. It is forbidden to establish Arab schools.
25. It is forbidden to establish Jewish schools.
26. Divorce is permitted once every four years.

27. All the flags will be abolished. In official ceremonies and at sports competitions, white flags will be flown.
28. The name of the state will be changed.
29. The anthem will have no words.
30. The social workers will start to get real salaries.
31. All the children will learn one historical narrative.
32. Lying to children is forbidden.
33. Politics will become a profession for which one will have to study.
34. Philosophers will replace the politicians.
35. A philosopher who believes in God is not a philosopher.
36. Journalists will report only the truth.
37. The hiring of media commentators will be forbidden.
38. The ultra-Orthodox and the Arabs will have to have an accompanying driver their whole life.
39. A fine will be levied on anyone who sends a package knowing that it will not fit into the mailbox and that the recipient will get a note forcing him to go to the post office.
40. A citizen who considers himself superior to another will be deported to Siberia.

AMERICA

June 7, 2014

Last week I went with my wife to the U.S. consulate in Jerusalem. The nursery school teacher somehow managed to take a picture of the little one that was acceptable for the online visa application forms, so we were finally able to register and set a date for an interview at the consulate.

There were a few particularly scary items on those forms. I knew I could trust myself, but I had to ask my wife some things before marking "yes" or "no" in the security-related questionnaire.

"Tell me, did you ever take part in genocide?" I found myself asking her in the living room, with the children listening. "Were you ever a member of a terrorist organization?"

"No," she said. "Are you nuts?! What's with you?"

"I have to hear it from you," I told her, and went on: "Have you ever been in contact with anyone who was ever a member of a terrorist organization?" Here I looked her straight in the eyes to make sure she was telling the truth.

"No," she replied firmly, and I bought her answer.

"Is that what they are asking?" she wanted to know.

"Yes, you have to answer all these questions in order to enter America," I replied, and continued: "Do you intend to marry an American citizen and remain in the United States?"

"What?!" my wife snapped back. "I have to see that question."

"Forget it," I told her, and hid the forms. "I'll write 'no.'"

Armed with the right forms for applying for what is called an exchange visitor visa, we arrived at the consulate's entrance right on time. There was a long line leading to the outer booth, where a young woman seated behind glass, which I could have sworn was bulletproof, received the arrivals. We took our places in line.

It took me a few minutes to take in the fact that the uniformed security guards standing at the entrance to the consulate were speaking Arabic between themselves. It always surprises me, this thing with Arab security guards. True, I've already grasped that the guards in the malls, at the International Writers Festival last month at Mishkenot Sha'ananim, and in other venues in Jerusalem are from the eastern part of the city, but I can't quite grasp this situation.

I'm talking here not about Arabs who served in the army and were placed in security positions, but about Arabs like me who have never touched a weapon and are manning the security posts. They're never armed, it's true, but *rabak*! It rattles me when an Arab checks under the car hood and exchanges a couple of sentences in Hebrew with me in order to check out my accent. But I was happy now.

"Stand in a single line, please," the girl behind the glass requested through a loudspeaker, and we all closed ranks. My wife and I did likewise, because like everyone else, we wanted a visa to America. You know how it is in the West. Even though the clerk is an Arab, just like the guards, they have different rules, it's a different culture, and a line is a line—maybe it's some sort of an admissions test—and no one here wants to wreck his visa prospects because he didn't stand in line like a civilized individual.

"Did you notice that everyone here is either an Arab or an ultra-Orthodox Jew?" my wife whispered to me, and I replied, "This is Jerusalem—what else is there?"

The line advanced rapidly, and after we passed the polite young woman in the booth, we went by the Arab guards, too. You're not allowed to take in cell phones, so we left them in compartments at the entrance. For an instant I felt uptight, cut off, and frightened by the sheer fact that I was not going to be available. "I am available, therefore I exist"—in a twinkling I had grasped the meaning of life.

After security, you enter a large waiting room with seats and windows, behind which are more clerks. The long lines move along relatively quickly, and the clerks are unfailingly courteous and smiling, even though some of them are not Americans but Arabs and Israelis.

"This is what I call service," I whispered to my wife as we left our fingerprints in a machine and handed over our documents.

"You're right," she said, and told me about a girlfriend of hers who spent two years in America and related that "life in the United States is a lot more comfortable."

"What do you mean, comfortable?" I asked with discomfort.

"For example, if you go into a supermarket and there are no carts, they bring you one—there are workers whose job that is."

"Really?"

"Yes," she replied. "And she also told me that there are no lines at the checkout counters, because if there is pressure, they straightaway open a new counter. There's no waiting."

"So we're going to the United States because shopping in the supermarket is easier?"

"And for the children's English."

Unlike my wife and children, I am very anxious about the looming trip. We will be living in southern Illinois, where the winters are like the ones you read about in books. I imagine myself shoveling the snow off the driveway and trying to defrost the frozen windows of the car, and already I feel that all I want is to be back in my own home with a cup of tea with lemon and all the rest of it.

I will be teaching there, and that scares me very much; I have no idea what kind of teacher I will be. My tasks include teaching Hebrew, and when I think that I will have American students who go off speaking Hebrew with an Arabic accent, I get more than a little freaked out.

But my biggest worry about the United States is the kids. Right now they are enthusiastic and excited about the yearlong stay, but I sometimes suspect that they think it's like a family outing and haven't grasped the implications of a different language, a new culture, another type of society, and the inevitable acclimatization problems.

"It's easiest for the children," friends assure me, but I don't believe them. I've already enrolled the youngest in a preschool in the neighborhood where we've rented a place for the year, and I will enroll the older ones in public schools that are supposed to be good. I perused sites that rank schools and I contacted the local government for information.

Going through the visa forms beforehand, I had been thrown by the "race" rubric. I looked for Arab but could find no such category. There was white, black, Hispanic, and Asian, but no Arab. I looked on the Internet to find out what we are and discovered that in the United States, people coming from the Middle East or North Africa are considered whites. That really surprised me, because I never considered myself white. I remembered the moment when I checked the "white" box on the forms: I grinned with a leer and knew that I was going to be a racist—and how I was going to be a racist! Especially after forty years of experience with this.

"That's us," I said to my wife when our name was called through the loudspeaker: "Kasuha."

"Kasuha?" she asked, puzzled.

"Believe it or not," I said to her as we made our way to the clerk, "a white folks' name."

GOOD-BYE CIGARETTES, HELLO YOGA

January 31, 2014

Since my driver's license was revoked, I don't venture out much. In fact, for the past four days I've hardly crossed the threshold of the front door, except to throw out the garbage or check the mail. Most of the time I'm ensconced at the computer in my study, trying to write a few sentences between surfing Facebook, watching YouTube, and following the developments in the municipal election crisis in Nazareth.

Every half hour I light up a cigarette, and every hour on the hour I head for the kitchen and rummage about in the refrigerator to see what I can eat this time—usually a salami-and-mayonnaise sandwich. I eat in front of the television, watching reruns of comedy series and getting fat. Yes, it's been only two weeks since I lost my license, and the scale assures me that I've put on three kilos.

Between sandwiches and cookies, I wash dishes, clean the kitchen counter, and organize things. I hate washing the floor but I don't mind vacuuming, sweeping, and straightening up the perpetual mess in the kids' rooms.

Since my license was revoked you won't find even one dirty piece of clothing here. The amount of dirty laundry used to reach terrifying dimensions, but now I can't restrain myself and run the machine even with half a load. I put everything in the dryer right away and hang up the delicate things and the jeans. Afterward I fold everything and put it all back neatly in the closets. But I don't cook. Despite being preoccupied with housework, television, and sandwiches, I am pleased with the rate of progress in my work. In the end, it looks as if I wasted even more time at the television production company making coffee and gossiping incessantly with my colleagues; nothing really interesting happens at the office.

I am not suffering at home; on the contrary, I love our apartment. I've always loved it, and now that I am spending the whole day here I love it even more. The thought that we will have to rent it out in another six months, ahead of our stay in the United States, and the fact that some stranger will live in it, has started to bother me. But there's no choice—we need the money.

We have a big mortgage, and the place we will rent somewhere in Illinois is hardly going to be cheap. Actually, we've already found something, which is to say that a lecturer at the University of Illinois sent us photos of a truly American house close to the campus in Urbana. It's a fine place, with two floors, a fireplace in the living room, and a large garden. The children were delighted at seeing the snow that covered the garden. I checked the weather there and was glad to discover that it's getting warmer and is now only minus 14 degrees Celsius (6.8 degrees Fahrenheit).

I also regularly check out the websites of the schools I've marked out for the children. The schools were apparently closed for most of the last week because of the snow and cold, the sites reported, showing an image of a yellow triangle with the word "Alert" flashing in it.

If all goes well, we will be living in that house, which belongs to two lecturers who will be on sabbatical somewhere in Europe. The owners seem very nice. They told me about the nearby schools and transportation. They said they would leave my wife and me bicycles, and assured me that this was the most convenient and healthiest way to get to the university.

My wife laughed when I told her about the bikes, and in response I said, "Hey, who knows? Maybe someone over there will
have a good influence on me and make me a better person, one
who cares about the environment, and I will start to pedal to some
nice café every morning before going on to the campus, brimming
with good energy."

You can't smoke in the house, the owners told me, and I agreed
immediately. Not least because I have a hope that somehow the
tough regulations that say smoking is not permitted anywhere on
the campus will at last force me to overcome that filthy addiction.
Who knows, maybe I'll even go to a gym, do yoga?

The generous lecturers sent us photos of all the rooms in the
house. From time to time I go back to those images and gaze at
them in an effort to learn more about the place and the owners,
whom we will replace for a year. Simple, pleasant furniture; books
in every corner; a piano; lots of Legos; a radio in the room of one
of the boys, a baseball bat sticking out from under the bed, and a
stand for sheet music opposite an empty chair. Cello—this boy plays
the cello, I decided, even though I saw no sign of that instrument
in any of the photos.

What will they take with them, what will they leave behind?
I thought about the owners, and afterward about us. What will
we take? Clothes? How many? After all, the winter there is not
like anything we know here. And books? Yes, books, even a few
for the children to keep up their language skills. Arabic certainly,
but Hebrew—will we take Hebrew books?

Who will take care of my books back home? How can I let a
stranger sit in my study and touch my books? And my wife, well,
I know her; she will want to burn the mattress if she knows that
someone else slept on it. She's already declared that no matter what,
in Urbana we will buy new linens and mattresses for everyone.

"We'll take care of the house for you," I really wanted to tell the
lecturer couple we'll be replacing for a year, but I didn't say a word.

We will have to rent out our place, there's no other way: there are municipal taxes and other bills to pay, the house committee fee, and the mortgage—especially the mortgage, which, though it's been six years, hasn't been reduced by one shekel, and the monthly payments just keep getting higher. "It will start to go down one day," a friend assured me, but I remain a person of little faith.

We have a charming apartment, I thought after organizing the kitchen and folding yet another load of laundry. We will choose the renters carefully, I consoled myself as I made a cup of coffee and sat myself down in the spotless kitchen to read the paper at my leisure. It said on the front page that the mayor, Nir Barkat, is backing Rabbi Shmuel Eliyahu, from Safed, as Jerusalem's chief rabbi, and in light of what the rabbi has said in the past, I hoped that there won't be a law by the time we get back that will prohibit renting apartments to Arabs.

FAREWELL

July 19, 2014

Quite soon I am going away from here. In a few days we'll be leaving Jerusalem, leaving the country. Yesterday we bought little suitcases for the kids. No need to take a lot of clothes; we'll leave our winter clothes—in any event they won't be warm enough given the cold of southern Illinois, USA. We'll just need a few things until we get settled. Perhaps the kids should take some books, two or three in Arabic, and another few in Hebrew, so they don't forget the languages. But I'm already not sure what I want my kids to remember of this place, so beloved and so cursed.

The original plan was to leave in a month for a year's sabbatical. But last week I understood that I can't stay here any longer, and I asked the travel agent to get us out of here as fast as possible, "and please make them one-way tickets." In a few days we'll land in Chicago, and I don't even know where we'll be for the first month, but we'll figure it out.

I have three children, a daughter who is already fourteen years old and two sons, aged nine and three. We live in West Jerusalem. We are the only Arab family living in our neighborhood, to which we moved six years ago. "You can choose two toys," we said this week in Hebrew to our little boy, who stood in his room gazing at boxes of his toys, and he started to cry despite our promises that we will buy him anything he wants when we get there.

I also have to decide what to take with me. I can choose only two books, I said to myself, standing in front of shelves of books in my study. Other than a book of poetry by Mahmoud Darwish and a story collection by Khalil Gibran, all of my books are in Hebrew. Books that I started to buy from the age of fifteen that accompanied me wherever I moved over the years. Since the age of fourteen I have barely read a book in Arabic. When I was fourteen I saw a library for the first time. Twenty-five years ago my math teacher in the village of Tira, where I was born, came to my parents' home and told them that next year the Jews would be opening a school for gifted students in Jerusalem; he said to my father that he thought I should apply, that I should take the entrance examination. "It will be better for him there," I remember the teacher telling my parents. I did well on the test, I passed the interviews, and when I was the age of my daughter I left my home in Tira to go to a Jewish boarding school in Jerusalem. It was so difficult, almost cruel. I remember how I cried when my father hugged me and left me at the entrance of the grand new school, like nothing I had ever seen in Tira. I once wrote that the first week in Jerusalem was the hardest week of my life. I was different, other; my clothes were different, as was my language. All the classes were in Hebrew—science, Bible, literature. I sat there not understanding one word. When I tried to speak everyone would laugh at me. I so much wanted to run back home, to my family, to the village and friends, to the Arabic language. I cried on the phone to my father that he should come and get me, and he said that only the beginnings are hard, that in a few months I would speak Hebrew better than they do. I remember the first week, our literature teacher asked us to read *The Catcher in the Rye* by Salinger. There were no literature classes in Tira; we did not have a library in Tira—there still isn't. *The Catcher in the Rye* was the first book I read in Hebrew. It was the first novel I ever read. It took me several weeks to read it, and when I finished I understood two things that changed my life. The first was that I could read a book in Hebrew, and the second was the deep understanding that I loved books. From the moment that I discovered books, and that the sciences no longer interested me, I sat in the library and I began to read. Very quickly my Hebrew became nearly perfect. The boarding school library had books only in Hebrew, so I began to read Israeli authors. I read S. Y. Agnon, Meir Shalev, Amos Oz, and I started to read about Zionism, about Judaism and the building of the homeland. I very quickly understood the power of books and found myself reading stories about Jewish pioneers, about the Shoah, about war. During these years I also began to understand my own story, and without planning to do so I began to write about Arabs who live in an Israeli boarding school, in the western city, in a Jewish country. I began to write, believing that all I had to do to change things would be to write the other side, to tell the stories that I heard from my grandmother. To write how my grandfather was killed in the battle over Tira in 1948, how my grandmother lost all of our land, how she raised my father, orphaned at a few months old from his father, while she supported them as a fruit picker paid by the Jews. I wanted to tell, in Hebrew, about my father, who sat in jail for long years, with no trial, for his political ideas. I wanted to tell the Israelis a story, the Palestinian story. Surely when they read it they will understand, when they read it they will change, all I have to do is write and the occupation will end, I just have to be a good writer and I will free my people from the ghettos they live in, tell good stories in Hebrew and I will be safe, another book, and another movie and another column for the newspaper and another script for television and my children will already have a better future. Thanks to my stories one day we will turn into equal citizens, almost like the Jews.

Twenty-five years of writing in Hebrew, and nothing has changed. Twenty-five years clutching at the hope, believing it is not possible that people can be so blind. Twenty-five years when I had few reasons to be optimistic but continued to believe that it was still possible, that one day this place in which both Jews and

Arabs live together would be the one story where the story of the other is not denied. That one day the Israelis would stop denying the Nakba, the occupation, and the suffering of the Palestinian people. That one day the Palestinians would be willing to forgive, and together we would build a place that was worth living in, exactly like the stories with good endings.

Twenty-five years of writing and knowing bitter criticism from both sides, but last week I gave up. Last week something inside me broke. When Jewish youth parade through the city shouting "Death to the Arabs" and attack Arabs only because they are Arabs, I understood that I lost my little war.

I listened to the politicians and the media, and I know that they are differentiating between blood and blood, between peoples. Those who have become the powers that be say expressly what most Israelis think: "We are a better people than the Arabs." On panels that I participated in, it was said that Jews are a superior people, more entitled to life. I despair to know that an absolute majority in the country does not recognize the right of an Arab to live, at least not in this country.

After my last columns some readers beseeched that I be exiled to Gaza, threatened to break my legs, to kidnap my children. I live in Jerusalem, and I have some wonderful Jewish neighbors, and I have wonderful Jewish friends—writers and journalists—but I still cannot take my children to day camps or to parks with their Jewish friends. My daughter protested furiously and said no one would know she is an Arab because of her perfect Hebrew, but I would not listen. She shut herself in her room and wept.

Quite soon I am going away from here, and now I am standing in front of my bookshelves, Salinger in hand, the one I read when I was fourteen years old. I don't want to take any books, I've decided, I have to concentrate on my new language. I know how hard, almost impossible, it is, but I must find another language to write in, my children will have to find another language to live in.

"Don't come in," my daughter shouted angrily when I knocked on her door.

I went in anyway. I sat down next to her on the bed, and despite her back turned to me, I knew she was listening. "You hear," I said, before I repeated to her exactly the same sentence my father said to me when he left me at the entrance to the best school in the country twenty-five years ago. "Remember, whatever you do in life, for them you will always, but always, be an Arab. Do you understand?"

"I understand," my daughter said, hugging my tightly. "Dad, I knew that a long time ago."

"Quite soon we'll be leaving here," I said as I messed up her hair, just as she hates. "Meanwhile, read this."

And I gave her *The Catcher in the Rye*.